Making <u>Your</u> Film in the Digital Age

Now That All the Rules Have Changed

By Larry J. Gardner

ISBN 978-0-6152-2117-5

Printed in the United States of America

Published by Digifonics, Inc.
digifonics.com
and
lulu.com

*For Thea, Nancy and Lauren, my inspirations,
and for Lee Sedwick, my friend, collaborator, nemesis and
co-conspirator.*

Contents

Foreword

"Every artist was once an amateur."

Ralph Waldo Emerson

I started writing this book over three years before I finished it, mostly because I kept having to re-write it. Everything about the art, science and business of filmmaking is changing. I couldn't keep up with it all and write about it at the same time, and it's only recently that I gave up on that. Instead, I decided to make it shorter and concentrate on the fundamental things you need to know to make your film, because these are the salient points that don't change over time.

I'm a longtime writer, producer, director, shooter, editor, sound man, and do-everything-else kind of guy in the business of creating film and video. My career has given me the chance to be involved with a wide variety of projects ranging from ten-second commercials to feature-length films. I've worked on profitable corporate videos, advertising and promotional projects, and documentaries done just for the sheer love of the art.

As owner of a successful medium-size television production company for over 30 years, I've been in the business long enough to have used virtually every production format from 35mm motion picture film to digital video on a cell phone, and most of the tools of the trade. In short, I come from the "old school" of how film and video are done. But don't let that confuse you. Unlike a lot of us old timers, I am not put off by change. In fact, I embrace it. I thrive on it. Give me a new way to do something, and if it's better than the old way (I keep an open mind), I'll jump on it. In the case of filmmaking, I never liked the old way, but I love the new way. Being detached from the Hollywood way, I have been trying to do it a different way for a long time, so maybe I've been doing it different longer than almost anyone else. That's why I decided to write this book.

My company was not in Los Angeles or New York; it was in Raleigh, North Carolina. While I've shot all over, including both LA and New York and had a fair amount of exposure to those cultures, most of my work has been on projects far less ambitious and with vastly lower budgets than blockbuster movies or network TV. So, I've learned how to cope with a low budget and carefully design my projects to get the most bang for the buck.

One of the most important and surprising things I have learned is this: the intrinsic quality of a film has very little to do with either the technology or the budget. Regardless of the tools used or amount of money available, the film has to be conceived, researched, written, performed, shot, edited and distributed. All of these require unique skills and abundant human brainpower, the so-called "wetware" on top of the hardware and software that makes it all come together.

Some skills can be learned and some can't. You can learn about technology from a book, but some would say you can't learn art at all. I agree with this proposition, and for that reason I won't be intruding upon your artistic sensibilities any more than I feel I must. Instead, I'll concentrate on the steps you must take to bring your very personal artistic vision to the screen.

Although film production is a very technical business, this book does not concentrate on the latest technology. There are several reasons for this. First, the technology is changing rapidly. What's the latest and greatest today might be a dinosaur two years from now. Secondly, the hardware and software needed to create a video project have become ubiquitous. Almost any personal computer and video camera can be used together (along with some more-or-less inexpensive software) to create a finished project that would have required rooms full of equipment and hundreds of thousands of dollars to create just a few years ago. In the right hands, the image and sound quality possible with modern "prosumer" equipment can rival or exceed what was not long ago attainable only with the most expensive professional gear. The equipment is not only affordable, the technology is increasingly easier to use.

Unfortunately, it's a lot easier (and probably more fun) to just take a camera out and start shooting than it is to design, plan and execute a good piece of film or television. That's what this book is mostly about – all the things that apply regardless of the technology. They are the foundation of the art, whether you're making a 30-second commercial or a feature-length film. Armed with this knowledge, your own vision for your film, and the amazing new digital technology, you can make your film, and it can be good.

Your audience (intentionally or not) will compare what you do to things they've seen before. They hold unwritten expectations of sound and image quality, storytelling, talent, pace, flow, drama – the factors that combine to create the final "viewing experience". Every production must meet these expectations if it is to be successful. These qualities are often called *production value*, and have little to do with the content, the delivery system or the budget. A good example might be the experience you have when you watch a good movie on your bedroom TV. Although the movie was created to be shown on a 50-foot screen, the production values and the story come through virtually undiminished.

Someone has said, "Content is king". As a kid, I spent an hour every Sunday night watching *Disney* through the snow from a distant TV station, since it wasn't carried by a local broadcaster. Though the sound was sometimes garbled and the picture often barely recognizable, I squinted my way through every program for the sake of its content. Likewise, your audience will forgive you many sins if you've done your homework and created memorable, engaging and compelling content.

I won't talk much about high-budget productions or how Hollywood makes films, because the affordable new digital technologies are opening up the field to newcomers who may have the tools, but don't have the high budgets. The genius that will go into future digital production will be grounded in the filmmaker's ability to engineer a way to "make it work" with the technical and financial resources available. I'm convinced that there has never been a strong relationship between quality and budget, and the new technology further weakens that relationship. There's absolutely no doubt that exceptional work can be done on a low budget. Besides, there are a lot more low-budget films being made than high-budget ones, and that trend will only continue.

This book is not about someone else's film. It's about *your* film, the one that you haven't yet made. Its purpose is to help you make it and to help you make it better. When I use the word "you", I mean the person, *you*, but also whoever may be doing any particular part of the production process. Filmmaking is always a collaborative process, sometimes involving hundreds of people. Traditional filmmaking courses and books will spend a lot of time on the formal structure of the collaborative hierarchy customarily used in the film industry. They ask if you want to become a producer, director, actor, or cinematographer. In the Digital Age, the many roles required to make a film become simultaneously blurred and fluid. It's now quite possible (even common) for one person to be writer, producer, director, cinematographer, makeup artist, editor and caterer on the same film.

A major part of the film business is not about filmmaking at all: it's about getting funding and distribution. As one filmmaker put it, "The hard part isn't making the film, it's making the *deal*." That's a very different subject, and Hollywood wants you to believe that without their big production budgets, massive marketing and expensive distribution your film will never be seen, much less make money. The Digital Age is having profound effects here also, by making very inexpensive, high quality production possible, and by opening up digital distribution avenues undreamed of in the past. This is a profound change. Who would have believed that the average person would ever spend more time exploring YouTube than watching films in theaters?

Don't expect to find all your technical answers in this book, either, although I'll describe a lot of techniques sprinkled with what I hope are helpful hints and tips, and some technical details that may be hard to find elsewhere. And don't expect to find a formula; every project is different and good production design demands that techniques be adapted to fit the concept. Don't look to this book to be an exhaustive or definitive treatment of the subject of filmmaking; at best, it is a very limited overview. I only hope that it will be a useful introduction that can help make your work more professional, even if you're a rank amateur.

I've also decided not to put in many pictures, just those that relate directly to the topic. To save you and me money, I elected to print the book in black and white, too. And pictures are a lot prettier in color. You can find a lot of them on the internets.

Finally, I'll only touch on the "rules" of filmmaking, as taught in film schools. The new generation of filmmakers is learning that rules are there to be broken. Nonetheless, I'll introduce a few rules here and there, the ones that you break at your peril.

Digital technology literally unshackles the intrepid filmmaker, stripping away limitations of the past. It allows him or her to have a freedom of expression previously unknown, because it was financially and technologically impossible. The high costs and complexities of the past made it necessary for filmmakers to pursue a safe path, minimizing the possibility of making expensive mistakes. Today's freedom means you can afford to make mistakes and to pursue new ways of doing things, to experiment, and create new forms and techniques. You can do it your way, to make your film very personal in an unprecedented way.

Throughout the book, I've thrown in a little about the history related to some of the topics. I think this is important, because it's always good to understand how things got to be the way they are, and because knowing where you've been helps you understand where you're going.

This book is about seizing opportunities and running with them. I hope it will give you a jump-start toward learning the basics you need to know to make a quality film, regardless of your budget or experience level. But remember, it's merely a primer. It's intended for the impassioned beginner and aspiring filmmaker, but maybe it can also be of some help to the experienced professional in making the transition from traditional filmmaking into new and better digital ways of doing things.

Larry Gardner

May 2008

"In feature films, the director is God; in documentary films, God is the director."

Alfred Hitchcock

Introduction

Digital filmmaking has been a long time coming. It began with the invention of photography in the 1800s. A few decades later, mechanical sound recording and the motion picture became realities. Electric power was wired to businesses and homes around the world. The electronics age dawned in the early 20th century with the development of the vacuum tube, bringing with it radio and sound-on-film – the "talkies". Experiments with television led to a major new industry and commercial broadcasting in the 1940s. By the 1950s, the small screen gained glorious color and recording video on magnetic tape became possible.

Paralleling these developments was a stream of innovations in the field of computing, with the first electronic digital computers appearing in the 1940s. These behemoths performed scientific calculations in minutes that before would have required rooms full of mathematicians and years to complete.

The introduction of the transistor in the 1950s and integrated circuits in the 1960s paved the way for fantastic increases in the complexity and simultaneous dramatic reductions in cost, power consumption and bulk of electronic equipment. Solid-state devices reduced the venerable vacuum tube to a dusty relic and brought a torrent of new capabilities to computers, audio and video.

By the 1970s, portable video recorders and lightweight cameras began to displace motion picture film for television production. At the same time, digital audio recording became possible, leading to the development of the Compact Disk, the first widespread application of digital technology to media, which rapidly became the new standard for audio. With the dawning of the 1980s, digital video recording became a reality, and by the end of the decade, computers had gotten powerful enough to capture, store and manipulate digital video. Cameras, too, moved beyond the vacuum tube age, creating images with tiny chips called *Charge Coupled Devices* (CCD).

Suddenly, there was a major milestone in filmmaking history: digital technology became capable of encompassing virtually all of the previous technologies involved in filmmaking. The camera was in reality a computer, turning pictures and sound into streams of bits, ones and zeroes, ready to be processed and edited in another computer. Once there, the functionality of myriad other devices like video switchers, audio mixers, recorders and processors could be emulated in software – no "outboard" equipment was necessary.

To complete the digital chain, the DVD provided a distribution medium capable of holding two hours (or more) of pristine video on a single shiny disk. The 1990s added digital broadcasting via satellite, cable, and local television stations. High

Definition Television (HDTV) became a reality as thin, flat-panel displays began to displace "the tube". Digital photography also matured and created a viable alternative to film in both professional and amateur picture taking.

By the turn of the century, perhaps the most startling trend was more significant economically than technologically: the cost of digital cameras and computers plunged miraculously. Memory chips and disk drives increased in capacity by a thousand times. Suddenly video's copious demands for computing power and storage space turned from overwhelming to near trivial. Every new home computer had the speed and storage necessary to handle video and even consumer camcorders were digital and could transfer their video and audio data to a computer through a single cable. Audio and video quality of low-cost equipment became fully "professional", even when compared to the best high-end gear of a few years earlier. Capabilities of a modest computer for editing, special effects and other post-production processes rivaled those of systems costing hundreds of thousands of dollars as the digital age was dawning.

Innovation and mass production set the stage for the upcoming revolution: for the first time, filmmaking was becoming democratized. No longer were the tools of the trade in the domain of large corporations, film studios or very wealthy individuals. Now, they were within the reach of the independent filmmaker. In real dollars, the cost of a complete arsenal of production equipment for a project became comparable to the financial outlay once required for the purchase of only the film stock and processing for a typical production. The actual recording media (tape or disk) costs only a tiny fraction of a comparable amount of film, and it's mostly re-usable. Already "broadcast quality", this level of equipment quickly became capable of creating full high definition images.

The same technological forces came to the expansion of broadband connectivity; video communication was becoming as universally possible as telephony had been before. For an increasing number of people, the Internet became the new post office, library, theater, telephone, newspaper, TV station, cable system, and it is becoming the new Hollywood.

In spite of all this progress, however, no technology can replace the human forces, talent and sheer brainpower that must be brought to bear on writing, producing, directing, acting and myriad other skills that are at the core of the creative filmmaking process. What technology can do, however, is open up new ways of working and new ways to get digital films in front of an audience. Ultimately, these new freedoms are creating a new culture, with the potential to foster a breed of filmmakers capable of flourishing independently of the movie studios and television networks that have long maintained a stranglehold on both production and distribution. This will certainly happen, even in the face of (and perhaps in spite of) the ongoing "megamedia" mergers.

The fantastic new artistic freedom leads to the development of a grassroots, "bottom-up" production community that has the potential to displace the traditional "top-down" architecture that has been at the foundation of both the film and television industries since their inceptions. Hollywood and Big TV have served their functions well in creating in America a highly profitable and world-dominant system of content creation and delivery. At the same time, new technologies like Internet video sites, file sharing, video-on-demand, IPTV and ubiquitous CD and DVD "burners" are threatening the established industry giants and forcing them to lobby for severe legislation, incorporate complex digital rights management mechanisms and instigate massive litigation aimed at protecting their "intellectual property".

Independent digital filmmakers will have a profound impact on the culture of the 21st Century. For this to happen, however, it is important for the aspiring filmmaker to understand that in spite of the "newness" of the technology, the art form of telling stories with sound and pictures is not new. It is, in fact, mature. Having developed over more than a century, it is based largely on other, much older forms. Its traditions derive from the epics of Greek drama, the composition, light and shadow of Renaissance art, the music of Bach and Beethoven. Its heritage is rich and deep, but new minds yearning to create and innovate can keep it forever fresh for audiences yet unborn. For this maturity and for the development of the art of filmmaking, we must credit Hollywood.

However formal or casual the approach, every film goes through the distinct phases of pre-production, production and post-production, followed (hopefully), by distribution. This book is loosely organized into parts related to the three production phases, plus another section that's about choosing your technology.

Over most of the history of filmmaking, the technology was a given: you shot film with a motion picture camera. In the Digital Age, you have more choices. There are multiple image formats, a plethora of recording methods and media, and a bewildering array of tools available to help or hinder the adventure of making your film.

"A movie studio is the best toy a boy can have."

Orson Welles

PART I - PRE-PRODUCTION

Pre-production is critical to a successful outcome for any film, digital or otherwise. More than any other part of the process, it separates the professionals from the amateurs. It requires firm discipline and extreme attention to detail, traits that are sometimes lacking in creative types. Most filmmakers consider it difficult and frustrating; doing too little is common while doing too much is impossible. Although digital technology has helped make pre-production a little easier, it has had far more impact on production and post-production.

Be prepared for this essential phase to take more work, time and brainpower than you ever expected. Good planning, research, writing, script editing, production design, casting – the list goes on and on – don't come easy, but will pay huge dividends in the later phases of making your film and getting it seen.

In this part, you'll find little talk about techniques or technology. Those subjects come later. Pre-production is like piano lessons. You have to learn a lot about notes and scales and staffs before you can play a Mozart sonata. Grin and bear it. It's important – trust me. That's why they concentrate on it so much in film school.

Keep in mind, too, that there's a lot more to it than in this brief overview. My goal here is just to get you thinking.

1.1 What's The Story?

"Stories tell us of what we already knew and forgot, and remind us of what we haven't yet imagined."

Anne L. Watson

A quick answer to the question: The story is *everything*! Humans want and need stories. They're how we understand the world. Stories have no particular length, they are as long as it takes. Your story can be an epic or a one-liner. Whether your subject is exciting or dull, your film can and must tell an interesting story.

Feature films and dramatic television can be the ultimate storytellers because their creators have the freedom to enhance and change the story at the whim of their imaginations, and in these media (especially in the Digital Age), anything is possible. Documentary film is a bit different, since the subject matter (of necessity) drives the story. A documentary tells a story nonetheless, and creating an effective documentary can be as daunting a creative challenge as making a dramatic movie.

Classic storytelling demands a clearly defined beginning, middle and end. Your story must have characters, antagonists and protagonists. There will be a plot with interesting twists and turns. Add to these a sense of place, an environment in which the story takes place. All dramas use these age-old elements to create the fabric of story, and there is no reason why a documentary shouldn't use them with equal effectiveness. After all, a documentary is nothing more than a drama that takes place in the real world. Any drama, whether presented on stage or screen (or even on radio), should contain these elements.

The beginning, middle and end might be rigidly divided into Act I, Act II and Act III (on the stage) or simply flow smoothly through the transitions (a movie). The beginning sets the scene, establishing a sense of place; it introduces characters and the conflicts between protagonist and antagonist. The middle plays out the conflicts and includes tension, suspense, humor and perhaps most importantly, the unexpected. The end presents a resolution: they lived happily ever after – or not. These principles are certainly time-proven; they go back to eras long before Shakespeare, all the way to the ancient Greeks, or even before. They are also the subject of many other books, and far beyond the scope of this one.

So back to the question: What's the story?

Choosing the Story

If you're lucky, you'll have the luxury of choosing the story you're going to tell. If you have this freedom, be realistic about it, keeping in mind that the cost and time as well as the knowledge required to create your film will be dependent on the story. Writers are advised to write about what they know. The same is true for filmmakers.

Obviously, if you're planning a film, you have an image of what the story is going to be – *The Concept.* Maybe you don't know exactly how the story will unfold. If, for example, your film is about a day in the life of a celebrity, you won't know the story until you've accumulated the footage you shot during that day. On the other hand, if you're doing a video biography of the same person, your research will tell you most of what you need to know about her before you begin to shoot. In either case, the nature (and much of the excitement) of making a documentary lies in the fact that you continually add to what you know about the story as the process moves toward a conclusion. Some documentarians have called this natural evolution "finding the film".

As the *storyteller*, you *must know* the story. This means research, the more the better. It may be formal or informal, written or unwritten, but it's absolutely necessary. Fortunately, researching for a film in the Digital Age has been made much easier by the ultimate digital library: the Internet. Google it.

No matter how much homework you have done or how well you know the subject, you learn a lot more as you go along. Whatever the subject, when you arrive at the location for your first day of shooting, your knowledge will begin to multiply. Equally important, you will develop a "feel" for the story. In the back of your mind, you will become increasingly comfortable and familiar with the characters, the plot line, and the places where the action happens.

The Treatment

Whatever the genre of your film, at some point, the story needs to be defined. It's helpful to start by creating an informal outline, dividing it at least into beginning, middle and end segments. The outline should include a cast of characters (real or fictitious) and a list of locations. From this outline and other information, create a *treatment*, a short narrative that is an overview of the entire project.

A treatment can be used to show others what the project is all about and where they might fit in. It's easier to read than a script and is the best kind of document to use when you're trying to raise funds, assemble a cast and crew, or otherwise going about mustering resources for the project.

Treatments don't need to have a particular format; every project's treatment is pretty much a custom job and every filmmaker has his own way of doing it. In addition, unlike a script, a treatment will often contain information that is not a part of the story but is important in making the project happen.

The treatment will evolve as the pre-production process continues. Below is a list of some of the things you may want to think about including in your treatment:

- A synopsis of the story including character sketches and the reasons you think it will make a good film.
- A description of the target audience and/or market.
- A list of the people who will be working on it, including cast (if any), crew, subject matter experts (including interviewees), writers, narrators, artists, editors, etc.
- A brief statement of how you'll go about making the film, where it will be shot, the equipment to be used.
- A short explanation of the visual style.
- A summary of key expense items, possibly including a detailed budget.
- An estimated timetable or production schedule.
- Ways the film will be distributed.

No matter how simple your film, creating a treatment is a useful exercise to help you get started. It's the launching pad for your project and will be a key element in determining whether the film has what it takes to actually be finished.

The Script

Unlike dramatic films where the script is the "bible", some will argue that a documentary doesn't have or need a script in the traditional sense; it's been said that a documentary is "a tale that only comes together in the telling." While a script that actually reflects what a documentary film *is* may never exist, it's still helpful to create one knowing in advance that it will be a dynamic document, constantly changing throughout the production process.

Documentaries or informational films often contain interviews with subject matter experts or personalities, or may include impromptu dialog. What these people might say on camera won't be known until the scenes are shot, but at the outset, you may have a good idea of what you may *want* them to say. Other subjects are better covered using a narrator whose words you must anticipate. Most documentaries include all of these elements.

The first script effort should contain as many as possible of the story elements that will be in the finished piece, even though it may end up having little similarity to what actually ends up on the screen. If project has strong dramatic elements or is actually a drama or feature film, the script must be much more complete and thought out, including full scene descriptions and dialog – it will become "The Bible".

Clearly, too, many projects you may be interested in are not documentaries in the strictest sense. These might include such genres as corporate videos, training films, and a wide variety of broadcast television fare. The very popular "reality" TV shows, for example, are quasi-documentaries with a lot of show biz added.

A corporate video may be a documentary in the sense that it *documents* how a product is made or how a company performs a business service. Even so, it will likely be 100% scripted from the beginning. It is communicating facts and information to the audience, but everything about it can be known in advance. As with a drama, for this kind of project it's necessary to write the complete script before anything is shot. At the other end of the spectrum, a film covering an expedition to the Amazon jungles would be expected to be very different from any script that could be written before the shooting takes place.

Remember, these elements are the same for any film, from a 20-second comedy bit for *YouTube* to a Hollywood epic. It's only a matter of size.

The Vision

The treatment and script together convey your "vision" of the film. Creating these documents will be a brain-stretching exercise that will force you to confront not only the subject of your film, but also help you visualize what the film will look like. Unlike feature films, documentaries rarely make use of *storyboards* as visualization aids. Still, having a clear vision of the film as a whole will be a guiding light that will help with the many decisions you'll have to make throughout the production process.

Your vision is the key to your project's communicating with the audience, to telling a good story. Whatever the subject, the film has the potential to bring the audience drama, suspense, surprise, humor, delight, shock, distress, horror, amazement, satisfaction, knowledge, persuasion and even enlightenment. Your vision is a very private, inexpressible incarnation of the film and your passion for it. It must be thought about, cultivated and nurtured to ultimately be expressed in the finished product. While it's almost impossible for one person to create a film working alone, *good* films are the product of *one clear vision*.

Filmmaking is inherently collaborative, involving groups of people working closely together toward a common goal. Being able to clearly communicate your vision to others can be your most important skill in moving the project smoothly toward completion. Remember: collaboration is not the same as democracy – someone must always make the final decisions.

"You can't truly teach without entertaining and you can't truly entertain without teaching."

Anonymous

1.2 Who's Your Audience?

"Condense some daily experience into a glowing symbol, and an audience is electrified."

Ralph Waldo Emerson

In the television business, there used to be an easy answer to this question: Whoever's watching when the show hits the air. Not anymore. Today, the question has gotten harder to answer. The digital age has brought with it a plethora of new ways to get your film in front of an audience. Viewership is becoming increasingly fragmented as channels and delivery mechanisms proliferate and more and more "niche" audiences are being carved out. The Internet has added new pathways to audiences with streaming video being made available to a vast number of potential viewers. Because the proliferating sites offering video also offer search capabilities, viewers are increasingly able to find the kind of content they personally prefer.

Thus, your subject matter will directly affect what kind of viewer might find your film interesting and entertaining. A documentary about a celebrity, for example, may have very wide, general audience appeal and be suitable for broadcast, satellite, cable, DVD and/or Internet release. It may work locally, nationally or internationally. If your subject is more esoteric, you will need to focus on designing it with a more targeted approach to reach an audience of more exotic tastes.

Dramatic films could find their way to television or theaters; they are also viable for DVD and international release. Corporate and training videos generally have pre-defined (and sometimes captive) audiences: stockholders, employees, customers, and potential customers. Music videos could end up anywhere, even on your iPod or phone. Programs in any of these categories require the same creativity and storytelling skills, whatever the audience.

What's the Right Length?

Alfred Hitchcock simplified the answer to this question: "The length of a film should be directly related to the endurance of the human bladder."

I'll add my own quotation to this: "It's a rare film that can't be improved by making it shorter." As an editor, one thing I've always wanted to do (but haven't – yet) is to cut *Gone with the Wind* down to a normal two-hours. While I have always thought it's a remarkable piece of work, in the many times I've watched it I haven't once gotten through it without thinking at some point, "Is this thing *ever* going to end?"

The enigma of length becomes especially acute when you have a personal involvement in the project. Sometimes it's tough to make the decision to leave things out that you worked so hard to get in the first place, and the closer you are to the project the more difficult these decisions become. So we come back to the story: If it doesn't advance the story, leave it out.

For several years, I had the task of producing a film for the employees of a large corporation. This annual show was a "State of the Company" message from management, intended to covey news and information about recent developments, products and services as well as some human-interest stories. The target length was fifteen minutes and time was reserved in each of the company's many facilities for employees to watch – a captive audience. Management attached great importance to its message and scheduled viewings by all the employees on the same day.

The first few years, the film came very close to the target length, running twelve to fourteen minutes, but one time the final cut came out at eighteen. I showed it to the client for approval, and he seemed delighted with the way it turned out. Then he asked, "How long is it?" When I told him, he immediately retorted that it must be cut to no more than fifteen minutes. I reassured him that the extra length wouldn't affect the cost of making copies and that I really didn't know what could be cut, continuing to suggest that we go with it "as-is". "Can't do it," he replied. "Do you have any idea what it costs to pay 80,000 people for three minutes?" Needless to say, we found the three minutes to cut.

Sometimes program length is even less flexible. For PBS broadcast, for example, a nominal 30-minute show is specified as 26:46, or 56:46 for a 1-hour slot. Other broadcasters have similar requirements and it's obviously important to be aware of these and other technical requirements before you start production.

Other considerations about program length have to do with attention span: How long can you retain your audience's attention? How compelling is your content? How interested is the audience in your subject? A sales video can rarely run more than five minutes; a program for kids longer than three minutes might be too long or may need to be divided into digestible "chunks". Feature films can be two or three hours, but still can rivet their audience's attention. If you're lucky enough to be working on a subject that holds a lot of appeal for a large audience segment, the best rule for length might be: "It's as long as it needs to be, but *no longer.*"

Then, the question becomes: How long does it take to tell your story? Remember, shorter is better. You want to leave the audience begging for more, not praying for the end.

I have a pet theory that there is a right size for just about everything. Chairs, tables and doors are about the same size wherever you go just because they are the size they need to be to fit the human scale. Drinking glasses tend to hold about eight ounces; novels are around three hundred pages. In the film business, Thomas Edison's choice of 35mm as the right size for film has stuck with us for over a century; it is used for probably 95% of film projection all over the world in spite of the availability of larger and smaller gauges, simply because it is the right size. Feature-length films average around two hours, TV sitcoms and game shows are usually thirty minutes and most commercials are thirty or sixty seconds. True documentaries seem to cluster somewhere between a half hour and an hour.

Going back to the concept that shorter is better, on several occasions, I've had the opportunity to create two versions of a film, the original longer one and a "condensed" version. Almost without exception, audiences have seemed to give more enthusiastic reception to the shorter one. While making two versions will obviously take more time and effort, it can be a good exercise in giving your audience "the best of the best" and helps you view your project from a more detached perspective.

The Viewing Environment

Where is your epic going to be seen? Perhaps it will be enjoyed in the comfort of an evening living room or home theater experience. Maybe it will be shown in theaters. Corporate videos are often seen in conference rooms or classrooms. Maybe it will be seen only on a computer screen. Films are also watched in unpredictable places, using portable media players and mobile phones.

Keep in mind that if the viewing environment includes distractions, it will be hard for your audience to find the time or maintain the attention span to watch a long film. A dark, moody film may be hard to watch in a brightly lit room. By considering the viewing environment, you can better tailor the length and look of your film to fit the audience.

1.3 Adopting a Style

"Never offend people with style when you can offend them with substance."

Sam Brown, Washington Post

There are almost as many styles as there are films. Inevitably, your subject matter will have a bearing on the style you select. The styles covered here are only the basics, and any of them can be serious, light-hearted, comedic, scholarly, highly structured or free form. They aren't based on textbook definitions, but are merely broad categories; you certainly don't have to choose any one of them. In fact, many of the best films will use a mix, choosing what's appropriate for any particular part of the subject matter.

Driving with Narration

In the days when 16mm film was the dominant medium for non-theatrical films, the cameras were fairly portable and easy to handle, some comparable in weight and size to current video camcorders. Early sound recording equipment, on the other hand, was bulky, required power and introduced the then-difficult requirement that the camera run at a constant, precise speed to maintain lip-sync. The simple and popular spring-wound 16mm cameras weren't suitable for sound work because of their imprecise speed and, even more importantly, the amount of noise they made. Recording sound in the field also required more people, often a sound recordist, a boom operator and possibly an assistant responsible for doing the "slates" and "clap sticks". While a few cameras were capable of recording sound-on-film, higher quality sound required an external recorder that was capable of maintaining "sync" with the film. During editing, each take had to be "synced-up" with the picture, a long and laborious process.

To overcome these obstacles (and because of the costs), sound was often an afterthought; footage accompanied by narration became the norm. Interviews (if done at all) were shot in a controlled location where lip-sync sound recording could be easily done. Due to the lack of location sound, music became an important sound element, along with enough sound effects to give some impression that sound had been recorded on-location. Documentaries made this way became a unique art form and an enduring part of film culture, largely made possible by the skill of the sound editor, perhaps the most underrated artist in the business.

Even with today's excellent digital camcorders with high quality audio capabilities, sound recording in the field can still be problematic. The chapters on sound will cover these issues in more detail, and experience will teach you that there are many cases where sound recorded in the field is far from ideal.

Subjects requiring archival footage or still images also lend themselves to being narration-driven. Often the footage may have no sound or what's there is inappropriate. Some great films have been made using mostly still images and carefully crafted narration and music tracks; Ken Burns' *The Civil War* is an excellent example.

Knowing in advance that a large part of your story is to be told by a narrator will guide you in choosing what to shoot. Strive to get footage that tells the story as visually as possible, minimizing what the narrator has to say. Give your editor as much good material as possible. While film can cost $100 a minute or more to shoot, digital video is extremely cheap.

In the chapter on writing, we'll discuss some narration "dos" and "don'ts".

The On-Camera Guide

Sometimes called "on-camera narrator", this documentary style uses a personality or "presenter" to carry the audience through the story and it has become popular in the video age. Using an on-camera guide is a great way to handle subjects that don't involve many people, or are about dead people of whom there is little or no footage. By putting the narrator in locations that are significant to the story, you can gain a "sense of place" as well as exploiting the talents of the presenter. This technique can open up an otherwise dry subject and give you footage to cover information that you might not be able to easily illustrate otherwise.

On the down side, a presenter must be exceptionally talented to pull off the role of on-camera guide. Ideally, you should use an experienced actor who is willing to do a lot of rehearsal, and who is able to memorize long monologues and deliver them convincingly. If you choose to use this style, be very careful in choosing the talent because the entire film's success depends on him or her.

The Interview

Most documentaries include interviews in some form, and these often serve as the foundation for telling the story. The interviewees should be experts on your subject and should be chosen for their knowledge, intelligence, clarity of expression, appearance and, of course, their willingness to be in your film. Time spent in finding the right subjects for your interviews will pay off handsomely. It's helpful to do interviews as early as possible in the shooting process because of what you'll learn from your interviewees. If you've chosen them well, they can point you in the direction of new information and more things to shoot.

The interviewer is rarely shown in the classic documentary, unless he happens to be a celebrity. In fact, seeing the interviewer and hearing his questions might be a distraction.

In addition to the obvious logistics necessary to shoot an interview, preparation of questions and background ideas is essential. If you haven't met the interviewee before the shoot, it's helpful to learn something about him or her personally. Whether used in the film or not, it is good to start the interview by asking about some personal details. This can help make the person feel more comfortable with you (or the interviewer) and with the camera. It's also a good opportunity to be sure you have the right spelling of the person's name, his or her title and organizational affiliation. Also ask how he would like to be identified – wound he prefer "William K. Smith, Jr." or just "Bill Smith"?

Let the person know that he's part of the effort to make the film as good as possible, and ask him to suggest questions that he may think would contribute to the story. Also, it's good to help him understand that he should try to make his answers as concise as possible. Here are a few things interviewees often do that can be avoided with a little coaching before the camera rolls:

"Yes" and "no" answers don't help. Ask them to include the question in their answer. For example, if you ask, "Do you think Thomas Jefferson was a major driving force in making this country a democracy?" a good answer (instead of just "no") might be, "Thomas Jefferson was not a major driving force in making this country a democracy. In fact, Jefferson has been quoted as saying, 'Don't ever let this republic become a democracy.'"

In most cases, it's best to have the interviewee directly address the interviewer, *not* the camera. The interviewer should be seated a bit to the left or right of the camera and the subject should maintain eye contact with the interviewer. If his eyes wander around, especially looking at and away from the camera, he will look uncomfortable and perhaps even "shifty-eyed".

Ask the person to try to avoid phrases like "as I said", "as you said earlier", or "as I mentioned before". Whatever these phrases refer to may not be in the finished film, or may actually be heard later by the viewer, and thus can be confusing for the viewer and a nightmare for the editor.

Sometimes two or three people are interviewed at the same time – husband and wife or tennis doubles champions. In these cases, it's good to instruct the subjects on what to do when they're not the one answering a question. They should look at whoever is talking, either the interviewer or the person answering. It can make them look disinterested or even dumb to be looking at the camera or out into space. Of course, the camera operator should try to cover the person speaking individually, where possible.

Drama

While it's far beyond the scope of this book to attempt to teach you how to make a feature film, it's important to understand the dramatic film and be able to use some of the techniques that have been established over the hundred-plus years of its history.

The Hollywood studio "system" was developed and exquisitely refined to create dramatic films, movies developed as screenplays and using actors to portray the parts of characters. Early motion pictures trace their history to stage plays or skits that were simply performed in front of a fixed camera. Over time, editing became a critical part of filmmaking and directors developed more-or-less "standard" ways of covering scenes and interpreting screenplays. To teach aspiring filmmakers these methods, film schools were established and feature filmmaking became a true art form. With the coming of sound, the motion picture was able to encompass a variety art forms; it required writing, acting, music, graphic arts, painting, sculpture and many other creative elements. Most of the traditions of dramatic filmmaking were firmly established by the 1930s.

Early features were shot on great sound stages, cavernous warehouse-like structures with thick, soundproof walls. Here it was possible to create huge sets to simulate almost any environment and provide a great deal of control over the entire shooting process. The film stocks available at the time required huge amounts of light and the equipment was bulky and heavy. Cameras were enclosed in lead-lined "blimps" to make them quiet enough for sound recording. One popular model was so heavy that it took four strong men just to put it on a tripod. Over many years, equipment became more lightweight and portable, film stocks became more light-sensitive, and shooting "on-location" became more practical. Even today, many upscale features are shot (at least partially) on sets and sound stages, because of the total control this gives the filmmaker.

In the digital age, we have cameras that can work in very low light levels and still produce pictures of excellent quality, and high definition cameras that provide quality that can (debatably) match motion picture film. Equally important, the new generation of cameras provide CD-quality sound recording capabilities and multiple soundtracks. These developments have the potential to greatly decrease the logistical complexity of the technical side of the production process.

Still, a feature-length dramatic film is a complicated piece of work. It must be guided totally by a shooting script that conveys every element of the setting, characters, scenes and dialog. As we see in the chapter on writing, a dramatic script format has evolved that is easy to read, contains all the necessary information in narrative form, and helps the reader visualize the final film.

A large part of any dramatic film consists of scenes with actors and dialog. In most cases, these scenes are shot using the classic "master and close-up" structure. In a typical scene, the characters (say John and Marsha) may be seated at a table having a conversation. The director will usually shoot the entire scene from a camera position that includes both characters – this is called the *master shot*. Then, he'll shoot the entire scene again for each character, a series of *close-ups*. He may further augment the scene by shooting over-the-shoulder shots of each character, or perhaps moving camera shots to point up key elements of the scene or to follow the action. This fundamental method of shooting dramatic content gives the editor great flexibility in how the scene can be assembled into a flowing series of shots that tell the story.

The Music Video

MTV and VH-1 have made the music video a very popular form, a unique genre with its own subculture. The music itself is the foundation and story; the film must support and enhance the musical experience. It is a visual interpretation of a song, but the music always comes first. Music videos have an enormous range of styles and possibilities subject only to the collective imaginations of filmmaker and musicians. Perhaps the first collection of music videos was Walt Disney's animated classical musical extravaganza, *Fantasia*, produced in 1940.

Since the song will always have been pre-recorded, creating a music video requires playback on the set or on-location so the performers can lip-sync, maintaining continuity and tempo. The logistics of playback have been made a lot easier in the Digital Age. A simple way to handle it is to burn a CD of the complete song along with tracks that are individual song segments (first verse, second verse, bridge, etc.). An audible countdown or click-track at the beginning of the song, and a few beats before and after each verse are helpful for performers to get the tempo of the playbacks.

A well-designed CD and a simple boom box are probably all you need for playback, or use your iPod (or other MP3 player) and an external amplifier. Because CD or iPod playback speed is inherently very accurate, you should have no problems maintaining sync with the video. Don't use that old cassette player for this purpose. They're notorious for speed variations, especially as the batteries begin to approach the end of their life.

When shooting, be sure the camera has a microphone attached so the editor has a record of the playback for reference purposes, and be sure the editor gets a copy of the CD. This will help make sure your editor doesn't need the additional skill of lip-reading.

You'll want to shoot a variety of angles of each segment, stretching your creativity and, most importantly, giving your editor a wide range of choices. In many ways, the editor makes or breaks a music video, so get one with a good sense of rhythm and who is willing to experiment and try a lot of different ways to do the cut – a lot can be gained by "cut and try".

Other Styles

There are countless other styles and sub-styles, of course – travelogues, infomercials, panel discussions, comedy, sitcoms, how-to guides and varieties of so-called "electronic journalism", not to mention films that could simply be classified as "TV shows".

Of course there are also "styles without a style", such as Cinéma Vérité, Direct Cinema, Method, Guerilla and Zen Filmmaking. While some (wishfully) think these styles don't require pre-production and can be totally spontaneous, any film can benefit from careful planning.

Commercials (or TV *spots*) represent an art form that has evolved quite independently from the rest of the industry; indeed spotmaking is an industry in itself. "Spotters" will be the first to tell you that a commercial is, in fact, a "mini-movie" with the mission of communicating, influencing, motivating, enlightening, informing and entertaining in sixty seconds or less. Thousands of commercial-makers have used the genre as a steppingstone to the film business; thousands more have made it a fulfilling and lucrative career.

Choosing a style could also mean creating your own style. Digital filmmaking is in many ways a new art form, distinctly different from legacy art. By all means, experiment!

"In matters of style, swim with the current; in matters of principle, stand like a rock."

Thomas Jefferson

1.4 Legal Issues

"Lawyers spend a great deal of their time shoveling smoke."
Oliver Wendell Holmes, Jr.

I feel compelled to begin this chapter with a disclaimer: I am not a lawyer, and nothing written here should be construed by the reader to be legal advice. Any information about legal issues contained herein should be strictly considered to be nothing more than the author's humble and non-expert opinion.

Consult your attorney for legal advice when and where you may need it, and if your project is at all complex or intended for distribution to the general public, at some point you *will* need a lawyer. You are also going to need insurance--unless you are so poor as to have no assets to protect, and simultaneously have no desire to become otherwise. Because this book is about filmmaking and not about law, we can only scratch the surface of this complex field.

Frankly, I would have preferred to leave this chapter out altogether, but legal issues have become so important to filmmaking, I felt compelled to put up a few warning signs at the beginning of the road.

You Must Be This Tall to Ride

Be warned that there are myriad potential legal pitfalls ready to wreck your film and negate your hard work. Paralleling the technological progress of the Digital Age, the legal areas of filmmaking have become increasingly difficult, murky and complex. In today's climate, litigation is always a possibility and becoming increasingly likely to occur. The lack of clarity in copyright laws, in particular, makes it virtually impossible to avoid potential legal entanglements. If your film is unsuccessful, you have little to worry about, but if it happens to be a major success, a hoard of lawyers will most certainly be beating a path to your door. The more success, the more lawyers.

Most of your legal worries will be about liability with regard to "intellectual property" – copyrights, and (to a lesser degree) trademarks and patents. Since 1989, fixing anything you create in tangible form (on paper, tape, disk or any other physical medium) makes that work your copyrighted property automatically, and the same is true for everybody else. Every note you write, every email, every picture you take, and every frame of video is technically copyrighted, whether you want it to be or not. No longer is it necessary to "register" your work with the Copyright Office, although it's still possible and desirable to do so. No longer do you need to attach a copyright notice to your work, though it is certainly advisable to do so.

Suppose you wrote a long letter to a friend ten years ago describing a movie plot and characters. Now suppose that note fell into the hands of a Hollywood screenwriter, and a blockbuster movie was made using your story. In that case, it is quite possible that you would have a claim against the writer or studio for copyright infringement. Because of possibilities of this kind (and myriad similar ones), Hollywood maintains armies of lawyers who spend their expensive time trying to make sure that every detail of every production is properly cleared and intensively researched to avoid such litigation. Simultaneously, other lawyers are scrutinizing everybody else's work to be sure the studios' intellectual property is protected from possible infringement. Concerns in this area represent the main reason why Hollywood studios will rarely even read unsolicited scripts.

Amazingly (and sadly), the legal aspects of a production can absorb a substantial portion of the available financial resources. Yet, in spite of lawyers' best efforts, it is utterly impossible to completely protect intellectual property and it is equally impossible to avoid potential infringement of someone else's intellectual property. All you can do is try to minimize the risk. How you do that depends on your ability to balance the amount of money you want to spend on lawyers against how much risk you're willing to take. Sometimes failing to take risks can compromise the artistic integrity of your film. Taking blatant risks (like trying to do a re-make of "Star Wars") could make your film a legal nuclear bomb.

What Are The Intellectual Property Risks?

Unfortunately, the risks are everywhere and it's very hard to tell which ones are real and which ones are not. One of my favorite illustrations of how outlandish copyright claims can sometimes get comes from the third page of my very old and tattered office dictionary. It reads, in part:

"Copyright © 1984 ... All rights reserved. No part of this work...may be reproduced or copied in any form or by any means--graphic, electronic, or mechanical including photocopying, taping, or information storage and retrieval systems...without written permission of the publisher."

What does this really mean? Do I need written permission to use words from this book? Does it mean what it literally says, that I cannot write any of the words in this dictionary in any order (reproducing the book "in part") without infringing the copyright on this "work"? Does it mean I'm committing infringement of the worst kind because every word I have used here is also in (and presumably copied from) the aforementioned copyrighted publication? Can I legally use dictionary words in speech if I don't write them? Can I use them in my film? Is a recording of the spoken words a violation? How about the glowing words on my computer screen? And have I violated the copyright because my brain is an information storage and retrieval system (well... sort of)?

It gets worse. There's no end to the questions that can be raised. It's obvious that certain sequences of words (like the ones in this book, for example) can be copyrighted. Music is copyrighted, so are works of art. Trademarks and service marks can be both registered and copyrighted. Then, buried in copyright law and court cases is a thing called "derivative works" – the idea that a copyright can be infringed by something similar that may have been derived from a work. Yet the law doesn't say in concrete terms what "derivative" really means. (Is the ABC Network aware that their evening news theme is remarkably similar to the Circus March used in Disney's *Dumbo*? Since Disney owns ABC, does it matter?)

Is a photograph of a building a derivative work and therefore infringes the architect's copyright on the design, even though the photograph is clearly neither an actual building nor a blueprint? Am I ever given notice that the design is copyrighted? These points may seem argumentative or trivial until you realize that we are surrounded by objects covered by copyrights. The designs of the clothes you're wearing are probably copyrighted, and possibly protected by trademarks and patents as well. So are virtually all of the publications on your library shelves, as are the thousands of product slogans (and they're covered by trademark law, too).

The filmmaker's problem is both acute and overwhelmingly complex. Any story you decide to use in your film will be "similar" in some way to one or more other stories. Almost anywhere you try to shoot will potentially have copyrighted "works" in the foreground or in the background. (Your actors will be wearing clothing, won't they?) Fortunately, this kind of "incidental" and "potential" copyright infringement is *usually* harmless. "Usually", because in copyright law there are always exceptions.

Under current law, your script is automatically copyrighted as soon as you write it; your film is copyrighted as soon as it is shot. Still, it is worthwhile to register the copyright on your script with the US Copyright Office, or at the very least send a copy of it to yourself registered mail, return receipt requested. These steps will let you prove in court (should it ever be necessary) that your film is, in fact, an original work and your property.

What is Fair Use?

Incidental appearances of copyrighted elements in another work are often covered by what is called *Fair Use*. Under Fair Use, courts and judges take into account four aspects of use:

- The purpose and character of the use,
- The nature of the copyrighted work,
- The amount and sustainability of the portion taken,
- The effect of the use on the potential market.

Each of these points merits some discussion. Courts rely heavily on whether a work is simply copied or used to create something new, so they look closely at the "why" factor: Why did you use the work? If it was to enhance a concept, especially one that was not possible without the use of the copyrighted work, it may influence the court to consider it a fair use. If you are simply copying a work and selling the copies, that's obviously not fair use.

The nature of the copyrighted work also has a major bearing on whether your use is fair. Informational content is of greater value the more it is disseminated to the public, so drawing from such content is more likely to be ruled fair use than using portions of fictional works. In addition, using published material is more likely to be fair use because an author is always entitled to control the *first* public use or publication of his expression.

The third point simply means that the less you take the more likely your use is fair. On the other hand, it may not be fair use if you use the "core" of a work. If Charles Dickens still held a copyright on "A Christmas Carol", you'd dare not use the phrase, "God bless us, every one." Parodies have been considered exceptions to this rule, however, since parodies are aimed at the heart. "God bless us, every one--except you, Scrooge!" might very well be fair use.

The fourth point essentially asks the question, "Does your use adversely affect the copyright owner economically, or affect the economic *potential* of his work?" If the answer to this question is "yes" then the use is probably not fair. Certainly, if the copyright owner perceives that he is harmed by your use, he is entitled to defend his rights and seek damages from you. For example, if you make a film from a short story, your film may not adversely affect the sales of a book containing the story (you may even enhance those sales). By adapting the story, however, you may have deprived the author of the potential to sell the screen rights and you may deprive him of royalties he may have received from another filmmaker. Thus, this is not fair use.

There is also a concept called "de minimus", referring to content too small or distorted or shown for too short a time to be recognizable, like inclusion of a beverage can in a shot that might be a Coke or a Budweiser – all you can tell is that it's mostly red, unless you look at individual frames. Fleeting and unclear images *usually* constitute fair use.

Remember, too, that judges and courts are human beings. As such, they unavoidably have a sense of what's good and what's bad. If they think your use is bad, you are at a distinct disadvantage. If they perceive that your heart's in the right place, they may be inclined to be more lenient and understanding. Hopefully, of course, your case will never get to court. Unfortunately, however, only a court can legally establish whether your use is legally fair, and by the time it gets to court, it may be too late.

While a film producer must be very careful about depending on the Fair Use as a defense for using copyrighted material, common sense tells you that copyright infringement must probably be blatant and voluntary for the copyright owner to consider legal action. Remember, though, that some copyright holders defend their property vigorously while others may take a more permissive attitude. When in doubt, it's probably best to secure a license from the copyright holder, but always be aware that merely seeking permission can sometimes backfire.

Permissions and Clearances

Getting permission to use copyrighted material can be hard work, and carries its own risks. First, you'll have to locate the copyright owner, and since a work doesn't have to be registered, that may prove difficult. Every work is covered by copyright law, but there is no useful central registry or database to search. Copyrights can also be transferred, sold and re-sold, so there's no assurance that the original author is still the owner. Remember, too, that a work is likely protected whether or not there is a copyright notice. There are firms out there whose specialty is locating copyright owners and getting licenses, so if you can afford their services it's a relatively painless way to go. Remember, getting formal clearance to use a work and properly licensing it is the only *safe* way to use any copyrighted work. Equally important, if you don't have proper clearances on everything you use, you may have difficulty getting insurance, financing or distribution for your film.

Don't think that you can't be sued because your film is for non-profit or educational use. The likelihood that a copyright owner will seek damages from a non-commercial infringer is lower than from someone who is using their work to make a profit, but the rights of the owner and the fact of infringement are no different.

Some people believe that if they acknowledge or attribute the use of a work they can use it, that this is automatically fair use or automatically cleared. Not true. Attribution is a courtesy only, unless the copyright owner has specifically provided otherwise. An acknowledgement does, however, indicate your good faith and that you're not attempting to hide the fact that you're using a copyrighted (or potentially copyrighted) work. On the other hand, it's an admission that you know it is copyrighted and that you knew to whom it belongs. It's a balancing act, and you're wise to tread cautiously.

The Public Domain

Eventually, copyrights expire, and every published work will someday become part of the "public domain"; it will belong to the public and be usable by anyone. Lawmakers seem to be in the habit of extending the term of copyrights, however. In the United States, copyrights have expired for all works published before 1923, so there is a wealth of material that has entered the public domain – material that is free for anyone to use any way they want. There are also some works published between 1923 and 1964 that have fallen into the public domain because their copyrights were not renewed under the law in effect at the time. Once in awhile an author will decide to simply give his work to the public, and will include a statement such as, "This work is dedicated to the public domain." Any of these works are fair game. In 2019, works published in 1923 will fall into the public domain, those published in 1924 will be free in 2020, and so forth – until Congress decides to change the law again.

Be aware that just because you are able to get a work "for free" doesn't mean that it's in the public domain. It may still have copyright protection and you could still be sued for using it. An exception to this is anything published by the US Government. Ordinarily, Government documents are automatically in the public domain.

Sometimes filmmakers fall into a copyright trap with music they want to use. For example, the works of Mozart are in the public domain, since he was certainly not an American citizen and died in 1791. While the music itself might be free, it's quite likely that any *recording* of the music is *not* in the public domain, since recordings and performances are covered under a separate area of copyright law. If you must use Mozart, it's perfectly fine for you to include your own kazoo rendition of *Eine Kleine Nacht Musik* in your film, but don't use the Chicago Symphony's recording of it.

Releases

If you use a person's image, name or voice, you may need a formal release from that person. A release simply means that the person agrees not to sue you. If you're making a film for commercial purposes, you almost certainly need a release from each person who appears in it. The law makes exceptions for so-called "informational" use, so a person's image may be used on a newscast, for example, without a formal release. As with permissions, it's better to be safe than sorry. Since the people in your film will be available during the shoot, getting releases from each of them is a worthwhile investment of a little extra time.

When releases are not obtained and things get sticky, courts have sometimes ruled in filmmakers' favor because of "implied consent". This means that the very fact that the person appears in the film in a way that it was obvious he was aware he was being photographed and recorded, he must have consented. In spite of this, however, many distribution organizations will require signed releases before they will take your film.

You will often need releases and/or permits for locations, too.

Insurance

Like the subject of intellectual property, insurance for film and video is a very complex field and many volumes have been written about it. Here are a few hints about the insurance that you might need to cover yourself while making a film. Being mindful of the need for various kinds of insurance will help you determine what kinds of coverage you require and how much risk you will have to take. Just as it's almost impossible to cover every possibility of copyright infringement, you simply cannot buy enough insurance to cover every possible risk or contingency.

Insurance is not just for your protection, either. Locations where you may want to shoot often require certain minimum levels of insurance, and may require you to contact your insurance company and have them named as the "loss payee" or "additional insured" in the event insurance coverage is actually needed. Equipment rental houses also have similar requirements.

The insurance you may need to carry includes some or all of the types described briefly here.

- Workman's Compensation Insurance -- protects people working on your film in the event of personal injury.
- Employer's Liability -- protects you as the employer from liability should an employee claim damages from your negligence or other causes. It also protects you from liability created by an employee working on your behalf.
- Commercial General Liability -- protects you from liability from other potential damages, such as your accidentally blowing up the wrong car while shooting your big chase scene.
- Automobile Liability – Required in most states just to legally operate an automobile.
- Errors and Omissions – Protects from potential intellectual property issues, for example. You could be sued because you got permission to use a photograph and it turns out the one you used and the one you licensed were actually different pictures.
- Umbrella Liability – An extra policy that essentially covers "everything else" in the event damages exceed those covered by other insurance.
- Negative Coverage – Protects your original film negatives, tapes, disks, etc., in the event of loss requiring a re-shoot or abandonment of the project.
- Property of Others – Provides coverage, for example, of the valuable fur coat you borrowed from your neighbor to be worn by your leading lady.
- Valuable Papers and Records – Protects valuable documents and computer files related to your production.

- Key Personnel – Life and/or health insurance that may be needed to cover people like the director or key cast members whose death or disability could wreck the film.

There are many more kinds of insurance and other instruments related to filmmaking, such as performance and completion bonds. You can contact your local insurance agent for information about most of these products, but if you're getting serious about filmmaking, you would do well to contact a broker who specializes in insurance for the motion picture or television industry.

If your film is simple and self-financed and you're not rich, you may want to consider foregoing extra insurance and taking your chances. While I can't recommend that you proceed that way, many beginning filmmakers have gotten started by taking the risks. The choice, of course, is up to you.

"Kill all the lawyers!"

William Shakespeare

1.5 What Will it Cost?

"Money never starts an idea;
it is the idea that starts the money."
W. J. Cameron

Since you've gotten this far, the preceding chapters have probably started you thinking at least a little about money. The coming of the Digital Age has certainly made the technology required for filmmaking much more affordable, but the costs of many of the other pieces that go into the production puzzle have increased.

It's been said that the hardest part of making a film is not making the film. It's making the *deal.* In other words, coming up with funding to cover production and especially distribution can be the most difficult and time-consuming part of the process. Every completed film, no matter how simple or complex, has been funded somehow, by someone. Feature films can cost in the hundreds of millions of dollars and it's not unusual for network TV shows to cost millions for a single one-hour episode. At these production levels, costs work out to be somewhere in the range of $15,000 and $1 million plus *per screen minute.* Documentaries tend to cost less, maybe $3,000 to $15,000 per minute, although it's certainly possible to do quality work on much lower budgets, sometimes even a budget that approaches zero.

Costing-Out and Budgeting

Before you can go looking for money, you need to have some idea of what it's going to cost to make your film, so you will need to go through the process of "costing-out" the production. No production company would ever commit to creating a film without knowing how much it's going to cost, and certainly no bank or investor will offer you money without knowing how much you need and what you need it for.

It's also true that everyone wants the most for their money; the lower the production cost the more likely it is that your film can be funded and completed. This isn't to say that you should cut costs to the point that your film is seriously compromised. Certainly, you wouldn't want to take people off the street and try to use them as actors just because professional actors can be expensive. Still, you can intelligently minimize costs by good design and being realistic about your expectations. There are minimum levels of quality and production value that must be met if your film is to be successful, either commercially or artistically.

So how do you cost-out your production? How do you arrive at a realistic budget? You can begin by dividing your expenses into manageable categories. Traditionally, expenses are first divided into *above-the-line* and *below-the-line areas*. The "line" itself is a broad one, but here's how it usually falls:

Above-the-line costs include the elements of producing and performing, such as the primary talent (actors), script, director, music, office services, lawyers, clearance costs, accountants, etc.

Below-the-line items include the physical and service elements of the production, such as sets, props, wardrobe, transportation, equipment, supplies, facilities, editing, etc. Also in this category are production technical personnel (cinematographer, camera operator, sound recordist, grips, gaffers and other support labor). Sometimes supporting actors, extras, stunt people, etc. are also included in below-the-line expenses.

Once you have a general idea of what the above- and below-the-line items are, you can break the costs out into more succinct sub-categories.

Here's a list of many of them; your list will be longer or shorter:

- Writing and script acquisition
- Producer, director, art director, creative
- Research
- Legal costs
- Insurance and permits
- Production office expenses
- Location scouting and related costs
- Location expenses
- Set design and construction/studio facilities
- Props
- Wardrobe
- Tape, disk and/or film stock
- Production crew costs
- Equipment rentals
- Editing
- Graphics and animation
- Special effects
- Soundtrack production
- Music
- Advertising and promotion
- Miscellaneous and contingencies

Once you have assembled an appropriate list of expense categories, you can put them into a spreadsheet and begin to develop a more-or-less reasonable production budget. From there, you will see which items are reasonable and which must be cut.

The objective of costing-out your film may be different for one genre of film than for another. For example, if you are doing a documentary, you may have to design it around a fixed budget amount that you might be receiving from a grant. Similarly, a training film might have to fit into a budget based on how much the company commissioning the film has historically paid for similar productions.

For the rest of this chapter, let's assume your goal is to make a high-quality low-budget film – isn't that what everybody really wants? To realistically reach this goal, let's retrieve our list and talk about some of the items in more detail.

Writing and script acquisition
Producer, director, art director, creative fees
Research

The cost of these items can range from zero to millions of dollars. At the low end, you could write your own script, do your own re-writes, do the research, be the producer/director, and waive any fees for your work. At the high end, you could budget to acquire rights to a best-selling novel, hire a high-paid Hollywood screenwriter to create a screenplay adaptation, and hire the best talent in Hollywood to do the rest. The truth must lie somewhere between these two extremes.

I have worked on several documentaries on which I was the writer, producer and director, personally did all the research (with a little help from my friends) and even edited the film. Even so, these important aspects of the productions weren't accomplished at zero cost. My production company paid me a salary while I was doing all this work, and I had significant expenses for travel, lodging, meals, books, and lots of other little things that all added up. The company also provided the equipment and facilities, booked for times when they weren't otherwise occupied. This was a viable way to get the work done because I was lucky enough and experienced enough to do a reasonably professional job in these areas.

On other projects, I've taken a hybrid approach. I might create a first draft or outline of a script, and then turn it over to a writer skilled in the subject matter for "polishing". Sometimes I have had an assistant gather research material for me to simplify the process and give me more time for the actual work. I've also found subject matter experts (in some cases the authors of some of my research materials) who have been willing to help for a small honorarium or even just for a screen credit. Of course, volunteer production assistants, usually students interested in getting a "feel" for the business have always been welcome – and they are inexpensive or free.

Sometimes you will need to separate the "mission critical" jobs from the not-so-essential ones. The integrity and quality of your film rests squarely on the shoulders of the producer and the artists. If you don't have (or can't acquire) the skills you need to perform any of these functions, hire someone who can. Follow the old rule: Hire someone better than yourself to do a particular job. Keep in mind that there are ways to pay people besides cold cash. Sometimes a division of shares or profit sharing arrangement can be negotiated to let you be able to acquire really good people without a heavy up-front expenditure.

Legal costs
Insurance and permits
Production office expenses

In any serious production effort, it's difficult to eliminate these costs, but there's a lot that can be done to reduce them. Most of these issues are covered in the preceding chapter.

One way to reduce legal and insurance costs is to form something called a "sacrificial corporation". Your lawyer can help you form a "Limited Liability Corporation" (LLC) to help protect your personal assets from liabilities associated with producing the film. The LLC becomes the entity that both produces and owns the film. As such, it assumes any liabilities incurred in the process. Generally, the LLC will have limited assets, often only the film itself, so the worst-case scenario might be that the corporation is sued and loses the film because of a judgment or settlement. Since liability is limited and personal risk is nearly eliminated, the LLC can carry substantially less insurance than would be required to adequately protect a larger entity with other assets. In other words, the LLC can afford to take more risks than an individual or company with other assets and interests. In some cases, the corporation can be designed to be a non-profit educational entity, possibly enhancing fair-use rights to intellectual property. Of course, there will be some legal costs in establishing the LLC in the first place, but it can be money well spent.

Acquiring permits may be hard to avoid, but it's possible to choose shooting locations where no permits are required. If permits are necessary, be aware that in order to get the permit, you may be compelled to provide proof of insurance. There are even ways around these issues. For example, suppose your script calls for two actors to be having a conversation on the Brooklyn Bridge (a location that requires a permit for shooting). If the scene is short and simple, it may be better to pose as a tourist and get some footage of the bridge as a "background plate", and then add your actors to the scene during editing – a special effect that might be much more affordable than actually shooting the scene on location. The technology of the Digital Age comes to the rescue.

Technology can also help with the production office item. You can form a "virtual office" so the people working on your film can collaborate via the Internet from almost anywhere, potentially a big money-saver. I have done a number of projects where essentially all of the "officing" can be done with email, file transfers and "instant messaging", even video conferencing.

In the Digital Age, of course, most of your documents will be electronic, even though you'll be printing a lot of them. If you aren't there already, you are going to want to "get geeky".

Location scouting and expenses
Set design and construction

For each of these categories, it's hard to beat a professional who has built a career dealing with one of these specialties. Still, costs for these items can be minimized with a bit of creativity and ingenuity. The locations chosen, of course, will depend on the story you're telling. Public locations like airports, museums, libraries, theaters, hotels and supermarkets will usually require a permit, or at least written permission to be used for shooting, and will often charge fees – sometimes steep ones. To avoid these locations, sometimes you can find another spot that can "double" for the real thing. An independently owned grocery store (or almost any kind of small business) can easily double for a large corporate-owned facility, and the owners may welcome the opportunity for a little excitement and a small gratuity for their trouble. Owners of private homes, too, are often amenable to opening their houses to a considerate and thoughtful film crew, sometimes even for free (especially if they've never hosted a film shoot before!)

Churches, too, offer opportunities; they are often used only a few hours a week. I've used the front entrance of a church to double as a courthouse, and I've shot in church offices. Private schools and colleges can also provide great settings, as can country and golf clubs, private hospitals, medical clinics, doctors', lawyers' and dentists' offices.

Sets and studios are often avoided entirely in low-budget productions, and certainly digital technology helps make it possible to do without them. Some projects, however, need sets to create the required imagery. Again, if you can afford it, you should hire a professional set designer, construction crew and sound stage. If that's not possible, local theater groups may be able offer attractive alternatives. They often have extensive prop-shops, shooting space and, sometimes, enthusiastic crews anxious to try their hand at film set construction. Using theater groups will require some educational efforts and attention to detail on your part since theatrical sets are rarely as realistic as film requires. Some theaters have adequate shooting space, too, or a carefully selected warehouse can double as a sound stage.

Remember, too, that digital technology can do a lot in helping with sets and locations. A very small set can be extended to be part of a much larger scene with skillful compositing. New software makes it possible to create a "virtual set", too – quite possibly a viable alternative to "real" sets.

Props
Wardrobe

Again, your story will dictate what props and wardrobe you'll need. For high-budget productions, props will be purchased or designed and built to the script's requirements. Costume designers can create wardrobe for all the actors – at great expense. If your film's timeframe is "present day", things get a lot easier. Everyday items ranging from beer cans to firearms to furniture can be obtained with relative ease, being either available for purchase or rental. Wardrobe, too, is easier, and often your actors can use their own clothes.

One of the greatest tricks I've ever learned may not be strictly ethical, but it's paid off for me on several occasions. It's simple: just purchase the necessary items a day or two before the shoot using your credit card. Then, a few days later, return them to the store for credit. It works great as long as the merchandise is undamaged and you carefully keep all the packing material (if applicable). If you want to be entirely up-front, make your purchases from small, independent retailers and tell them exactly what you're doing, even agreeing to pay a small "re-stocking" fee on the returned merchandise. If the re-stocking fee is about the same as the net profit a store might make on the items, it's a great deal for everybody. Merchants will often enjoy the opportunity to (in effect) sell merchandise twice, making a profit on both transactions.

For larger props, such as furniture, I've had great luck using furniture rental stores. You can simply rent the furniture you need and they will usually deliver it and pick it up when you're done. Usually there's a one-month minimum rental, which will cover most shooting schedules. Furniture stores, too, are sometimes open to short-term rentals if they understand what you're doing.

Vehicles are a special category of props, and in Hollywood and other film production centers, there are companies specializing in period and antique vehicles. Elsewhere in the country there are antique and classic car clubs whose members would love to see their prized cars used in a movie, usually for a modest fee, or even free. Sometimes owners of valuable classic cars don't want them to be driven by your actors, so you can design your shots so that the owner can be a double for your characters, or maybe the script can be "tweaked" so they can actually perform in the film as an extra or "bit" player.

Tape, disk and/or film stock

In the days when a film was really a film (shot on that stuff with sprocket holes in it), film stock was an expensive part of any production and careful consideration was given to the *shooting ratio* – the number of feet of film shot divided by the number of feet in the finished film. Since 35mm film runs through the camera at ninety feet per minute, the cost of film stock, processing and printing or transfers will be upwards of $100 per minute of film shot. For a modest shooting ratio of twenty to one (twenty minutes of film shot for every minute used in the final production), just the film can cost $2,000 per finished screen minute, or $240,000 for a 120-minute feature. A low-budget film producer needs to keep an ever-watchful eye on film stock consumption.

The Digital Age has virtually eliminated this burden. Even the most expensive digital videotape costs no more than about $1 a minute; DV or HDV-format tape costs less than .10 per minute – a 10,000% saving compared to 35mm film! Granted, 35mm film provides the ultimate in image quality (although some are beginning to argue this point), the quality difference is getting harder and harder to see, especially on the small screen.

This is a truly revolutionary change. Digital filmmakers can almost ignore the cost of "stock" on their overall bottom line, even for very low-budget productions and with high shooting ratios. At a shooting ratio of twenty to one, tape costs can be under $100 for a 120-minute finished film. Of course, digital tape, disk or memory can be re-used, so the net cost is potentially zero.

Production crew costs

Unlike the amazing cost savings the Digital Age has brought to the area of the recording medium, the crew is human and hasn't changed much over the history of filmmaking, except they (like everything else) have gotten more expensive.

While the producer, director and cast are not usually considered part of the production crew, almost everyone else is. A bare-bones crew might consist of three people: a videographer/director to do the shooting, a sound person to take care of recording the audio, and a gaffer/grip to do essentially everything else. Capable crew people to fill these positions can be found around the country, though rates can vary widely. Hollywood-level people will cost more. A crew list for a higher budget film might include (in addition to the three mentioned above) a director of photography (DP), camera assistant, microphone boom operator, makeup artist, wardrobe person, hair stylist, one or more additional grips, electricians and gaffers, dolly grip, several production assistants and more. The list could grow much longer for complex productions.

The best way to minimize crew costs is simply to keep the crew small, not by paying people less, unless you can find capable people who are interested enough in your film to be willing to work on your film for free or for below-market rates. Using inexperienced people with the intent of providing "on-the-job" training can also work, but it will certainly make your shooting schedule longer and could lead to mistakes that can cost you days of shooting, or worse.

I learned a valuable and expensive lesson about the importance of qualified crew people once when I was working on a film shoot. My assistant cameraman became ill, and I needed a replacement. Because of where we were shooting, I had the option of using a relatively inexperienced local person or flying in a more qualified assistant. I chose to use an inexperienced local who seemed bright enough and who had been around the business enough to seem confident in his abilities. During the shoot, he appeared to be doing well, loading the camera quickly and always ready to help in any way he could. But when the film came back from the lab, it was completely useless. Every time he had loaded the camera, he had done it incorrectly. As a result, we lost a full day of shooting and a lot of film stock, at a cost of thousands of dollars – all because I thought I was saving a few hundred dollars. In the filmmaking business, crew mistakes can be very expensive.

Equipment rentals

Depending on the scope of your project, you may choose to rent all the equipment you'll use. Every project, of course, requires a camera, and it makes no sense to buy one if you're only going to use it for a few days. For extended or multiple projects, however, purchasing a camera may make sense. Digital standard definition (SDTV) or high definition (HDTV) cameras come in an enormous range of prices and quality levels. Recent offerings from the major manufacturers in the sub-$5,000 range can deliver fully professional quality within their capabilities and are suitable for many projects. Even those with price tags under $1,000 can deliver acceptable pictures and excellent sound. For top-flight quality, however, you can spend $100,000 or more on a camera, and for some projects, it may not only be worth it, it may be a necessity. (In the chapter on technology, we'll discuss the ins and outs of choosing a camera.) In deciding whether to rent or buy, keep in mind that while a good camera can provide many years of excellent service, it will probably be obsolete long before it wears out. Consider whether it will be adequate not only for your current projects but for future projects as well.

In addition to the camera, some other equipment will be required for the duration of your shoot: a tripod, microphones, headphones, an audio mixer, a field monitor, and a complement of lighting instruments. For these items, you'll also need to make the purchase-or-rent decision. Almost certainly, however, there will be some items you'll want to rent. These will include specialized equipment that may be used only once or a few times during production, such as dollies, camera booms, Teleprompters, large lighting instruments, camera car rigs and the like. Early in the pre-production process, it's a good idea to form a relationship with one or more rental companies that specialize in the level of production you're contemplating. If you're lucky, you can find a local rental house that can give you a package deal on either on these extra items, or possibly on every item on your equipment list.

Editing

Editing and the other areas of post-production have historically represented a substantial portion of any project's budget. In the Digital Age, the cost of editing hardware has plummeted. Nevertheless, editing continues to be very labor-intensive and time-consuming. This means that whatever technology you choose, a lot of somebody's time will be required to complete your project, and time will be the biggest cost. For small projects, it's not unusual for the producer/director to become the producer/director/editor. Larger projects will need an editor and one or more assistants.

Traditionally, the editing process has been divided into two phases: *offline* and *online*. In classic motion picture production, offline is the process of assembling the elements of the film by an editor, using a *workprint*, a positive print of the original camera negative. More recently, the workprint has been replaced with an *electronic workprint* – a video transfer of the original negative.

Once the workprint has been edited, an *edit decision list* (EDL) or *cut list* is developed. A cut list contains the original film's *edge numbers* for each scene. (Edge numbers are printed on the edge of the film during manufacturing, and corresponding edge numbers appear on the workprint.) The original negative is cut to match the workprint, a process called *conforming*, *no*, or simply *negative cutting*. Final cutting of the negative is the online part of the process.

In the digital world, offline is the editing of some kind of reduced-quality version of the field footage. Online (or conforming) is the assembly of the program using full-quality versions of the original footage, using the EDL created during offline.

Separation of online and offline was mandatory in traditional film production, since cutting an original negative finalizes editorial decisions; it is very difficult to change your mind after your negative has been cut. In the digital world, the original footage is never physically cut, but is copied instead. Thus, the choice of creating separate offline and online versions of a program is determined by the cost (and to some extent other technical considerations).

In the Digital Age, the line between offline and online has become blurred. With computer editing systems, it is now feasible and preferable to simply edit the film in full resolution, so "when you're done, you're done." For most low-budget projects, all the editing can be done on a computer using low-cost software. (More about this in the chapter on editing.)

The final result of the editing process is some kind of "master". For an old-fashioned film, it might be the cut negative, a special copy called the "master positive", and one or more duplicate *internegatives* from which the final "release prints" are made. In the digital world, the "master" will be some kind of digital files, usually delivered on an appropriate disk or tape medium.

Graphics
Special Effects
Soundtrack Production

Even the simplest projects will need at least a few graphic elements – titles, credits, etc. At the other extreme, animated films (the subject of another book) are 100% graphics. For many projects, the titling tools included in the editing software are adequate, allowing for a do-it-yourself approach. Attractive, well-designed and animated graphics, however, can contribute to the "look" of your film and can take a significant slice of your budget.

Special effects can also add both production value and cost. Like most other elements of your film, effects require good design and pre-production planning. Mechanical or *practical* special effects are performed during shooting and include any effect that is complete once the shot is "in the can". Stunts can be considered special effects, and *stuntmen* (or women) and their equipment and props are included in this category.

Digital special effects (usually called *visual effects*) are created during post-production, and include compositing processes such as *bluescreen* or *greenscreen*. Again, recent software has the capability to accomplish a wide variety of tricks, and designing effects that can be easily created is key to keeping costs low.

Editing software (and complimentary audio processing software) comes to the rescue again in the area of sound. In many cases, the entire soundtrack can be edited, processed, mixed and output without leaving the editing environment. Some packages also allow narration recording and dialog replacement. While the production tools may be adequate, sound design is a specialized skill and bad sound is probably one of the most frequently encountered shortcomings in low-budget productions. These problems range from bad dialog recording to relying too much on "natural" sound effects recorded during shooting. My advice: don't shortchange your soundtrack in planning your budget. Corresponding to the improvements in digital video, sound equipment has become better and cheaper, but there are still skills required and experience is worth paying for.

Music

Budgeting for music is problematic, especially if you want to use popular songs or famous artists. Acquiring rights to use such material can be a very expensive and time-consuming proposition. Another option is original music, and the sky's the limit on what that can cost. Still, in the Digital Age it's possible to create excellent original music on your computer with software like Apple's *Logic* and *Garage Band*. Stock music is also a possibility. Many stock music libraries can offer low-cost music clearances with special rates for non-broadcast projects. Harking back to the legal issues, remember that use of a pre-recorded piece of music is almost never fair use, even for films for "in-house" use or created for non-profit organizations. Get proper clearances or don't use the music, and include the costs in your budget.

Advertising and promotion

This category usually applies only to feature films, but may also be included in a budget for syndicated television shows or videos intended for the home market. Proper advertising and promotion can be critical for success, though it's often not in the filmmaker's purview, since completed films are often sold or licensed to distributors who handle these areas.

Miscellaneous and contingencies

Once you have completed your budget, you can think of this category as the "fudge factor", a way to cover costs not covered in other categories. Cost estimates are rarely 100% accurate, so a contingency of ten to fifteen percent is customary in budgeting a film. Since few films really come in "on-budget", be sure to include a contingency in your fund-raising efforts.

Where Will the Money Come From?

No matter how much the Digital Age has reduced the cost of filmmaking, it certainly is not and will never be free (as in free beer). Once you've gone through the exercise of costing-out your film, you'll have a good idea of how much money will be needed to complete it. Actually, you should have two ideas: how much it will cost if you do it the way you really want to and how much it will cost if you do it as cheaply as humanly possible. If you're lucky (and smart) the real cost will lie somewhere between these two. One factor influencing your budgeting will be whose money you're spending. If you're spending your own (self-financing the film), you are likely to be more frugal than if a major corporation with lots of money is funding your project. This isn't necessarily a good thing, but it's human nature.

Like so many other things, there are as many ways to finance a film as there are films. The first and most obvious way is self-funding. This simply means you don't use any outside sources of financing. Many low-budget productions are made this way, often relying on the help of friends and colleagues, with or without giving them an interest (or percentage) in the completed film. Sometimes self-financing is looked upon as an investment – "I'll come out way ahead and make some money once my film is sold." This can certainly be true, but filmmaking is (and always has been) a very risky investment. Things can and do go wrong. Film industry investors expect a very high profit from films because statistics have shown that most films will lose money. They must make a lot of films, knowing in advance that the ones that make money must make enough to cover the cost of the ones that don't. You probably think your film will be good, good enough to make a profit, but the first rule of funding a film is: be prepared to lose your entire investment. In other words, don't risk more than you can afford to lose. Unfortunately, the statistics are clear: Just like gambling in Vegas, you are more likely to lose than to win, whatever your investment.

It's probably more realistic to consider self-funding documentary projects or programs designed for the home entertainment market. Dramatic features are more complex and therefore more expensive to make in most cases. Obviously, too, short films are easier to self-finance than long ones.

A Scenario

Below is a hypothetical description of how a simple film might be approached by the self-funding independent filmmaker as compared to how a similar film might be produced by a production company or TV network.

Suppose, for example, you are very interested in skateboarding and the skateboarding sub-culture. There's an active skateboarding group in your neighborhood, some of the members are damn good at it, and they have a regular schedule of activities. You have a good consumer-level digital camcorder, and recently bought a Macintosh computer, which comes pre-loaded with an entry-level editing package, iMovie. After getting the written permission of your skateboarding friends, you shoot a documentary about how they got into the sport and how they learned to do their tricks. Maybe one of your friends is in a band and agrees to create the music to accompany your film in return for a screen credit. With these resources, you are ready to go. Keeping in mind the limitations of your equipment package, you adopt a style that lends itself to the subject: you choose to shoot everything hand-held, use only existing light, and to record the natural sound with the camera's built-in microphone. Your narrator is also your featured character and you decide to record his narration in a quiet corner of your living room, still using the camera's microphone, but up close for an intimate effect.

Since tape is cheap, you acquire footage of a wide variety of skateboarding activities in your neighborhood, say ten hours of it. The tape will cost you about $50. To accommodate all this footage, you may have to add an external hard drive to your computer, maybe another $200. And maybe you need to buy some kind of animation software to do your titles and some explanatory graphics to explain some of the skateboarding tricks. Add $300. Not counting the cost of your camera and computer (we'll assume you had those already) the film has cost you $550 so far. If you don't count your time, that could be your total investment, and of that amount only the $50 for tape stock is applicable only to this project – the other items can be used again for future projects. (Actually, the tape can, too.)

After you've spent countless hours learning to use the equipment with a high level of proficiency, you'll spend many more hours learning software and completing your editing, graphics and soundtrack. At this point, you'll have a master of your show that's as good as your creativity and skill can make it. Depending on your abilities and luck, it could be very good. It could also be awful.

Approaching the same project from the point of view of a production company, the costing-out for this project might look like the budget on the next page. The company will use paid professionals for all production tasks. They'll need to pay someone to create the program concept, someone else to do research to find out where the skateboarding activities are taking place, and find locations to shoot. They may also want to build sets to get the best shooting conditions and hire a composer to create an original music track. They'd hire an animation company to create the graphics and do their editing in a post-production house, at rates from $150 to $250 per hour, or more. Of course, they'd have their lawyer along to be sure everything was properly cleared and all releases are signed. When they're done, the money they have spent will have helped insure a successful outcome for the project. Again, it could be a very good film. It could also be awful.

Production Budget – "Skateboarding" – 1/2-hour Special

Writing and script acquisition	10000
Producer, director, creative fees	10000
Research	5000
Legal costs	5000
Insurance and permits	3000
Production office expenses	1000
Talent Fees	3000
Location scouting and related costs	2500
Location expenses	1000
Set design and construction/studio facilities	10000
Props	1000
Wardrobe	1000
Tape, disk and/or film stock	1000
Production crew costs, including travel	24000
Equipment rentals	10000
Editing	20000
Graphics	10000
Special effects	10000
Soundtrack production	5000
Music	20000
Sub-Total	**152500**
Miscellaneous and contingencies (15%)	22875
Total	**175375**

Not every project will have such a wide range of possible costs, but the point is good design and ingenuity can open up opportunities to create a good film on a modest budget.

It's beyond the scope of this book to describe the myriad ways money can be raised for a film project. Forming a production company and soliciting investors is one way, getting a grant is another, selling the rights to your script is also possible. It's all part of putting together the pieces of the puzzle.

One thing to always remember: Whoever controls the money makes the deal. When investors fund your film, expect them to want some level of control – hopefully as little as possible, but that's wishful thinking. They are going to want to get their hands into the project if for no other reason than to protect their investment.

"Lack of money is no obstacle. Lack of an idea is an obstacle."

Ken Hakuta

1.6 Writing and Visualizing

"There is nothing worse than a sharp image of a fuzzy concept."

Ansel Adams

Writing for film is the subject of hundreds of books (at my last check, amazon.com listed 2,133 of them) and a smaller but impressive number about writing for TV are also in the bookstores. Books on screenwriting for feature films are loaded with ideas about dramatic structure, character development and conforming to the "Hollywood Style". Screenplays have a complicated and uniform style and structural protocol that must be adhered to by any writer who is attempting to get a dramatic script read, bought or produced in Hollywood. This is a subject beyond the scope of this book, but it deserves serious study if learning to write screenplays is your objective.

Outside Hollywood, writing in the Digital Age is becoming free-form but scripts still broadly follow the two classic script formats: the "Hollywood" or narrative style and the two-column "Video" style. In this chapter, you'll see a short example of each to give you an idea of which one best suits your film and your writing objectives. Your choice will (maybe surprisingly) affect the way you think about your film and how you are able to convey your vision to the reader.

Narrative or "Hollywood" Style

The "Hollywood" form usually requires a strict adherence to various scene description, capitalization and typeface rules, and it's designed to be read in a linear way, like a stage play. The "rules" of this style are intended to help maintain a level playing field: all scripts are presented in the same format, with the objective that readers will consider only the content of the script and not be influenced by the presentation style.

Here is an example of a section of the script for the hypothetical "Skateboarding" film we talked about in the preceding chapter.

EXT. A HILLSIDE STREET - DAY

FRED rolls to a stop on his skateboard as BILL approaches. Heavy rock music in the background

BILL
Hi, Fred. Looks like you're getting some good runs in today.

FRED
So far, so good. But I lost a really nice board this morning.
(frowning)
I slipped off the damn thing and it rolled right under a bus.

TITLE - "FRED SMITH, REGIONAL CHAMPION"

BILL
Bummer.
(looking at FRED's skateboard)
That one doesn't look so good either.

FRED
Yeah, it's kinda beat up, but it's my old favorite.

EXT - A BIG SKATEBOARD RAMP - DAY

We see FRED doing a series of tricks on the ramp.

FRED (V.O.)
I used it in the competition in Los Angeles last year. It kept me going and I came in third place. I didn't expect to win.

2-Column Style

This style traces its history to the time when TV was mostly "live". Since the sound and picture were always handled by different people, the two-column orientation made the script easier to follow during actual production. It's also an easier format for talent like newscasters or narrators to read, and thus it is better suited for documentary films. Its main disadvantage is that it's not as easy to read for content as the narrative form, so it's not as good for conveying your vision of the film.

Here's how the same "Skateboarding" script might look in a "Video" 2-column format:

Video	**Audio**
FADE IN – HILLSIDE STREET – WIDE SHOT	Heavy Rock Music – Fade under dialog
FRED rolls to a stop on his skateboard as BILL approaches.	BILL: (On Camera) Hi, Fred. Looks like you're getting some good runs in today.
SUPER TITLE: "Fred Smith – Regional Champion"	FRED: So far, so good. But I lost a really nice board this morning. (frowning) I slipped off the damn thing and it rolled right under a bus. BILL: Bummer. (looking at FRED's skateboard) That one doesn't look so good either. FRED: Yeah, it's kinda beat up, but it's my old favorite.
DISSOLVE TO: Shot of Fred doing tricks on big skateboard ramp	Music up for a few beats, then under FRED: (V.O.) I used it in the competition in Los Angeles last year. It kept me going and I came in third place. I didn't expect to win.

It's relatively easy to format the 2-column script in standard word processor software (like Microsoft *Word*). As production goes along, it's also easy to add columns for additional information, such as scene numbers, timecodes for various scenes, location notes, and the like.

The narrative format can be painful to work with in "off-the-shelf" software, so most screenwriters prefer to use a specialized application. My favorite is *FinalDraft*. It features some very powerful formatting tools and allows you to switch through the various styles with a simple tap of the "Tab" key. It also includes some great utilities that help you carry a script through the changes that always take place during production. For example, you can add A and B pages and A and B scenes so the page number a particular scene falls on never changes as the script is revised and re-written. This avoids a lot of confusion; it also means that you don't have to print new copies of the whole script after changes are made.

In spite of the popularity of the 2-column format in the video world, I am partial to the narrative style for a variety of reasons. First, your film is *not* live TV, so the advantage of the two-column scripts for the separate operations of audio and video is not an important consideration. Second, the narrative style script is more flexible, especially if you don't feel it necessary to abide by all of the strict rules of the format as applied to dramatic screenplays. It allows you to put in as much or as little screen direction as you'd like, use scene numbers or not, and generally add readable commentary anywhere in the script, helping the reader to *get* your vision. Third, the narrative style is more "literary": if a reader is accustomed to reading plays (or screenplays), your script can become almost as easy to read as a novel. It's also easier to edit; there is no problem with keeping the two columns of audio and video properly aligned with each other.

A script has three main purposes: it will help you sell your film idea, it will serve as the roadmap, the final authority about what cast and crew will be doing during production and post-production, and, perhaps most importantly, it will convey your vision of the film to others. Whether you write your own script or hire or partner with a writer, your film will be first judged by the script. The more clearly your script can help the reader visualize your film, the better your finished product will be.

Creating a script can be a big part of clarifying your vision, discovering its strength and weaknesses. It's very much like putting together a jigsaw puzzle, as you figure out the best way to organize your film, how to introduce places and characters, what the action will be, how the elements will come together to tell the story. You'll find yourself juggling the order of scenes, figuring out how to create special effects, and usually trying to design scenes you can shoot on a minimal budget.

Whether it's a five-minute experimental film or a full-length feature, dramatic films are either created from the beginning as screenplays or adapted from a book or short story. In an adaptation, characters, places, plot elements and basic story are defined in the underlying work, but the process of creating the script is nearly the same in both cases. The important thing is to have a plot that is cinematic, believable and holds together.

Once the story is developed, the two most difficult aspects of writing a dramatic film are creating good dialog and making the script visual, or cinematic. While many screenplays include a narration, most of the story is told with dialog and images. This is significantly different from novels and short stories which are largely narrative. It's also different from a stage play, because a good film exploits the ease with which film can take an audience from place to place in an instant.

Dialog

Amateurish dialog can ruin a film. Dialog must be believable for a character to say and always reinforce the character's development. It should be written so that an actor can handle it in a convincing way. In a science fiction script (for a movie I won't name here), a writer had the man from Mars saying, "I come from the planet you call Mars."

Upon first reading this line, a director sprang from his chair and shouted, "A Martian wouldn't say that!" Of course, none of us has any clue what a Martian would say, but we all have very strong cultural ideas of what is natural for characters to say and what is not. A farm hand wouldn't say his overweight boss is "corpulent", either.

By definition, dialog is a conversation, not one person talking *at* another for the audience's benefit. In a conversation, there is always the implied idea that the participants have shared knowledge, whether the audience members do or not.

Good dialog is *conversational.* It also has undertones, meanings implied partly from what is said and partly through how it is said or the actions surrounding it. If a character is trying unsuccessfully to unlock a door, she could say, "I can never seem to get this door unlocked. Can you help me with getting the key in the lock? It's too tight or something." That would be fine on radio, but in a screenplay, it would be much better if she simply said, "I keep having trouble with this!" or simply "Dammit!" and let the action clearly show that she is having trouble with the lock and key. This not only shortens the dialog, but makes it much more natural. It also gives the other character a chance to be responsive and understanding of the implied call for help. Simultaneously, it helps make the characters in the scene more multi-dimensional; they are allowed to flow through several different situations in a single short scene.

Sometimes it's necessary for a character to do a detailed explanation of something, some kind of long speech. In bad scripts, it's often one character telling another what the second should already know, just for the benefit of the audience. This is called *exposition*, or *expository dialog* and it should be avoided where possible. When a long monolog is necessary to develop the story, it's often done in some kind of "meeting" setting, like a group of people being briefed on important information. One of the best examples of *good* exposition is George C. Scott's speech to the troops in the opening scene of *Patton*. The speech is so compellingly written and performed that the viewer hardly notices that the troops he is addressing are neither seen nor heard.

Finally, dialog should avoid the use of clichés. I'm not beating around the bush when I say that, you know. After all, dialog can't be all things to all people.

Narration

Some dramatic films and almost all other genres are likely to use narration, and writing it is another challenge. Unlike dialog, narration is always expository. (Otherwise, why would it be there?) Personally, I like to minimize narration, even in a documentary. Narration is, however, a necessity in many films, and it is easy to find plenty of droning, boring and pompous examples of doing it badly.

Like dialog, good narration should sound conversational. Watching a film is a very personal and up-close experience, and the narrator is practically whispering in your ear. When writing narration, keep in mind that it is going to be perceived by the ear, not by the eye. It must be comfortable to *hear*, if not necessarily comfortable to read. Unlike the printed word, where the reader can easily go back and re-read a sentence or paragraph, once a sequence of narration passes there's no chance to review. It must be clearer and more concise than prose, using simpler language and generally shorter sentences and phrases. It's also vital that the narration and visual elements complement each other; the narrator generally shouldn't be talking about one thing while the audience is seeing another.

Narration should be written (or re-written) with a firm knowledge of the visuals that will be used with it. A common problem in documentary filmmaking is the need for the editor to scamper to find enough footage to "cover" a particularly long piece of narration. As with dialog, narration should be used to convey only information that can't be adequately covered by your images. If a picture is really worth a thousand words, it should be easy to keep the narration short and succinct.

Screen Directions

Writers, producers and directors differ about how much screen direction should be included in a script. Directions like "CUT TO: CU FRED" (cut to a close-up of the character, Fred) should normally only be included if it's the easiest way to describe the necessary emphasis for a particular shot. Whether the camera directions are there or not, directors will make their own decisions about how they want to shoot a particular scene.

Better screen directions describe the scene from the point of view of the audience. Instead of "TRACKING SHOT OF JOHN AND MARSHA WALKING DOWN STREET", try something like, "We follow JOHN and MARSHA as they walk down the street."

Storyboards

Feature films usually make use of detailed storyboards, and sometimes they can get very elaborate, with carefully drawn images of every shot. Documentaries, on the other hand, rarely use them. Like so many things in filmmaking, every production is different.

Storyboards can be a great help in conveying your vision, especially in a dramatic film, music video or commercial, even if they're just quick-and-dirty stick figure drawings. Sometimes you can combine snapshots of locations with sketches to create a hybrid storyboard. This can be useful in working out blocking and camera angles. It can also help alert you to possible lighting problems with a location. The ultimate, of course, is to hire a professional storyboard artist to work with the director.

"I like a film to have a beginning, a middle and an end, but not necessarily in that order."

Jean-Luc Godard

1.7 Talent

"Talent is like electricity. We don't understand electricity. We use it. You can plug into it and light up a lamp, keep a heart pump going, light a cathedral, or you can electrocute a person with it".

Maya Angelou

I am seldom awed by anything, but I have come to realize that if anything in this world can be awesome, it is talent. In the film business, the word *talent* is used both in its ordinary sense of inborn abilities, and to refer to anyone whose image and/or voice becomes a part of a film. Actors (amateur, professional, good, bad) are referred to as *talent*, as are non-actors who may play the roles of characters – even themselves. Both veteran and beginning filmmakers have a tendency to underestimate the enormous value good talent brings to any production. Every film needs talent, whether actors for a dramatic piece, narrators, or on-camera interviewees. Your choice of talent will make or break your film.

Talent falls into these broad categories:

- Principals – The major or "lead" parts
- Supporting – Actors in major scenes
- Bit players – Also called "day players"
- Cameos – a short appearance of a celebrity
- Extras – for crowd scenes, parties, etc., usually non-speaking roles.

Some years ago, I was fortunate enough to win a New York Art Directors Award for directing a commercial for a major bank. Going into the production, I had felt the spot was a bit lame, a little too simple. It was a single-shot standup based on the premise, "I'm worth a lot to my bank." I had the good fortune to cast a delightful lady for the role, Portia Nelson, who had played Sister Berthe in *The Sound of Music.* Portia's elegant turn of phrase and Mona Lisa smile made a plain vanilla idea into a delightful piece of television. Actually, I was completely satisfied with the first take, but she'd have none of that. She wanted more, doing take after take, each a little better than the one before. Finally, after about fifteen takes, she sighed, "Well, I guess that's the best I can do. I'm sorry." In spite of her apology, the spot was perfect, and I, as director, didn't do anything but watch. Portia made the spot.

Great talent is not always so humble. In my first working experience with Charles Kuralt, the distinguished CBS News commentator and brilliant journalist, we were recording narration for a fundraising film. The show was about fifteen minutes long, and he had volunteered to do it for his alma mater, the University of North Carolina. Because he didn't have much time, we arranged to do the recording in a hotel room. He hadn't seen the script before, so he looked it over while I unpacked the recording equipment.

After I asked him to read the first paragraph to set levels, he said, "Let's give it a go." I started recording and began following along on my copy of the script. As he read, I noticed that he changed a few things, but I didn't stop him. About halfway through the first page, he slid it aside and dropped it silently on the floor, the words still flowing into the microphone. He was delivering the copy from the first page as he read the second page! Halfway through the second page, he did the same, and kept doing it throughout the script. When he finished he asked, "Is that OK?" Without giving me time to answer, he said, "I think we're done." In fifteen minutes, in one take, Kuralt had performed a beautifully interpreted and flawless read, and simultaneously re-written the script, vastly improving it.

In your filmmaking, you probably won't often be working with celebrities, but if you carefully seek it out, less-than-famous but highly skilled talent is out there. If you have the budget for it, a good casting agent is worth his weight in gold. Some of the best talents are members of the *Screen Actors Guild* (SAG) and/or the *American Federation of Television and Radio Artists* (AFTRA). While union talent (SAG/AFTRA members) may cost more than non-union actors, the unions bring benefits to producers as well as members. More than one producer has had the experience of having an actor tell them, in the middle of a production, "I think I'm going to be sick tomorrow unless I get more money." Sure, it's unethical, but it happens. For SAG/AFTRA members, however, it is unthinkable – at least it is if they want to continue their career.

If you live in a so-called "right-to-work" state, you can use both union and non-union talent in the same production, but be aware that in most cases if you use any union talent, all players must be paid union scale. If you are not a SAG/AFTRA signatory, you can sometimes use a talent paymaster service to hire union talent for you.

About Casting

Whatever class of talent you plan to use, you will probably be going through one or more casting (audition) sessions, either set up by an agent or conducted independently. If you've never had the pleasure of choosing talent this way, you are in for a unique experience. Every casting session is different, and some can be brutal, although good taste and common courtesy demand that the brutality is concealed from the talent. Prospective cast members read parts of the script, and sessions are videotaped. The tapes are screened later and the decision makers pick the actors for each part (if they are found), and the "winners" are notified. It's during the screening that the brutality seems to emerge. It's not unexpected to hear things like "her nose is way too big" or "he looks like an ostrich," or "he looks ok, but he sounds like Elmer Fudd", or worse, sometimes much worse.

If possible, the director should attend the casting session and get the opportunity to work with the actors; a good working relationship with the director should be established as early as possible.

Sometimes *open calls* are held, where members of the public can come in to audition. Each is given a casting form for their personal information, the part they're reading, union affiliation (if any) and other data. These can be massive events, especially if publicized in the media, and some very fine talent has been discovered this way.

On a shoestring budget, you might need to get a bit more creative in finding talent. Unlike organized auditions where prospective cast members expect rejection as the most likely outcome, dealing with friends and neighbors can be much more emotionally sensitive. If you're not already sure that your friends can pull off particular parts in your film, it's probably best not to ask them. Some very good films have been made with volunteer talent, particularly short films. A feature-length film using volunteers, however, is more daunting. The level of commitment and time required for such an effort is often beyond what can be asked of someone who has to earn a living otherwise. For actors doing major parts, feature filmmaking is a process of total immersion; while you are doing it, there simply won't be time for anything else. For bit parts, day players or extras, volunteers can be great resources.

Local amateur (or even professional) theater groups can be good sources of talent if you can be diplomatic and selective. Stage acting is, of course, very different from film acting. The ability to project from the stage is considered very important, but it is something you don't want actors in your film to do. When holding auditions of talent with lots of stage experience but little or none in the film area, be sure to get close to them (including video close-ups) to see if they can work "up close and personal" with the audience. Some adapt to it with only a tiny amount of direction; others never get it. Be sure anyone you cast from a theater group can get this vital point.

A word of caution: don't cast an important part without having the actor read for it. Even if you know the person well, or he comes highly recommended, you can't be sure he can do a good job in the part until you see and hear him do it. When auditioning, pick two or three key scenes that may be among the more difficult, give each participant a copy and a few minutes to become familiar with it. Always let each actor read in a room separated from where other actors are waiting. Otherwise, participants' performances will be influenced by the other actors' reads. An exception to this is when players must work together closely in a scene. In this case, you might want to audition actors in pairs, trying as many different combinations as you can. This can help establish if there is "good chemistry" between characters.

If you're having trouble choosing between several likely candidates for a part, have a *callback* – a second casting session, inviting the best two or three possibilities.

For some parts, it's important for the talent to have the ability to memorize long scenes. It can get very time-consuming and expensive to try to shoot a scene with actors who don't know their lines. Some directors will give the scenes to actors a few days before the casting session so they have time to memorize; others will give them the parts only a few minutes before the audition to see if they are "quick studies".

Obviously, when you select your cast you'll need to be sure their availability matches your shooting schedule and the schedule of other talents who will be in scenes with them. Once you've made your choices, you can book the talent for your project. It's a good idea, also, to keep the contact information for your second choices since conflicts can and do arise.

Directors differ on the issue of when (or whether) to give actors copies of the script. Some ask that all the actors get full copies; others prefer to give them only the scenes in which they appear. Another approach is to save the script for the day before shooting – actors receive their lines on a "just-in-time" basis, giving them just enough time to become familiar with bite-sized chunks of dialog.

Rehearsals

For dramatic films (and especially feature-length films), plan to have the actors available for extensive rehearsals. Again, each director will have his own style, but many like to take time to run through the entire film before breaking it down into scenes. This approach has the advantage of allowing the actors to "get the vision" and how they fit into it. Since films are shot out of sequence, rehearsals that proceed in linear fashion, beginning to end, can help preserve the integrity of the film as a whole.

After these full run-throughs, additional rehearsals should be scheduled for the principal players, to polish their performances and to facilitate possible re-writes of some scenes. Never forget: resolving script or performance issues during rehearsal instead of on the set is going to be far easier and less expensive!

"Talent wins games, but teamwork and intelligence win championships."

Michael Jordan

1.8 Producing and Directing

"Thinking ahead. That's what producing is. It's like being a plumber. You do your job right, nobody should notice."

Dustin Hoffman in "Wag the Dog"

"A director's most important job is to direct the audience."

Steven Spielberg

The hardest part of a producer's work is finished before the cameras roll, during pre-production. Production is the phase when the director has the biggest part of his job to do. So why would I put directing together with producing in the pre-production section? It's because good pre-production (and a good producer) makes the director's job a whole lot easier when it's time to shoot. And, the more the director can participate in the pre-production process, the more he can share the vision and make the film his own. Taking ownership of a film is an important aspect of directing, so it's always best if the director can be involved as early as possible in the process.

In the Hollywood model, the roles of producer and director are sharply defined. As filmmaking becomes democratized in the Digital Age, the line (like most of the others) becomes blurred. Nevertheless, these two critical jobs must be done on every film, even if the producer and director happen to be the same person. Unlike the more technical aspects of digital filmmaking, however, the jobs of producer and director aren't made much easier by the technological revolution.

Hollywood pictures usually have Executive Producers (the ones who made the deal and /or provide the money), one or more producers (they line up the key players and resources and figure out how to make it happen), a few associate producers (they help the producers), one or more line producers (they wrangle the crew, cast and facilities before and during the shoot), and a gaggle of production assistants. There may also be separate producers for graphics, music, special effects, or other aspects of the film. Together, the producers form a team or department with a structure designed to fit the requirements of a particular film. This team will usually pick the director, negotiate a deal, decide when he'll come into the project and determine what his level of pre-production participation will be.

When a director comes into the process early, he'll want to work with the writer in polishing the script and adapting it to his style – those sometimes unending re-writes. He'll participate in the casting decisions (perhaps making final decisions), select locations, help pick appropriate artists and technicians, and help coordinate the myriad details. Very often more re-writes are needed to adjust for casting decisions or to change a script locale to match available locations. Early involvement can also help with set design, art direction, props and wardrobe selection.

Decision-Making

One of the most important aspects of pre-production is the opportunity it gives the producer and director to make good, informed decisions as early as possible in the process. Decide how your film is going to play, incorporate those decisions into your vision and your script, then, stick by them. One of the most expensive things you can do is to postpone decisions until you're on the set. Still more expensive is making the decision that starts with, "Let's shoot it both ways."

One director gave this tongue-in-cheek advice: "Don't shoot anything you're not going to use." Of course, that's impossible, but it's a worthy goal to pursue, and it is approachable.

I once had the occasion to have lunch with an editor who had worked with Alfred Hitchcock, whom he accused of taking over his job. Hitchcock had a reputation for planning his films so thoroughly that they were edited in his head long before the camera ever rolled. He also was known for never going for another take once he had one that satisfied him. Further, he rarely shot entire scenes from multiple angles; he would only shoot those segments he *knew* he wanted. As a result, his editor told me, there would always be an edit just a few frames before the Master called, "Cut!" Hitchcock consistently used careful planning to make great films, not necessarily to save time and money, although it did. It's a good lesson to take to heart.

The Schedule

Ideally, the production team can do a script breakout (or breakdown) – a day-by-day and hour-by hour listing of when, where and in what order the shooting will be done, including the necessary people and resources. For dramatic films, a production board is often used, with scenes, talent and locations laid out in shooting order. Of course, it's far more efficient to shoot all the scenes that take place in a particular location at the same time, and to group scenes based on the characters (actors) that appear in them.

I've found it helpful to prepare the script so that a new page starts at each change of scene, then put together a script notebook for each of the key people. The book contains two copies of the script: one in normal order and a second with the pages arranged in shooting order, with a divider for each shooting day.

In documentary production, the process becomes more fluid and less predictable, with the producer and director concentrating on very different considerations than with a feature film. Scheduling seems to be the biggest logistic puzzle – how to get the crew where they need to be when they need to be there. Since you are usually not hiring the subjects of a documentary, you are often at the mercy of their schedule, and it's in your best interest to make things as convenient and painless for them as possible. In documentaries, the schedule becomes much more of a "bible" than the script, and keeping the crew flexible and mobile is a big part of the battle. Often, the producer becomes a travel agent, and (again) the Internet is a great resource for booking low-cost travel. Real travel agents are also making a comeback, too, faced with the competition of online services. A good one is a great asset to your production team. Often they are glad to get an account where a substantial amount of airline travel and hotel rooms are involved, and are willing to understand the need for flexibility and last-minute changes in itineraries.

Integrity

It's your film. Stay true to your vision. A lot of the problems you'll encounter in making your film will be related to *creative control.* There will always be pressures to compromise the integrity of your film, for myriad reasons. Your vision will certainly change as you go along. Carefully consider each change on its merit: Will it help or hurt the film?

"I made some mistakes in drama. I thought the drama was when the actors cried. But drama is when the audience cries."

Frank Capra

1.9 Production Design

"Luck is the residue of design."
Branch Rickey

Production design is all about the "look and feel" of your film. In a Hollywood feature, it's respected and becomes a major part of the pre-production process, but in lesser films, it's often sadly neglected or even treated as an afterthought. Effort spent in good production design will do a lot to make your film more professional and definitely give it an edge over other low-budget productions. A film can gain a great deal of production value, integrity and continuity by carefully designing the overall "look" and sticking with it throughout.

Art Direction

This area covers everything from design of titles all the way through sets and wardrobe. Needless to say, a major Hollywood production could have an army of people in this area alone, but even a simple documentary should have a carefully designed "look", extending from good choices of type faces for titles to choice of backgrounds and wardrobe for interviews. A film about coal miners in West Virginia might have a dark, low-key look and a certain "grunge factor"; one about the New York fashion scene might be high-key and be shot in opulent surroundings.

Having a low budget doesn't mean you can't be creative; there are plenty of low-cost or no-cost ways to up your film's production value. One filmmaker I've worked with did a wonderful documentary in which he carried around a wrinkled, painted canvas background that he used everywhere he shot interviews. It gave him a consistent look and it served a signal to the audience that some key point was about to be made. He improved on the payoff by using unconventional shot composition on this big background, sometimes handholding the camera and doing deliberate abrupt *jump-cuts* of his subjects. Good use of shot composition can be a very powerful way to create thought-provoking scenes.

If you're shooting on location instead of on sets, it's amazing what a little paint can do – if you can get permission to use it. In one case, the production crew gave a homeowner a free interior makeover in exchange for using the house for a few days. Sometimes the right choice of paint colors can completely change the feeling of a room and make it match the mood of the scenes being shot there. Carefully selected furniture can make a huge difference, too.

If you're building sets, art direction will involve their design and ultimate construction. This can get especially difficult and expensive if you are doing a period piece or if the required sets are large. In the Digital Age, it's certainly worth investigating ways of creating "virtual sets" using computer graphics imagery (*CGI*). While it's not necessarily cheap, it can often allow you to make your sets a lot smaller and present opportunities for shots that wouldn't otherwise be possible. A word of warning here: convincingly marrying live action with computer generated backgrounds can be daunting and requires a very high level of expertise, even if the computing power and software are readily available. Don't count on being able to do these *process shots* unless you are certain you have the resources to pull them off. As has been said, "Bad special effects are worse than no special effects."

For documentaries, music videos or other non-dramatic genres, many digital filmmakers are using more abstract computer generated backgrounds or animations, shooting their subjects in front of a blue- or green-screen.

All this is to encourage you to do a lot of thinking and planning about all the aspects of the artistic look of your film. Will it be brilliant and colorful? Dark and menacing? Soft and pastel? Warm and rich? Bright and misty? Decide early in your planning.

Lighting Design

Lighting style will be a vital part of the look, too, and is an important aspect of production design. Some more radical filmmakers eschew any kind of artificial lighting, insisting "available" light gives a more believable look – the ideas of "shoot what you see" and "if you can see it you can shoot it." While this works for some subjects, it's one of those rules that are made to be broken – there are many occasions when some tastefully added light will make a world of difference. The fact that digital cameras can work in very low light and create recognizable pictures doesn't mean the pictures are of an artistic quality good enough to be called professional (unless, of course, you choose this look and are consistent with it throughout your film).

Being consistent with lighting is important to the integrity and unity of any film. This is not to say that you can't have more than one style within a film, but it's important to keep the lighting style uniform within a scene or sequence. You would not, for example, intercut scenes with very soft, bright light on one character and dark, contrasty light on another. Of course, the lighting should be consistent with the time of day or night.

In the world of lighting, there are definitely two distinct schools: film and television. At the risk of generalizing, traditional film lighting tends to be "contrasty" with more shadows, while TV lighting is more "flat" and shadow-free. These differences derive largely from the fact that film scenes are usually lit for a single camera position while TV lighting has traditionally been designed for the need to accommodate shots from multiple cameras and angles simultaneously. Also, TV lighting tends to be from above to allow the cameras freedom of movement; film is more often lit from the floor, with the lights mounted on stands.

Traditionally, TV lighting has been a bit hotter too, to compensate for the lower sensitivity of cameras, to make it easier to keep shots in focus, and sometimes to make up for the light lost in the Teleprompters that are often mounted on studio cameras. Even outside the studio, some believe that soft, shadow-free lighting looks better on television. This is certainly true when a show is being watched on a TV screen in a fully-lighted room, but it is very limiting if you want to convey a look or mood for a more theater-like viewing environment.

For much of the history of TV, electronic cameras have not been able to deal with high-contrast scenes very well, so it was common practice to use enough *fill* light so that image detail in the shadows wasn't lost. Since early cameras could only handle a contrast ratio of about 10 to 1 (compared to film's ability to handle 40 to 1 or more), such low-contrast lighting was a necessity. Current digital cameras, however, can handle far more scene contrast and thus are able to function very well with film-like lighting styles. Thus, this long standing difference between film and video becomes more of a historical footnote than an obstacle.

Like other members of the creative team, your Director of Photography (videographer, cinematographer) should be included in the pre-production phase to actively participate in the design of your film's visual style. A strong DP can also work toward making choices of equipment that will be able to implement the style within the contemplated budget.

Wardrobe

If your film is set "here and now" or is a documentary, wardrobe shouldn't be a serious problem, but should certainly be thought about during pre-production. Many dramatic films (especially period pieces) will require custom-made costumes, and designing them is the subject of another book. In any case, however, choice of wardrobe is a production design decision. What your actors wear will say a lot about your story: is it casual or formal, hip or gritty, colorful or drab? The classic westerns didn't have the good guys in white hats and the bad guys in black hats for no reason. The choice was made to help tell the story.

Wardrobe can also help develop your characters. Seeing a man in a tuxedo immediately implies to the audience that he's either a wealthy man-about-town or a waiter. A woman wearing an apron is stereotyped as a housewife. Uniforms also help establish characters. Bargain shops and formal wear rental companies can be your best friends, as can uniform rental organizations. For more unusual wardrobe requirements, most major cities have costume rental houses. Local theater groups, also, often have extensive costume collections and may be willing to rent or loan them.

Television also creates a few special demands on wardrobe. Because the image is made up of "pixels" (picture elements), it's best to avoid very fine patterns in clothing – these can create annoying moiré artifacts. Also, it helps to stay away from excessive contrast – a dark-skinned person's features can disappear if they are dressed in brilliant white. Adjacent saturated colors (such as bright red and blue stripes) can become "fuzzy" because of the way the video system handles color. Some colors, too, can end up looking very strange if you're shooting black-and-white.

Makeup

While makeup artists rarely need to participate in the pre-production process, films using specialty makeup can require extensive preparation. Examples of this need might include films in which the characters are shown from youth through old age, or science fiction or horror genres. In these cases, makeup and prosthetic design becomes an important pre-production consideration.

At the other end of the spectrum, some low-budget films forego makeup altogether. It's easy to rationalize that eliminating makeup can save time and money while somehow making the actors appear "more natural". In the real world, this simply is not true. Actors' appearance and character development can be enhanced in subtle but very important ways with good makeup. *Subtle* is a key word in film makeup. Your eyes are your best guides for film makeup; if you can see the makeup, so can the camera. Your actors will look much better with makeup, but it should be invisible – they should look like they aren't wearing any.

Props

Props (properties) are usually considered anything a cast member touches or manipulates in a scene. These would include things like dishes, guns, books, eyeglasses or sometimes vehicles. (Other objects included in scenes for visual appeal are more properly referred to as *set dressing*, not props.) Larger cities have prop rental houses and, once again, local theater groups may be good sources for props. Design of special props can be an important consideration for dramatic films, particularly those in the science fiction or fantasy genres.

Special Effects

The range of special effects in film is so vast that many books have been written about them. I can't anticipate what effects your film will need, but one thing is certain: special effects add expense – sometimes a lot of it. It's also true that almost every film will include at least some effects. The points here are that all effects require very careful and informed planning and design, and that doing a bad job on this important area of pre- production has been the downfall of many films. We'll get more specific on how some common effects are done in the production section; here we'll be a bit more general.

Feature filmmakers tend to split up this category into *special* effects (those that are accomplished during shooting) and *visual* effects (those that are finished during post-production). During pre-production, we'll think of them together since both require careful design. For the low-budget film, it's even more important to think through ways to accomplish the required effects simply, quickly and inexpensively. Sometimes, too, you may have to re-work the film to eliminate as many of them as possible, hopefully without compromising artistic integrity.

Rule #1 for effects is that they be *convincing*. Bad effects are so common that a word has entered the language to describe them: *fakey*. Good special effects are invisible; the audience isn't aware that they've even seen an effect – they accept what they see as reality within the world of the film, without question. It's also arguably true that some the best effects are the simplest ones. Who can forget *The Three Stooges* hitting each other over the head with balsa wood hammers, or the appearance of Marley's Ghost in *A Christmas Carol*, or the shower scene in Hitchcock's *Psycho*? You'll probably remember Charlton Heston's parting of the Red Sea as Moses in *The Ten Commandments*. I bet you also remember that one as being fakey.

Music

Creating a music score for your film can also be considered a part of production design. While the actual recording of the music is generally considered part of post-production, it's helpful to begin the process of creating a score as early as possible. (Obviously, if you're doing a music video, the song will have already been chosen and probably recorded in its final form before you start shooting.) I've found it helpful to locate music that conveys the "feel" I'm after and to play it often during pre-production. Having a sense of how music will underscore scenes can enrich and stimulate the creative process and help convey your vision of the film to the production team. In the silent era, music was often played on the set during shooting to help the actors get in the mood for the scene, a practice that certainly could still be helpful today. If your budget requires the use of *stock* music, now is the time to begin selecting and using it. There is a wealth of royalty-free stock music available, much of it on the Internet. With royalty-free music, you purchase the music CDs or downloads; the purchase conveys the necessary rights for non-exclusive use.

Higher-budget films are often post-scored to match the final cut, though it's still important that the composer be brought in early enough to understand the vision and to begin working on an original score. Rough "demos" of the music can be developed and presented to the creative team during production design and used during editing.

Titles and Graphics

Good art direction can also pay off in titles and other graphics, so planning your graphic design should be an important consideration in pre-production. One example of creative art direction was used in a film about gambling, in which all the titles and credits were hand printed on playing cards that were carefully dealt before the camera in an extreme close-up shot. Another used handwritten titles on an ordinary legal pad, in keeping with the subject matter – how young lawyers get their start. In the classic *West Side Story*, the titles were in the form of graffiti.

Such novel approaches can work for some films, but most titles and graphics will be created in a computer – the Digital Age to the rescue. If your budget allows, find a good artist to create your graphic "look"; there are a lot of them around. You may have trouble finding one with film experience, but many capable artists accustomed to doing print and web design would leap at the chance to expand their skills. If your artist hasn't worked with creating titles for video, be sure your editor is familiar with the file formats needed and how to import them into your film. For simple titles, current editing software contains tools that can do an excellent job. Still, good choices of typeface and colors as well as deciding how the titles will be presented are important pre-production considerations.

"Many things difficult to design prove easy to performance."

Samuel Johnson

1.10 Who is the Crew?

"There are no passengers on spaceship earth. We are all crew."

Marshall McLuhan

The crew includes all the technicians, artists and administrators who'll be working during actual shooting, not including the director, producers, and other high-level members of the production team. Like everything else in filmmaking, crews vary in size over an enormous range – from one to hundreds, but for any film locating and booking a good crew is a vital part of pre-production. Low-budget films are most often shot with crews of three to twelve, perhaps with some added for the more difficult scenes. Generally, the larger the crew the faster you can move, and time is money. Still, filmmaking is an art form, so there is only so much you can do to accelerate the process. (No matter how hard they try, nine women can't make a baby in one month!)

Rather than try to list all the people you could put on your crew, below is a rundown of the specialties that are usually essential. Each specialty can include one or more people, depending on the requirements of the film. Conversely, it's common on low-budget films for people to wear multiple hats.

Director of Photography (DP)

One way or another, every film has a DP. In Hollywood parlance, the DP (or Cinematographer) is in charge of the camera, shot composition and the lighting, though he may not operate the camera and likely will never touch a lighting instrument. He'll be assisted by a Camera Operator, one or more Assistant Cameramen (AC) and a Clapper-Loader, along with the Gaffer, electricians, best boy and a variety of grips. In the video world, this person is called the Videographer. He's usually the camera operator as well, and only on higher budget productions will he have assistants. (At this point, I suggest we abandon the term "videographer", since we're making digital films, aren't we?)

Whatever the budget, the DP will be largely responsible for capturing your vision and creating the "look". While others on your crew could be beginners or amateurs, it's best to choose a DP is experienced and knows how to capture what you're looking for. He will also be in charge of the rest of your photographic crew.

Unless your film requires extensive lighting, there won't be many people on this part of the crew. Most low-budget crews are able to work with small lighting instruments that can be operated on the power that's available in the shooting locations, and a good DP will know how to take advantage of the wonderful sensitivity of the new digital cameras. In the production section, we'll discuss this school of lighting and how to "travel light". For lighting interiors, you'll probably need a *gaffer* to place the lights and a *grip* or two to carry things and to set up heavier equipment such as a dolly or camera boom. You may also need one or more electricians.

Often the photographic team will also include a video technician. This person will be responsible for setting up video monitors so that the director, DP or other crew can see what's being shot. Sometimes, too, he'll be making the recordings, either on tape or direct to a hard drive. Also, one or more video technicians may be needed for playback of any video elements that may be needed for TV sets or computers that may be in the scenes being shot.

Gaffer

This job has to do with placing the lights and getting power to them, again, something that has to be done on every crew. He'll be in charge of the electrical crew, too, under the direction of the cinematographer. His first assistant is the best boy/electric.

Key Grip

If any one person is "key" to making your production go smoothly, it's your *key grip*. It's his or her job to be sure all the crew resources are in the right place at the right time: cameras, lights, trucks, dollies – everything. He runs the grip crew, too, coordinating their activities. However small your crew, these responsibilities need to be covered. His first assistant is the best boy/grip, or just the *best boy*.

Line Producer and Assistant Director

These jobs are certainly separate in the world of feature film production, but overlap and sometimes merge for simpler projects. They often have production assistants assigned to them, or they may work alone. Usually, the *line producer* (LP) is responsible for having all the necessary physical assets (including the crew) in place for each shooting day, and staying a jump ahead of everyone else. Equally important, he'll need to be ready to accommodate the inevitable changes to schedule and crew. For example, there should always be a backup plan for every scheduled exterior shoot to minimize costly weather delays.

The *assistant director* (AD) (and sometimes 2nd or 3rd ADs and their assistants) will take care of the talent, getting them ready for each day's shoot. This will include distribution of current scripts, sometimes rehearsals, and coordination with props and wardrobe.

Sound Recordist

Before the Digital Age (and still for productions shot on film), sound was always recorded *double system*, with a separate sound recorder. With digital video cameras, the sound quality on tape (or disk) is extremely good; with some formats, four (or more) channels are available. Still, on many shoots a Sound Recordist or Mixer controls the audio feed to the camera, making sure the levels are correct and that the recording is clean, by monitoring a feed from the camera output on headphones. He may also mix multiple microphones, particularly when wireless systems are being used. Many productions still use double-system recording, for greater flexibility and for additional tracks. For music videos and some other productions, on-set playback of pre-recorded music will also be required. Often, the sound recordist also handles this task.

On most films, there will also be one or more boom operators keeping the microphones as close as possible to the actors while being careful to keep them out of the shot.

In the section on technology, we'll discuss ways the Digital Age has changed crew requirements and the way sound is recorded.

Sets

Once sets are designed, a construction foreman and crew will build them and in many cases will make modifications during shooting. On high-budget features, sets often will have special requirements such as *wild* walls that can be moved to make room for the camera or lighting instruments for some angles. Even when shooting on location, the shooting area is referred to as *the set* and a crew may be needed to adapt the location.

Props and Set Dressing

Except for documentaries, filmmakers will be required to provide *props* for the actors, such as guns, pens and pencils, watches, eyeglasses, telephones, food – anything they will handle. *Set dressing* includes a plethora of objects that enrich the scene – things like furniture, dishes, rugs, curtains, vases, potted plants, appliances, *practical* lights, and a thousand more. Even vehicles and animals are included in this category. Sometimes other specialties are also included, such as food or flower stylists, pyrotechnic artists, artificial rain or snow crews, and more.

As you can see, the film will dictate how many people are required to be sure all these elements come together at the right time and place on scheduled shoot days.

Makeup

This category includes *makeup artists* and *hair stylists*, and may overlap into special effects where character or "monster" makeup is required. The size of this department will depend on the style and look of the film, the size of the cast and the complexity of any makeup effects. On most low-budget films, a single makeup artist (and perhaps a hair stylist) can handle the job.

Wardrobe

Documentaries are "come as you are"; feature films can require an army of wardrobe assistants to be sure all the players are properly dressed. In the middle are the simple films where the director chooses suitable outfits from the actors' own clothing or makes a few purchases.

Script Supervisor (Continuity)

An important position for every dramatic film, the script supervisor takes careful note of the actors' performances and adherence to the script for every angle during a dramatic sequence to be sure the scenes will cut together properly. Continuity errors can easily ruin a scene – you'd never want an actor to be wearing one outfit when they enter a scene while wearing another later in the scene. Also, it's important to know which takes are good and which are bad. This can save a great deal of expensive editing time. The script supervisor is also responsible for being sure every scene is shot and that there is a good take for each. For each take, he'll record the timecode so that the shot can be quickly located by the editor during post-production. He will also make note of any script changes; these are going to happen a lot.

Special Effects

Additional artists and crew will be needed during shooting of special effects, or acquiring elements for visual effects to be added during post-production. These could be as simple as using a fog machine to make a smoky bar scene a little smokier all the way to greenscreen shots designed to make the superhero fly through outer space. Except for the simplest effects, it's important to pick crew members who have a thorough understanding of the specific effects needed and how they have been planned during production design.

Because digital technology has the potential to make effects easier and less expensive, most films include at least some of them. Good special effects are all about subtlety, so hire an expert if you can. If the budget doesn't allow that, be sure your director and DP are fully aware of the implications of any planned special effects. I stress this point because novice filmmakers often have the belief that effects are easier than they really are and will sometimes take shortcuts, tossing off possible problems with the infamous and dangerous line, "We can fix that in post."

Other Crew

There are hundreds of other categories of people who might be on your crew, depending on the complexity of the production. These might include carpenters, painters, greensmen, wranglers, drivers, food stylists, caterers, pyrotechnicians, special effects artists, even accountants and off-duty police officers. Every production is different, and the crew needs to be complete enough and flexible enough to cover every need.

"No member of a crew is praised for the rugged individuality of his rowing."

Ralph Waldo Emerson

PART 2
CHOOSING THE TECHNOLOGY

These days, choosing which technology to use in shooting your film can become a daunting task. There is no right or wrong. While choices of equipment are largely determined by budget, the Digital Age opens up opportunities to get more bang for your buck. It will be awhile before film is no longer an option for image acquisition, but for all but the highest-budgeted projects, it's not nearly as attractive as it once was.

Making equipment choices is actually a part of the pre-production process in the traditional sense. You obviously must know what technology you're going to use before you start shooting, but it's a moving target. New and better equipment hits the market almost daily. This is only an overview of the key factors you'll need to take into account in equipment choices. I have no allegiances to any particular manufacturers, nor do I wish to promote specific products, so I'll stay away from talking about brands or models except where necessary to describe a particular technology. If I did anything beyond that, this book would be obsolete before you get a chance to read it. Like everything else in the film business, equipment choices are a balancing act between capabilities, quality and cost. The objective is to choose intelligently and wisely.

"We live in a society exquisitely dependent on science and technology, in which hardly anyone knows anything about science and technology."

Carl Sagan

2.1 Film vs. Video: The Great Divide

Before we get into the technological options available to the filmmaker, it's important to understand that the film world has evolved a distinctly different culture from the video world, arising from very different histories and technologies. Filmmaking has a rich heritage extending back well over a hundred years. During most of that time, there was no such thing as *electronic cinematography (television)*, much less *digital cinematography*.

Some filmmakers, unfortunately, have adopted an elitist attitude, an unspoken confidence that film, with its amazing image quality, will *never* be approached by video (or digital) technology; only film is a *truly* professional medium. While most will deny that they embrace this mindset, it is still pervasive among some filmmakers. Strangely, too, many in television have the itchy feeling that they work in a second-rate medium – one day they might like to become "filmmakers".

Before you can make an intelligent and informed decision about the right technology for your film, you must put aside such cultural biases (should you have them). Television and film are both media that tell stories with sound and pictures. Digital technology has totally taken over the video world and it's rapidly doing the same for the film industry. In spite of film's (perhaps debatable) superiority for image acquisition, it has already been largely replaced in the film industry by digital technology, at least for all steps between the camera negative and the release print. Further, many major motion pictures are being shot with digital cameras, cinemas are exhibiting movies with digital projectors, and films are being delivered to theaters using digital transmission. In short, movies can and are being made totally without film. Like writers who cling to their manual typewriters, the days are numbered for filmmakers who don't embrace digital technology.

One significant difference between film and television culture arises from the fact that television has traditionally been a *real-time* medium – in the early days, most of the programs were "live", and those that were not originated on film. Film, conversely, always has a built-in and unavoidable time delay – the hours or days required for processing and printing – followed by the lengthy and laborious task of editing. Television was a major industry for many years before it was even possible to record the signals on tape; still more years elapsed before editing of that tape was possible. Decades passed before video could even approach the portability of film. Still more decades have gone by as we have watched electronic imaging technology incrementally edge closer and closer to the quality and versatility of film.

The physical processes involved in film and video are vastly different, too. Film works by photochemical reactions occurring when light strikes a photographic *emulsion* coated on a plastic strip, a process known for well over a century. Video works by exploiting the photoelectric effect, also discovered in the 19th century. Film cameras and motion picture projectors are essentially mechanical devices; video cameras and TV sets are purely electronic.

These technologies have followed parallel, but distinctly separate paths during most of their histories. A third field, that of digital computers, arose during the 1940s and has evolved quite apart from the television and motion picture industries.

Of these three, motion picture technology is the most mature. A film camera manufactured in the 1940s can still be used for production, and it's capable of yielding picture quality indistinguishable from the latest equipment. Likewise, it's common to see very old equipment still doing a great job in motion picture theaters. While video technology is less stable, a 10-year old camera or monitor can still produce very good pictures.

Digital equipment, in stark contrast to earlier technologies, seems to be doubling in its capabilities every eighteen months – a phenomenon known as *Moore's Law*. It means that a two-year old computer will be less than half as fast, have under half as much memory capacity and half the disk storage space as the most current model. Put another way, a new laptop computer will have more capability than a large corporate mainframe of ten years ago. In a nutshell, film and video technologies are going through continuing evolution while digital technology is in the frenzy of an ongoing revolution.

Technological revolutions are often sparked by what I call *breakpoints*. For example, when computers became fast and sophisticated enough that typing on a keyboard could instantly produce visible characters on a screen, the word processor revolution began. Suddenly it was possible to create text documents digitally instead of mechanically, bringing the many advantages of the word processor over the typewriter. In a relatively short time, typewriters became obsolete. Similarly, the capability to digitally record audio on CDs quickly drove the vinyl LP and the cassette tape out of the music business. There's been a similarly profound revolution in the tools we use for filmmaking. Digital imaging, recording, distribution and exhibition of motion pictures will drive all other technologies into museums, antique shops, and the shadowy back corners of eBay – like it or not.

System Design Criteria

Since the motion picture has never been a real-time medium, the emphasis in cinematography has always been on getting the maximum amount of information on the film. For this reason, feature films are universally shot on color *negative* film, as opposed to a positive or *reversal* film like *Kodachrome*. There is an exact parallel in still photography: If you want color prints (your pictures are intended to be copied), you use color negative film. The color negative itself, once processed, is ugly and orange; you can't look at it and tell very much about the scene. If you want color slides (transparencies), you shoot reversal film. The original film is processed and placed in cardboard mounts, yielding images suitable for direct projection. In the days when TV used film for news footage, it was usually reversal, as was the pre-video home movie.

The peculiar appearance of a color negative is indicative of its purpose. When the captured image is intended for copying and not for direct viewing, it's possible to enhance its performance in ways that improve the copying process and allow more control of color values and exposure. Color negative film has remarkable *latitude* – a rather large range of exposures can produce acceptable images. It can tolerate considerable overexposure, though underexposure can yield grainy pictures.

Reversal (transparency) film produces beautiful images, but copies suffer in quality. It also has narrow latitude and is intolerant of exposure errors, especially overexposure. In effect, it captures less information about the scene. Information is lost in exchange for a film that creates images suitable for direct viewing or projection.

Electronic cameras behave very much like reversal film. Their design has been based on the ability to use the camera output directly "on the air" with no further processing. This philosophy has resulted in cameras that throw away information about the scene (particularly details in highlights) before the signal is recorded. There is no real technological reason that video cameras can't be designed more like a film negative, allowing the recorded signal to contain more information, but the convenience and operational flexibility of having "ready-to-air" output have outweighed the possible quality advantages of a different camera design. Except for a few high-end systems, there are no cameras that are optimized for maximum latitude instead of directly viewable images. As we'll see later in the book, there are some creative ways to get around this limitation, improve the final image quality, and create "film-like" images from video cameras.

Is the Digital Motion Picture a New Medium?

I think it is. Film and television are both technologies to produce motion pictures, using totally different (but still analog) technologies. Digital video (or call it the Digital Motion Picture) uses devices and processes that have little similarity to those developed for either cinematography or traditional television. It's truly a new medium and a new art form, and deserves to be treated as such.

Digital production tools are exquisitely and deceptively complex. I would urge the aspiring digital filmmaker to gain a fundamental understanding of the basic *science* of television, of computers and of the motion picture before focusing on choosing a technology. Your knowledge should encompass the workings of light and sound, optics and imaging, of simple electronics and circuits, the principles of digital logic, a grasp of the technical concepts of television, and a solid mental picture of what goes on inside a computer. Only with an understanding of how your tools work can you make intelligent choices of which tools to use for any given task.

"I've come up with a set of rules that describe our reactions to technologies:

1. ***Anything that is in the world when you're born is normal and ordinary and is just a natural part of the way the world works.***
2. ***Anything that's invented between when you're fifteen and thirty-five is new and exciting and revolutionary and you can probably get a career in it.***
3. ***Anything invented after you're thirty-five is against the natural order of things."***

Douglas Adams

2.2 How Television Works

Digital filmmaking is based much more on television technology than on motion picture technology, so it's important that filmmakers understand the fundamentals of image capture, recording, transmission and display. While digital television is distinctly different from analog television, it accomplishes the same goal of transmitting (and/or recording) pictures and sounds electronically.

All television systems work through a process called *scanning*, whereby an image is effectively taken apart in the camera, transmitted or recorded, and re-assembled in the receiver. As a mental exercise, imagine that we want transmit a black-and-white picture from one person (the transmitter) to another (the receiver) over a telephone.

Here's how we might do it: The person on the transmitting end lays out a grid of rows and columns and lays it over the picture. He also informs the receiving party of the number of rows and columns in the grid he has chosen. The receiver then constructs a similar grid. Both parties create a gray scale – a shaded strip that goes smoothly from black at one end to white at the other – and they agree to a numeric scale, say 0 for black and 100 for white.

Starting with the upper left corner of the picture, the transmitter assigns a number on the gray scale to the average color of the first square in the grid and relays it to the receiver, continuing square by square across a horizontal line (*scanline*). At the end of the line, the sender tells the receiver he is beginning a new line. The receiver uses his gray scale and a pencil to shade each corresponding square on his grid to the corresponding color, starting a new line when he is told to do so. They continue this process, square by square and line by line, until the transmission of the image (*frame*) is complete, at which time the sender tells the receiver that he is starting a new image. With a small number of squares in the grid, the image would be very crude but perhaps recognizable. With a large number of squares and a large number of divisions on the gray scale, a very accurate reproduction of the original image could be transmitted. Also, if a numbered color chart is substituted for the simple gray scale, full-color images could be sent this way. The individual squares are analogous to the picture elements or *pixels* used in digital video.

What we have just invented is similar to a fax machine. It's a simple mental leap to convert the scenario into a television system that can transmit moving images – just make it fast enough to transmit 15 or more images every second. At that rate (or faster), the eye is capable of merging the images into what appears to be a continuous moving picture.

A television picture tube (*kinescope or cathode ray tube [CRT]*) is scanned in the same left-to-right and top-to-bottom fashion, laying out the picture information using an electron beam hitting a fluorescent screen. In analog color television, separate images for each of the three additive primary colors (red, blue and green) are encoded into a single *composite* signal. In the receiver, the composite signal is decoded into red, green and blue images that are displayed on a *tricolor* CRT in which three separate electron beams are arranged so that each of them is allowed only to strike fluorescent *phosphors* that emit only one of the primary colors. Since any color can be reproduced from a mixture of the three primaries, the result is a full-color display.

In the United States, a group called the National Television Systems Committee (*NTSC*) laid out the standards for the broadcast television system in the early 1940s; the standards for color broadcasting were added in the early 1950s. These specifications called for an image of 525 scanlines repeated at a rate of 30 frames per second. The other two major world standards are PAL and SECAM, both of which use 625 scanlines at 25 frames per second; they differ in the manner that the color information is encoded into the signal but are otherwise similar. NTSC, PAL and SECAM all use an *aspect ratio* of 4 to 3; the image is four units wide by three units high.

In the 1990s, a new group called the Advanced Television Systems Committee (*ATSC*) developed the standards for digital television (*DTV*), including digital standard definition (*SD*) and high definition (*HD*). These standards (and extensions of them) form the basis for all US digital TV broadcasting most digital filmmaking.

2.3 The Camera

"When cheese gets it's picture taken, what does it say?"

George Carlin

Certainly, the most critical tool in your kit is the digital video camera. The most important factor in choosing a camera is value – getting the most performance for the money invested. Before the Digital Age, I would have been the first to suggest that you consider purchasing a used camera, but imaging technology is progressing at such a rapid pace that even a one-year-old camera may be approaching obsolescence and prices are dropping every day. In today's world, look at the latest equipment; a $1,000 new camera may be better than a 1-year old camera that cost $2,000 new.

Image Format

The first choice you'll need to make is that of an image format. Are you going to shoot in one of the high definition (HD) formats or will standard definition (SD) be adequate for your project? Equipment for HD will be somewhat more expensive than otherwise equivalent SD gear, but that doesn't mean that HD production is out of reach for your budget. Remember, the fact that your primary release medium will be SD doesn't mean that shooting in HD won't improve the quality of your final product. The same idea applies to film; shooting 35mm film will yield better quality than shooting 16mm film even if the release medium is TV. Unless your release is only for Internet sites like YouTube, shooting in SD really makes very little sense anymore.

The table shows the most common currently used image formats in the U.S., Canada, Japan, Mexico and Central America.

1080i	HD	1080 active scanlines (image height=1080 pixels), 30 frames per second (FPS), 60 fields per second interlaced 2:1
1080p 24	HD	1080 scanlines, 24 FPS, progressively scanned
720p 60	HD	720 scanlines, 60 FPS, progressively scanned
720p 30	HD	720 scanlines, 30 FPS, progressively scanned
480i	SD	480 scanlines, 30 FPS, 60 fields per second interlaced 2:1 (Plain Old TV)
480p 30	SD	480 scanlines, 30 FPS, progressively scanned
480p 24	SD	480 scanlines, 24 FPS, progressively scanned

US Digital Television Formats

Note: The corresponding formats in Europe, Asia and Australia will differ in frame rate (50 instead of 60 frames/fields) and number of SD scanlines (580 instead of 480). For ease of conversion to the US-standard analog TV system (NTSC), the nominal 60 field rate may actually be 59.94, 30 FPS may be 29.97 and 24 may become 23.98.

About Interlace and Progressive Scanning

On conventional TV sets or computer monitors, the image is formed by a spot of light that scans the screen starting at the upper left-hand corner and proceeding left to right to form a scanline. It then “flies back” to the left and starts a new scanline, proceeding to fill the screen from top to bottom. This happens many times every second, one “screen-full” for every frame. The resulting light pattern on the screen is called a *raster.*

Early in the development of television in the US, it was determined that 30 complete images (frames) per second was a very good speed to create the illusion of smooth motion – even better than the 24 FPS commonly used in movies. The human eye, however, will see a 30 FPS image as flickering badly. To avoid the flicker, engineers came up with the idea of interlaced scanning. Instead of “painting” all of the scanlines in 1/30 of a second, an interlaced system lays out the odd-numbered lines from top to bottom in 1/60 second, then goes back an fills in the even-numbered lines in the next 1/60 second. The result is a 30 FPS display that doesn’t flicker, because it is “refreshed” 60 times per second.

All of the scanlines together form a *frame*; each top-to-bottom display of half the scanlines is called a *field*. Each field is actually a full-screen image with one-half the vertical resolution of a complete frame. (Motion picture projectors uses a similar trick: each frame is projected two or three times to minimize flicker.)

Since there are actually sixty images per second with interlaced scanning, motion rendition is smoother, too. Interlace is not without its disadvantages, however. It produces two common artifacts nicknamed "jaggies" and "twitter". *Jaggies* are the rough edges you can see on moving objects and *twitter* is perceived as jiggling edges on thin horizontal lines.

A *progressive scan* display (like a computer monitor) displays all the scanlines consecutively, creating 60 (or more) complete frames per second, fast enough to avoid flicker. It doesn't have interlace artifacts, but if the incoming signal has fewer than 60 frames per second it must have a mechanism for displaying the frames more than once to eliminate flicker.

All the formats are described by the number of pixels contained in the image. These are the rows and columns of dots that are converted to digital numbers and recorded or transmitted. Of course, a real picture doesn't have pixels, but pixels are used to create a digital representation of the image, a process called *sampling*.

Here's a brief rundown on each of the primary image formats to help with your choice (i indicates interlace, p indicates progressive).

1080i – (1080 by 1920 pixels) This is the most common format for HD broadcast production and distribution. It offers a good compromise between resolution and motion rendition, but does exhibit interlace artifacts under some conditions. Most HD cameras support this format; it is favored by several networks, including CBS and NBC, and it seems to be Sony's favorite format for HDTV broadcast. One variant, 1080p 30, eliminates interlace artifacts at the expense of somewhat inferior motion rendition. Even higher quality can be obtained with another version, 1080p 60, but because of the extreme bandwidth requirement, it is not widely used as of this writing. (The European version of 1080i 60 is 1080i 50, and is identical except for the frame rate.)

1080p 30 – (1080 by 1920 pixels) This is the progressive equivalent of 1080i and is supported by many digital cameras, though it is rarely used for broadcast. The difference has to do with the way images are captured and manipulated by the camera; there is actually no difference between the signal outputs of the camera in 1080i or 1080p 30, so the same recorders and editing systems can be used for either. In 1080i, the camera captures the images for the two fields in each frame at different times (odd field first, then even field), whereas a 1080p camera captures the image for all scan lines (both fields) simultaneously and reads them out at different times for recording. The net result is motion will be *smoother* in 1080i, but jaggies and twitter will be minimized with 1080p. Take your pick, depending on subject matter and the visual look you are going for.

1080p 24 – (1080 by 1920 pixels) This format was developed to provide electronic image acquisition for productions that will be released in theaters on 35mm film, and it's seeing more and more acceptance as a film replacement. It allows all-digital production and it can be printed to film with no frame rate conversion. For television release, however, it has inferior motion rendition when compared to the 30- and 60- FPS standards. Some filmmakers like to use it for television release in spite of this "shortcoming" because they like the "filmic look" it can impart. (The European version is 1080p 25, differing from the US version only in frame rate, 25 frames per second.)

720p 60 – (1280 by 720 pixels) Favored by ABC and Fox networks, 720p 60 delivers a full sixty frames per second and is considered by some to be the best HD format for sports or other live events. Panasonic and JVC have been proponents of this format. Although somewhat lower resolution than 1080i, subjectively the picture quality is nearly the same but with fewer motion artifacts. (One reason for the apparent near-parity with 1080i, however, is that many HD monitors and receivers do not have enough pixels to fully support the higher-resolution formats.)

720p 30 (1280 by 720 pixels) **–** Promoted by JVC, 720p 30 appears identical to 720p 60 for many kinds of subject matter, bit with half the data rate. Several moderately priced cameras support this format.

720p 24 (1280 by 720 pixels) **–** The 720-line equivalent of 1080p 24, supported primarily by Panasonic and JVC.

480i – (720 by 480 pixels) This is the digital form of "standard" NTSC TV that's been around since 1953, regular old SD. Until recently, most professional, semi-professional and amateur cameras use this format exclusively. Like 1080i, it is interlaced. (In Europe and many other parts of the world, the equivalent is 580i, based on the PAL and SECAM transmission systems that are SDTV there.) You may wonder why the vertical dimension is 480 pixels, when we said earlier that there are 525 scanlines in NTSC video. The answer: 480 is the minimum number of *active* scanlines containing picture information; the remaining lines are used for synchronizing, blanking and other signals.

480p 30 – (720 by 480 pixels) Some semi-professional and professional cameras also support this format, the progressive-scanned equivalent of 480i, or the SD equivalent of 1080p 30 or 720p 30.

480p 24 – (720 by 480 pixels) Supported by some SD cameras, this is the SD equivalent of 1080p 24, described above, also intended for transfer to film. Both these formats are called *24p*, which can sometimes become confusing. (Again, in PAL and SECAM countries, this rate is 25 frames per second, 25p.)

The astute reader may have noticed that the pixel ratio of some formats doesn't match the aspect ratio. 1920 divided by1080 (the 1080 formats) matches 1.77:1 (16 by 9), but 720 divided by 480 is 1.5 (not 1.33, the normal aspect ratio of SD.) This was a compromise – more horizontal pixels than needed for 4 by 3 (640 would be enough) but somewhat fewer than needed for 16 by 9 (the right number would be 850). The result is that SD formats have *non-square* pixels. This isn't a serious flaw – analog TV has always had discrepancies between horizontal and vertical resolution – but it can be an issue when using computer-generated graphics or when converting from one standard to another. More about this later in the chapter.

Extreme Formats

A few high-end cameras record at still higher definition than any of the ATSC standards, the most common of which are the so-called *2K* and *4K* formats. The 2K and 4K formats are approximations of 2,000 and 4,000 lines, or images in the ballpark of 2 million to 4 million pixels. While out of reach for most low-budget filmmakers, cameras supporting 2K and 4K resolutions are becoming more commonplace for major movies, and costs for these cameras is dropping rapidly.

About Frame Rate Conversion

Many of the formats described above will need to have their frame/field rates converted for display on a 30-frame (or 25-frame) interlaced monitor at some point. The most common of these *frame rate conversions* is from 24 fps progressive to 30 fps interlaced, something that has been needed since the first movies were shown on TV. The ratio of 30 to 24 (5 to 4) is equivalent to 5 video frames for every four film frames, or ten video fields for every four film frames. This is done through a process called *3:2 pulldown.*

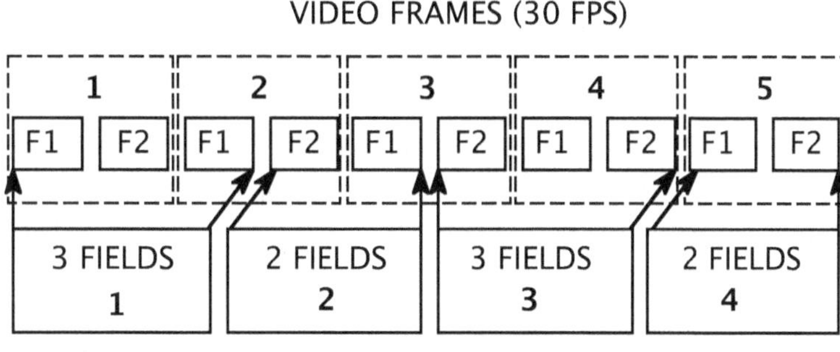

In conventional film-to-video transfer, film frames are alternately scanned into three or two fields of the 60-field per second video sequence, thus creating the necessary ten fields of video for each four frames of film. While 3:2 pulldown has been used successfully since the early days of television, it creates unique motion artifacts called *judder* on certain types of scenes, particularly fast-moving action or camera moves. Judder causes motion to appear jerkier than it would appear when shown with a film projector. With more sophisticated frame rate conversions, software has been developed that will look at the motion occurring within a scene and blend the film frames to display smoother motion and minimize judder. A similar process is used in converting other frame rates. Though conversion is likely to happen somewhere in the process and for some viewers, it's best to shoot using a format that's most likely to be used in the best final presentation of your film.

If you are shooting HD, the signals recorded will actually be in the format you have chosen; 1080i will be recorded at 60 fields interlaced, 720p will be recorded as progressive scan. If you're using SD with a tape-based camera, however, you may have the choice of shooting 480p 30 (30p) or 480p 24 (24p), in addition to "normal" 480i, but the footage will always be recorded as 480i. For 480i, each field of video is captured at a different point in time, 1/60 second apart. In the case of 30p, both fields of each frame will be captured by the camera in one "exposure" at the same instant in time (every 1/30 second, but they will still be recorded interlaced. If you're shooting 24p, the exposures will occur ever 1/24 second, but the video will actually be recorded on tape using 3:2 pulldown as shown in the drawing. Because of these recording techniques, 480i, 480p 30 and 480p 24 can all be viewed on a conventional SD monitor. In addition, editing of 480 p 30 can be edited on an SD editing system without changes. It's also possible to edit 480p 24 on a conventional editing system since the 3:2 pulldown conversion has already been done in the camera.

Important note: If you shoot 24p and ever intend to transfer your project to 24 fps film, keep in mind that using conventional 30 fps editing will "scramble" the 3:2 pulldown sequence – it can get "out of phase" at any cut. For this reason, it's preferable to edit 24p projects at a 24 fps rate; most editing systems allow this option. When it's used, the redundant (repeated) fields are simply dropped. Then, transfer to film will carry a one-to-one relationship of video frames to film frames. The 3:2 pulldown can be re-established on playback if necessary, with no loss of quality. With DVDs, this conversion takes place in the DVD player.

As a practical matter, if you *ever* intend to transfer your project to 24 fps film for theatrical projection, you will get the best image quality and a minimum of complications if you shoot and edit in a 24 fps progressive format (24p) from start to finish. 24p can be easily used in any release medium.

PAL SD cameras may offer 25i and 25p options, but not 24p. The PAL frame rate of 25 fps corresponds to the standard European film projection rate, so no frame rate conversion is necessary. Customarily, 24 fps is projected in PAL countries at 25 fps, creating a barely perceptible increase in speed. With this speed change, the pitch of the audio is also corrected. The same process works in reverse for playing 25 fps film in 24 fps countries.

Aspect Ratio

Early motion pictures standardized on an *aspect ratio* of 4:3 (or 4 by 3); the image was four units wide by three units high. Alternatively, the aspect ratio can be expressed relative to one: 4:3 is equivalent to 1.33:1, 4 divided by 3. With the arrival of television, the aspect ratio of 1.33:1 was chosen as standard, compatible with the motion pictures of the time that would often be used as program material on the new medium. In the 1950s, widescreen movies became the vogue, using wide aspect ratios such as 2.66:1, 2.33:1, 1.85:1 and 1.66:1. Over the years, the industry gravitated toward 1.85:1, the aspect ratio in which most films are produced today. Since movie audiences preferred a wide picture, with the coming of HDTV the video industry decided on 16:9 (1.78:1) as a good compromise. All current HD imaging formats use 16 by 9 as their aspect ratio and it is also an alternate standard for SD video (in addition to the more common 4:3).

So, if you choose to work in one of the HD formats, you will be shooting in 16 by 9, but if you are using SD, you have yet another choice to make. 16 by 9 programs (and widescreen movies) are often shown on TV in a "letterbox" format, with bands of black at the top and bottom of the 4 by 3 screen to accommodate the wider screen shape. Alternatively, your film can be shot using a "shoot and protect" philosophy – confining the important action to the middle 4 by 3 section of the screen, allowing the left and right sides of the image to be cropped away on SD displays.

For most projects, I prefer shooting in 16 by 9 for letterboxing on 4 by 3 displays. This approach tends to "future-proof" your film so it will look its best on 16 by 9 displays, which are fast becoming universal.

SD cameras capable of switching between 4:3 and 16:9 have their idiosyncrasies, using different methods to create the different aspect ratios:

1. The better cameras derive 4:3 by turning off part of the left and right sides of the imaging chips, thus slightly compromising the resolution in 4:3, but providing their full capabilities for 16:9.

2. Others turn off areas at the top and bottom of the chips to achieve a wide image, reducing the resolution available in 16 by 9.

3. A few simply insert black bars at the top and bottom to create a 16 by 9 letterboxed image in what is really a 4 by 3 frame – beware of this approach, since you can't create a true 16 by 9 picture from these images without quality compromises.

Camera instruction manuals might not reveal which approach they're using, but you can tell very quickly by connecting the camera to a standard video monitor and switching the camera between 4:3 and 16:9. If everything in the image gets tall and skinny and you're able to see *more* of the scene at the sides of the image, they're using approach #1. If everything gets skinny and you see *less* of the scene at the top and bottom, it's method #2. If you see black letterbox bars at the top and bottom, they're using the third (probably unacceptable) compromise.

What is Anamorphic?

Anamorphic lenses have been used for widescreen movies since the 1950s, with processes like *CinemaScope* and *Panavision*. Their optical function is to "squeeze" a wide image onto a narrower image format. In most anamorphic movies, the squeeze is 2:1, making it possible for a 2.66:1 image to fit into a 1.33:1 film frame. This makes the images actually recorded on the film appear tall and skinny (allowing a wide image to be fit into a standard film frame). During projection, a similar lens "unsqueezes" the image to create the original aspect ratio. On video displays, unsqueezing is accomplished electronically.

To shoot in an aspect ratio wider than 16 by 9, some high-end cameras (such as the Panavision *Genesis)* allow use of a full line of anamorphic cinema lenses. Some also allow cropping of 2K or 4K images to any aspect ratio.

Modern editing systems can work natively with either aspect ratio and allow you to convert 16 by 9 to 4 by 3 letterboxed, or *blow up* the central area of the frame to fit the 4 by 3 frame.

It's worth noting, too, that DVD players allow the user to specify the monitor aspect ratio. In this way, DVDs created in 16 by 9 can fill the screen on a 16 by 9 monitor or be automatically letterboxed or *zoomed* (by the player) for a 4 by 3 monitor.

How Many Pixels? How Many Chips?

Digital video (even HD) is relatively "low-rez" (low resolution) when compared to the images used by still photographers, just as 35mm film is low-rez when compared to the huge 8 by 10-inch negatives used in high-end still photography. In general, the more resolution you have in your original image the better your final product will be.

Digital cameras make images by focusing light entering the lens onto light sensitive chips. These chips are usually CCDs (charge-coupled devices) that are similar to the chips used in your computer except that they are affected by light in addition to electrical signals. A CCD chip consists of a large number of light-sensitive cells, representing pixels. (Some cameras use *complementary metal oxide semiconductor* [CMOS] or just MOS chips instead of CCDs, but for our purposes, they function similarly.)

During the time interval representing a frame (or field) of video, each pixel on the chip accumulates an electrical charge that is proportional to the amount of light falling on it during the *exposure time*. Following this accumulation of light, the charges are rapidly transferred (or "shifted") to a second set of similar pixels, which are not exposed to light. Then, while the first set of pixels is being exposed to light again, the charges are "clocked out" of the second set and are converted, one by one, to digitally encoded numbers by an *analog-to-digital converter* (ADC). The ADC measures the charge from each pixel and converts it to a digital representation (usually one byte, 8 bits) of the value of the charge – creating the raw data stream that comes out of the camera. (More on how the bits work in Chapter 2.4)

A typical HD (1080i or 1080p) image will be 1080 pixels high by 1920 pixels wide, a total of 2,073,600 pixels (roughly 2 *Megapixels*, 2 million pixels). Similarly, an SD image is 480 by 720 pixels, a total of 345,600 pixels (about .35 Megapixels). These numbers represent the minimum number of pixels to fully utilize the available resolution of the image formats, although some lower-priced cameras have been engineered to produce good pictures with somewhat fewer pixels.

It's important to understand that the number of pixels on the chip and the number of pixels in the image format are not necessarily the same. In fact, they usually are not. If the number of camera pixels is larger than the number in the output image, the image is said to be *oversampled*; if the number of camera pixels is less than the number in the output, the image is *sub-sampled* (or *undersampled*). Of course, oversampling is better and most current cameras have enough pixels to take advantage of it.

In most professional or semi-professional cameras, separate chips are used for each the additive primary colors (red, green and blue, *RGB*) with an optical system of prisms and filters being used to send the appropriate light to the correct chip.

Single-chip cameras, once considered only good enough for consumer cameras, are coming to the forefront. Digital still cameras have proved that single chips can create remarkably good images—so good, in fact, that virtually no 3-chip still cameras have been manufactured in recent years. Several manufacturers offer high-end single-chip HD cameras. These chips have color filters built-in, as part of the individual pixels; each pixel is designed to be sensitive to only one color, though not necessarily red, green and blue. With sufficient pixels and oversampling, a single chip can offer some significant advantages over a 3-chip design. For one thing, there are no additional optical elements (filters, prisms, etc.) between the lens and the imager, creating potentially sharper pictures, less distortion and fewer surfaces to get dirty. Increased sensitivity is another bonus – no light is lost in a beam-splitter and filters. Because the color filters are a part of the design of the chip, the design of the camera itself becomes simplified. A one-chip camera also can help with lens designs, making interchangeable lenses easier to accommodate. This idea has been exploited by Panavision in their *Genesis* camera; it accepts their full line of lenses designed for their 35mm cameras, giving cinematographers the same flexibility in lens choices they formerly had only with film cameras. The *RedOne* camera offers similar choices.

For maximum quality, a 3-chip HD camera should have a minimum of 2 Megapixels per chip; a 3-chip SD camera should have no less than 370,000 pixels per chip. A single-chip HD camera should have at least 6 Megapixels (the Panavision Genesis has over 12 Megapixels), with 1 Megapixel being about the minimum for a single-chip SD camera. More pixels are definitely better – with a few caveats.

Chip Size

Chips with more pixels are bigger, right? Not necessarily. As imaging chip fabrication technologies have improved, the number of pixels per square millimeter has continued to increase. The large chips used in the "extreme format" cameras are nearly the same size as a 35mm motion picture frame. Other pro cameras use 2/3-inch (10.66 mm) chips (measured diagonally), creating an image size about the same as 16mm film. 1/2- and 1/3-inch chips are also popular in professional and prosumer cameras. In general, chips smaller than 1/2-inch are in cameras with fixed (non-interchangeable) lenses, and these go down in size to 1/6-inch or even smaller. Because larger chips can have better light sensitivity, they are preferable.

You can get an idea of a camera's chip size by looking at the lens – big lens, big chip. For example, camera with 2/3-inch chips will have a rather large interchangeable lens that takes filters and lens accessories with a 72mm diameter; a prosumer camera using 1/4-inch chips may have a fixed lens, using 37mm filters.

More important that the chip's size is its pixel count. The performance of a 1/6-inch 1-Megapixel chip can be about the same as a 2/3-inch 1-Megapixel chip, and may have the advantage of requiring a smaller, lighter (and likely less expensive) lens and camera. In this case, the advantage of the 2/3-inch chips might be the ability to use interchangeable lenses, and somewhat better light sensitivity.

Speaking of sensitivity, it's worth mentioning that current cameras have amazing performance in low light, though some are much better than others. Single-chip cameras may be superior to their 3-chip cousins in this performance area. Camera sensitivity is often specified in *lux.* One lux equals about 1/10 *foot-candle,* the amount of light produced by a single candle at a distance of one foot. An approximation of one foot-candle might be the minimum amount of light under which someone with normal vision can comfortably read a newspaper. (Technically, 1 foot-candle = 1 *lumen* per square foot; 1 lux = 1 lumen per square meter, therefore 1 foot-candle = 10.76 lux.)

The published specifications are not a very good indication of usable camera sensitivity, so if low-light performance is an important consideration for your project, it's best if you can try out the actual camera to judge its performance. In the real world, you will probably not be able to get professional-quality pictures with any camera under illumination less than about 100 lux, or 10 foot-candles.

Resolution

In looking at camera spec sheets, you'll find something called *resolution*, specified in *lines* or *tv lines (TVL)*. Simply stated, it's the number of vertical lines that a particular camera can resolve. If, for example, a camera is specified as having 600 lines of resolution, it means that it could barely allow you to see individual lines in a shot of vertical lines of a size that 600 of them would fit in the width of the image. Actually, the resolution of a camera is a measure of the combination of the image sensor and the optical system. In the early days of television, resolution was measured with a standard test pattern, an example of which is shown below.

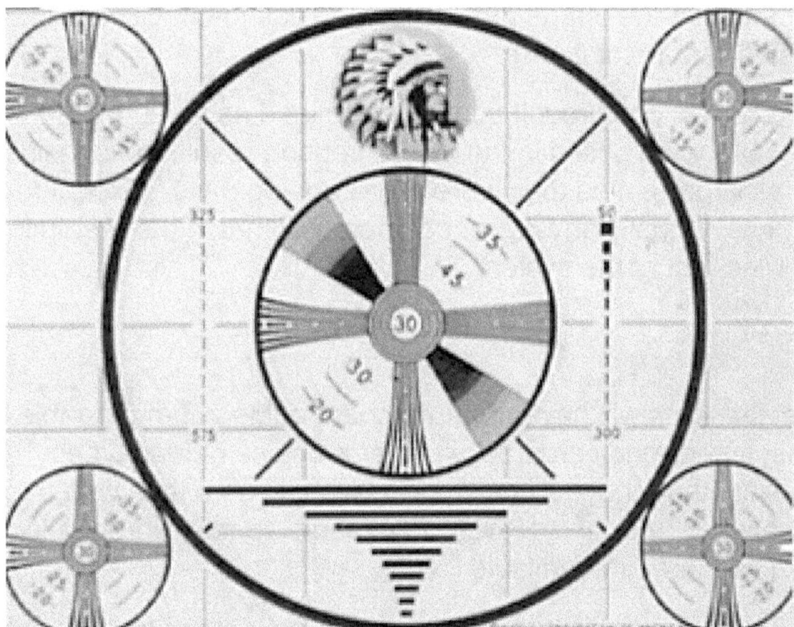

The numbers indicate tens of lines – 30 means 300 lines. By observing where the lines run together, the approximate resolution of the system (lens, camera, transmission chain and monitor) could be measured. Here's a more modern version:

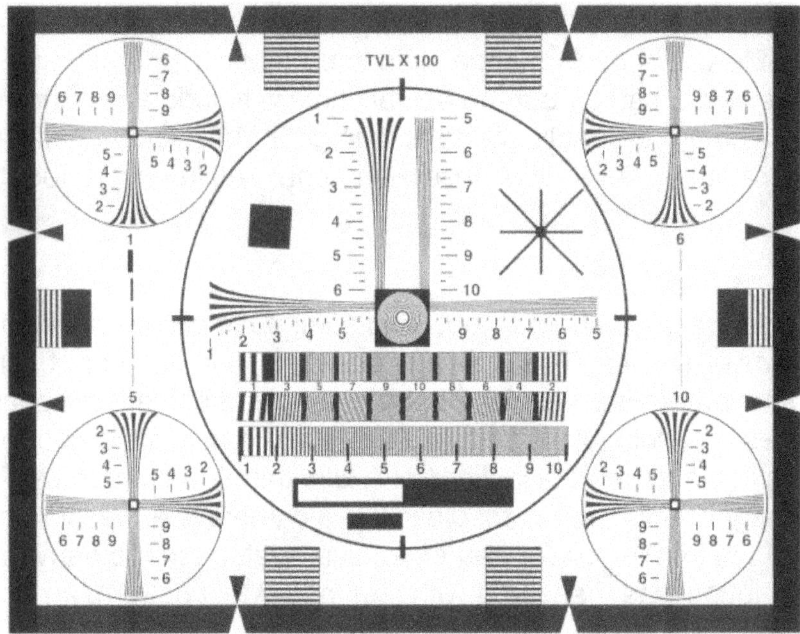

(Note: don't try to use the charts printed in this book to check your camera – they do not have sufficient resolution!)

Because a digital camera's resolution is determined as much by the recording format as the number of pixels in the image sensor, resolution specifications aren't nearly as important as they were in the analog days. Except for very inexpensive units, virtually any current camera will match the resolution capabilities of the rest of the system.

Lenses

Most low-cost cameras will have non-interchangeable zoom (variable focal length) lenses; higher-end cameras will offer a choice of lens types. Almost without exception, though, you'll be working with a zoom lens with a range of somewhere between 10:1 and 15:1, though some special-purpose lenses with ranges of 50:1 or more are available.

A zoom lens' range (*zoom factor*) is the ratio of the longest focal length to the shortest focal length. Sometimes the lens range is specified by the minimum and maximum focal length, i.e. 10-150 mm. Alternatively, the same lens may be described as 10 x 15, which is the minimum focal length and zoom factor.

The focal length is the distance between the optical center of the lens and the image the lens casts, when focused on an object at infinity. Of course, a zoom lens has a continuously variable focal length. A short focal length creates a *wide-angle* view; a long focal length gives you a *telephoto* effect. A zoom lens allows a continuous adjustment of the focal length. Fixed focal length lenses (often called *prime* lenses) are available for some high-end cameras. Because they have a simpler optical design and fewer glass elements, they can (at least in theory) produce higher quality images. Their disadvantage is, of course, that you must use a different lens to get a different focal length.

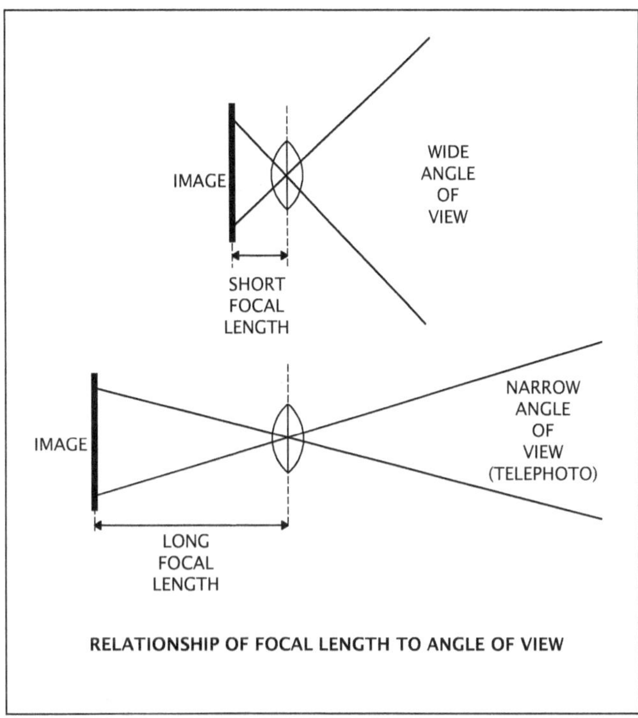

RELATIONSHIP OF FOCAL LENGTH TO ANGLE OF VIEW

The optical quality of modern zoom lenses can come very close to the performance of prime lenses, and for most purposes, they will be more than adequate. Perhaps surprisingly, the permanently attached lenses on some of the better prosumer cameras may actually be better than the "standard" interchangeable lenses provided in higher-end camera packages. This is true because it is often possible for designers to create a less expensive but high-performance lens system if they can design it as a part of the total optical system of the camera, instead of having to deal with existing lens mounts and other variables. Of course, high quality glass will do a lot to get the most out of any camera, especially if you're shooting in HD. With the exception of consumer or ultra-miniature cameras, optical quality should be good or excellent with lenses from any of the major manufacturers.

Many prosumer and consumer camcorders have a feature called *digital zoom* in addition to the optical zoom capabilities of the lens itself. Digital zoom works by turning off some of the pixels of the imaging chip in order to effectively magnify the image, but this technique results in degradation of picture quality. Except for unusual situations, this feature shouldn't be considered a useful addition to a camera's capabilities. Fortunately, most cameras allow digital zoom to be turned off.

Zoom Lens Adapters

Although the zoom lens that comes with your camera may have a long range (e.g., 15:1), most have too long a focal length at the shortest setting. In other words, full wide angle isn't wide enough. Lenses designed for general-purpose use may not have a wide enough angle of view to get a full-length shot of a person in a small room – you simply can't get far enough away with the camera.

For example, a camera with 2/3-inch (17mm) chips may be supplied with a 15:1 lens with a minimum focal length of 10mm, about 60% of the diagonal measurement of the imaging chips. Such a lens might be fine for studio use or sports, but would not be wide enough for on-location drama or architectural shooting. Unfortunately, zoom lenses having minimum focal lengths less than 50% of the image diagonal tend to get expensive, but they're great if you can afford one. For interior or architectural shooting, I prefer a lens with a minimum focal length of about 40% of the chip size (6.8mm for a 2/3-inch chip camera). You can determine the equivalent minimum focal length for any camera simply by knowing the chip size and the shortest focal length of the lens. (No, I don't know why chip sizes are in inches and lens focal lengths are in millimeters!)

If you must use a lens with marginal wide-angle capabilities (as is true of almost all fixed lenses), there is a relatively inexpensive solution: a wide-angle adapter. It's a *must-have* accessory for any camera without interchangeable lenses. They are available to fit most camcorders, and with the better ones you can continue to use the zoom normally with the adapter attached. They are specified by a multiplier factor (such as 0.5, 0.6, 0.7, etc); they will multiply the effective focal length of the lens by indicated factor. For example, a 0.6 lens will turn a 10mm lens into a 6mm lens. I'd suggest an adapter with a factor of 0.6 to 0.7 for general use. A wider lens may cause straight lines to curve, a phenomenon called barrel distortion, giving a *fish-eye* effect. You might consider a 0.4 or 0.35 adapter for special effects shots. When you choose a wide-angle adapter, try to test it on your camera before you buy, since some of them will *vignette* (produce black shadows in the corners of the frame) at the full-wide setting of the lens. Another problem common in inexpensive wide-angle adapters is color fringing, a rainbow effect on objects near the corners of the frame. In general, the physically larger adapters will be less likely to exhibit these problems.

Telephoto adapters are also available, with factors of 1.5, 2, etc., and they are used in a similar manner. In addition, some interchangeable lenses are equipped with a built-in *extender*, usually with a telephoto factor of 2, that can be put into the optical path with the flip of a lever. Keep in mind that any adapter lens or extender will degrade the performance of your main lens (however slightly) so it's a good idea to use them only when you really need them.

Zoom Lens Control

Most camcorder lenses control the zoom function with a small rocker switch on the lens or camera body. The ability start and stop a zoom smoothly and accurately control the zoom speed varies widely from one camera to the next. The switch is pressure sensitive; push more for a fast zoom, less for a slow zoom. Professional lenses have a larger rocker with much more precise zoom control than prosumer cameras, but if you really want smooth zooms, nothing beats a separate zoom controller. These are available from a variety of manufacturers, and are designed to be mounted on the tripod pan handle. In addition to zoom control, many of them offer control of focus, turning auto-focus on and off, and starting and stopping the camera.

Controllers for pro lenses are usually available only for a specific lens, or a particular manufacturer's family of lenses, so they must be bought to match a particular lens. For many prosumer cameras, Sony's LANC protocol is used for lens control. LANC-based controllers vary in quality, but the best ones offer very smooth control of zoom and a relatively complete roster of other camera functions that are supported by LANC.

Pro lens controllers offer a continuously variable speed range, but the LANC protocol works on a series of discreet zoom speeds. Various cameras may support all of these speeds or only a subset of them. This means that your camera may or may not be able to realize a smoothly accelerating or decelerating zoom. Unfortunately, less expensive cameras may have only three or four speeds, which seriously compromises your ability to do smooth zooms. You won't find a listing of how many speeds your camera supports in the spec sheet, either. If you try the on-camera zoom rocker, however, you can get a sense of how many speeds are available – if you can see obvious, discreet speed changes, you don't have enough speeds available. While LANC-controlled lenses all have discreet speed settings, there should be enough different speeds that the zoom speeds appear to be continuously variable.

Whatever camera-lens combination you're using, you'll find a remote zoom controller a worthwhile accessory. I won't go so far as to say it's essential, because the style and subject of your film will determine whether and when zooms are appropriate or needed.

Extreme Closeups

Many zoom lenses (particularly interchangeable ones) have a minimum focus distance of three to four feet (3-3.5 meters. You can't get closer than this distance and keep your subject in focus, so if you're doing extreme close-ups, you'll have a problem. There are three ways to get around this shortcoming.

1. Some lenses have a *macro* function that allows them to focus much closer. Be aware, however, that when macro is engaged, you won't be able to use the zoom function without re-focusing.
2. There are supplementary lenses called *plus diopters*, usually available in sets of two or three (+1, +2, +3 diopters, etc., the higher the number the closer to the subject you can get and the greater the magnification). These lenses let you get much closer to the subject, but when they are

attached the maximum focus distance decreases. It is possible, however, to use the zoom function normally with plus diopter lenses attached.

3. Macro-focusing prime lenses are also available for some cameras. These totally replace the zoom lens; they are not adapters.

Close focusing is one advantage of camcorders with fixed lenses. Since the lens doesn't need to be removed, these lenses are often designed to focus very close and continue to keep the zoom functional, or to automatically invoke the macro function.

How Fast is Your Lens?

Lens *speed* is another important factor: fast lenses allow more light to pass through, thus increasing the effective sensitivity of the camera. Speed is specified by an *f-number* (factor), such as *f*1.8, also often written as a ratio like 1:1.8, because it actually is a ratio. The *f*-number is the ratio of the focal length to the effective lens diameter. For example, an *f*/2 lens with a focal length of 50mm will have an effective diameter of 25mm. All lenses contain an *iris* or *aperture* that adjusts the size of the lens opening to reduce the amount of light. Iris settings are based on standard *f-stops* in a series: *f/1, f/1.4, /f2, f/2.8, f/4, f/5.6, f/8, f/11, f/16, f*/22, etc. Each increase of one *f*-stop reduces the amount of light passing through the lens by one half. While an in-between *f*-stop (such as *f/2.4* or *f/14*) is certainly valid, you'll rarely need this level of precision.

With the exception of some special purpose or telephoto lenses, video lenses have speeds of between *f*/1.4 and *f*/2, a range of only one *f*-stop, but a factor of 2 to 1 in effective camera sensitivity. A faster lens is better, but it may also be bigger, heavier and more expensive. It's also important to remember that most lenses produce their sharpest images somewhere in the middle of their *f*-stop range – about *f*/5.6 or *f*/8.

You may also come across some high-end lenses that are calibrated in *T-stops* instead of *f*-stops. They work the same, but T-stops (the T stands for *transmission*) are determined by actually measuring the light transmission of the lens, instead of using calculated values.

Depth of Field

This is an important aspect of lenses, related to focal length and aperture. While mathematically complex, the concept is relatively simple. For a given focal length and focus setting, the image will appear to be in sharp focus over a range of distances. For example, for a particular focal length and *f*-stop, objects from 5 to 8 feet from the camera will be sharp, while objects closer or farther away will be more or less out of focus, depending on how close or far. Shorter focal lengths (wide angle) have greater depth of field, while longer focal lengths have shallow depth of field. Similarly, higher *f*-stops (e.g., *f*/16) allow greater depth of field than lower *f*-stops (e.g., *f*/2.0). Keeping these facts in mind can help you take advantage of the optical characteristics of your lens.

Wide-angle lens settings and high *f*-stops tend to keep everything in the shot in sharp focus, often having a depth of field from a few inches to infinity. Conversely, if you're using a telephoto lens "wide open" at a distance of ten feet, you'll find that the depth of field may be only few inches.

Cinematographers often make effective use of shallow depth of field to accent and draw attention to a subject, keeping the intended object in sharp focus while background and foreground objects become very soft. Sometimes they *follow focus* (sometimes called *rack focus*) during a scene; that is, they change focus from one object to another during a shot, or vary the focus setting to accommodate movement of the camera or subject. Whether follow-focus can be easily accomplished with a particular lens configuration is an important consideration. Sometimes it's done by turning the manual focus control from one marked point to another; with other cameras it's necessary to use the focus-distance display in the viewfinder. Accomplished shooters learn to follow-focus based solely on the amount of movement they need to give the focus control.

For a given shot, cameras with larger chips will have shallower depth of field. This may be very important for artistic effect, but with large-format chips it is more difficult to maintain sharp focus. I have seen more shots ruined by this problem than by any other, so remember this important point when choosing a camera. (To help solve this problem, you'll see someone called a "Focus Puller" listed in the credits of many Hollywood films. He's the person responsible for keeping the shots in focus, and doing follow-focus when needed.)

What is Infinity?

Related to depth of field is the optical concept of infinity. If you look at the focusing scale of a manually focused lens, you'll see a scale of distances (designated in feet or meters) with the symbol ∞, for infinity. For practical purposes, your subject will be solidly in focus when you set the lens to infinity for anything beyond about 10 feet with a wide-angle lens or about 100 feet for telephoto lenses. So, obviously, landscape, scenery, or shots of the moon will always be in focus with the lens racked to ∞. You don't have to worry about manually focusing on mountain ranges!

Autofocus Systems

In one form or another, autofocus systems are included on all consumer and prosumer cameras and on some professional models, and they are amazingly good within their limitations. Most work on the principle of maximizing fine detail in the image – a good indication that it's in sharp focus. They sometimes get confused when the object you want to be in sharp focus is relatively small in the frame or when the subject has low visual contrast.

In choosing a camera, it's important to be sure it is easy to lock the focus so it doesn't change while shooting when you might not want it to. The ideal way to use autofocus is to zoom in on the subject you want to be sharp, let the camera focus, then turn off the autofocus and zoom to the shot you want. Some cameras have one of a variety of focus assist systems to make it easier to see when a particular object is in sharp focus – sometimes a very useful feature.

One disadvantage of autofocus systems is that the lens is controlled by an electronic servomechanism, instead of a direct mechanical linkage. This means that the position of the manual focus control has no direct relationship to the lens' focus distance (in fact, there may be no manual focus ring at all) so it can be difficult to "follow focus". Manually focused lenses have a distance scale etched on the focus ring for this purpose. Some autofocus systems allow the focus distance to be displayed in the viewfinder to help with this problem.

Manually focusing in HD can be difficult because your recorded image contains more pixels than your viewfinder can display, so learn to use the autofocus, at least as a backup to be sure your shots are sharp.

Automatic Exposure Control

Standard equipment on all camcorders, these systems have become very good. It's important, however, to choose a camera that allows the user to override and lock the exposure during shooting. It's usually not a desirable effect if the camera reduces the exposure when the pretty girl in the white dress enters the scene!

With most cameras, the normal procedure is to let the automatic exposure control determine the proper exposure, then lock the exposure during shooting to avoid changes. Unfortunately, camera manufacturers' default automatic exposure settings tend to produce a bit of over exposure causing bright areas of the image to "burn out". The rationale behind this setting is that for "typical" scenes, it's more important to have good detail in flesh tones than in bright areas. While this is sometimes true, good lighting should eliminate the problem and avoid the need to compromise in this way.

Most cameras offer custom setup options that can, for example, allow you to continue to use the automatic exposure control system but to specify a bit more or less exposure on all shots. Unlike film, video cameras are very intolerant of overexposure, so highlight detail lost in the camera is not recoverable. Digital camcorders suffer from this shortcoming, but mildly underexposed shots can easily be brought up during color correction. Because of this (and unlike shooting negative film), it's better to underexpose than overexpose.

Cameras (especially consumer and prosumer models) often include a number of auto exposure "modes", too. Each manufacturer has its own versions of these and each is a bit different, so it's best to experiment a bit with your camera to see how they work. They're often identified with little icons representing people, scenery, sports, bright sun, etc. The "people" setting may brighten the mid-tones a bit while the "scenery" setting may brighten the shadows and darken the highlights. One particularly useful setting provided on most cameras is "backlight", a mode that works well for shooting subjects against the sky, a window or other light source. It's helpful to experiment with these settings to find the one that best suits the way you'll be working with a particular camera.

Some auto exposure systems allow you to assign either shutter or aperture *priority*. Shutter priority will keep a fixed f-stop (aperture) and adjust the shutter speed for the proper exposure. Aperture priority is the opposite – keeping the shutter speed fixed and varying the f-stop. Which to use is determined by scene content and artistic intent.

A word of caution about the auto exposure function of consumer and prosumer cameras: Some of these automatically invoke gain boost when light levels are low – without warning you. Be sure this function is turned off if the camera permits; it can lead to grainy, noisy pictures, and sometimes you can't see the problem in the viewfinder. (See Gain Adjustment, below.)

Automatic White Balance

White balance controls accommodate shooting under different lighting conditions. Sunlight, for example, contains much more blue than the light from a typical household lamp. (More on the differences in color of light sources and what to do about them will be found in Chapter 2.5.) The human eye-brain combination does a remarkable job of hiding these differences from us, even though the eye is exquisitely sensitive to differences in color. Instinctively, the eye seems to be able to pick an object of known color in a scene and adjust all the colors in the scene to match. The camera isn't nearly as smart, though automatic white balance is an attempt to accomplish the same thing.

I'm sure you've seen photographs of interior scenes that look very orange, or outdoor scenes that look strangely blue. These are the result of incorrect white balance. In the film world, film stocks can be balanced for exposure under daylight or tungsten (incandescent) illumination, and film cameramen have color correction filters to accommodate these differences. Digital cameras can compensate electronically, by varying their sensitivity to various colors.

With automatic white balance on most cameras, you aim the camera at a white object under the illumination you'll be using and touch the white balance button or control. When viewed on a monitor (or color viewfinder), the object should now appear white, not bluish or yellowish, indicating that the auto-white system is doing its job. Consumer cameras have "full time" automatic white balance that continually examines the average color of a scene and makes its "best guess" at the correct white balance. With most scenes, such systems are amazingly good, but in scenes where one color is dominant, they can produce unexpected and sometimes bizarre results. Where possible, it's best to white balance on a known-white object and then disengage (lock) the auto-white function.

Most cameras offer presets for known lighting conditions; there are usually two or three of them. There will be one for tungsten light and one or two for daylight use. There may also be one or two for fluorescent lighting. (See Chapter 2.5). Many professionals recommend using the presets rather than automatic white balance because the results are more consistent (and I agree). This is especially important where cuts from shot-to-shot within a scene must match. If the cameraman has done his job, the editor or colorist should be able to use the same color correction on all shots within a scene. The important thing is that color balance is "in the ballpark" and stays the same from shot to shot. Subtle color corrections can and should be applied during post-production.

Filters

Higher end cameras often have a filter wheel positioned behind the lens, providing optical color correction and *neutral density* (ND) filters that reduce the amount of light reaching the imaging chips. ND filters are useful when you wish to use the camera under very bright lighting conditions, such as outdoors on the beach. The camera's instruction manual will provide more detailed information on use of the filters, and later in the book I'll describe techniques for using them. If your camera doesn't have built-in filters, you can use standard screw-on filters over the lens, and there are hundreds of different kinds available.

Some cinematographers like to keep an ultraviolet (UV) filter (also called a *skylight* filter) on the lens at all times. These filters are optically clear for all visible colors, but sharply reduce invisible ultraviolet light. Film (and some video cameras) is sensitive to UV, so sources of UV light, such as a blue sky, will be rendered lighter on the film than they appear to the eye; a UV filter prevents this effect, resulting in deeper blue skies. Some digital cameras also have sensitivity to infrared (IR) light, which is also invisible. This sensitivity can cause errors in color rendition, so similar filters are available for cameras with this deficiency. Whether actually needed for its filtering action or not, one of these filters is still a good idea since it provides physical protection for your expensive lens.

Another useful filter is the *polarizer*, which is used to reduce glare. Light reflected from near-horizontal surfaces tends to be polarized (vibrate) horizontally so a filter that only passes vertically-polarized light minimizes the reflections. The light from the sky may also be strongly polarized, so a polarizer can deepen the sky's color. These filters are designed so that they can easily be rotated for maximum effect. They also provide about two *f*-stops reduction of light intensity.

A wide variety of fog and diffusion filters are also available, with effects ranging from subtle to extreme. Their main function is to reduce contrast in the recorded image and many shooters swear by them. One of the most popular filter lines in this category is the Tiffen Promist series.

Since video cameras can be white-balanced for most lighting situations, color correction filters are seldom used. Sometimes they are helpful for special effects, however, and a wide variety is available.

One popular special effects filter type is the *grad.* It varies smoothly in color from the top to the bottom, and is used to darken or colorize skies. Grads come in colors and neutral density versions, in both round and square. Square filters require a *matte box* for proper mounting.

Soft focus filters slightly blur everything in a scene, and are sometimes used for more flattering closeups. Star filters create a star effect around lights in a shot. Others can create ripples or concentric circles. A quick look at a filter catalog can give you a sense of the vast number of effects filters available.

Keep in mind that the effects created by these filters can usually be simulated during post-production, and many professionals prefer to shoot their footage "clean", depending on the editor for adding appropriate filter effects.

Image Stabilization

This is standard equipment on most consumer and prosumer camcorders and optional on professional models. Its function is to minimize shaky images resulting from hand-holding the camera. While the only sure way to get steady pictures is to use a tripod or other solid method of camera support, stabilization systems can do a lot to smooth out camera motion.

There are two common types of image stabilizers: optical and digital. Optical stabilization is generally considered the better of the two systems, although digital stabilization has the edge if the camera has multi-megapixel chips. Optical stabilization is accomplished by adding a moving glass element to the lens system and devices called *accelerometers* to detect camera motion, or they may derive equivalent information from the actual images. The accelerometers and an electronic servomechanism move the stabilizer element in the lens in a way that counteracts the camera motion.

Digital stabilization also uses accelerometers or digital motion detection, but instead of moving the image in the lens, it moves the area of the imaging CCD that is scanned, thus counteracting camera shake. When digital stabilization is used, it means that only about 80% of the available pixels are being used at any particular time, so you give up some resolution in exchange for image stabilization. Some cameras use the entire CCD when stabilization is turned off; others stay with the 80% in the middle of the CCD all the time.

Viewfinders

Most professional cameras use a black and white CRT (cathode ray tube) viewfinder for a very good reason: it creates a sharper image than the small LCD viewfinders found on most consumer and prosumer cameras. Get a CRT viewfinder if you can because it's very difficult to tell if your image is in pinpoint sharp focus on an LCD, especially if you are shooting HD. If you must settle for an LCD, try to find a camera with a black and white viewfinder since all of its pixels will be displaying useful sharpness information. Unfortunately, most manufacturers have gone exclusively to color LCD viewfinders in their consumer and prosumer lines, which means you'll have to learn to use and trust the camera's auto-focus system or double-check your focus on an external monitor. HD cameras usually have a viewfinder zoom feature, which magnifies the central part of the frame (only in the viewfinder) for critical focusing. These systems are a great compromise and work well.

Many cameras have a built-in LCD monitor in addition to the viewfinder, and these are larger and have higher resolution than the tiny LCD in the viewfinder. There are many compromises in their design to make them small, lightweight and consume modest amounts of precious battery power. As a result, they have a narrow viewing angle; the color only looks correct when they are viewed straight on. They're also not very bright, making them all but useless in full sunlight. Still, they are often better than the viewfinder for judging focus and shot composition, but they are not a substitute for a good external monitor.

With better cameras, the viewfinder is equipped to display *zebra stripes*, shaded areas in the picture that indicate a particular level of exposure. Basic zebra stripes show overexposed areas of the picture – those with video levels above 100%. Some offer a second level of stripes at 75 or 80% for better control. If you learn to use the stripes, you can often avoid the need for an expensive waveform monitor. Pro and prosumer cameras are also capable of generating *color bars*, a standard test signal (see Chapter 2.7).

You should also be aware that the viewfinders and LCD displays in most consumer cameras are *overscanned*. This means that on these viewfinders, you don't quite see all of the picture; about 5% of it is cut off, around the edges. The reason for this is that TV sets display a picture that is slightly larger than the screen. The amount of overscan in TV sets varies from one to the next, being greatest on smaller, cheaper CRT sets.

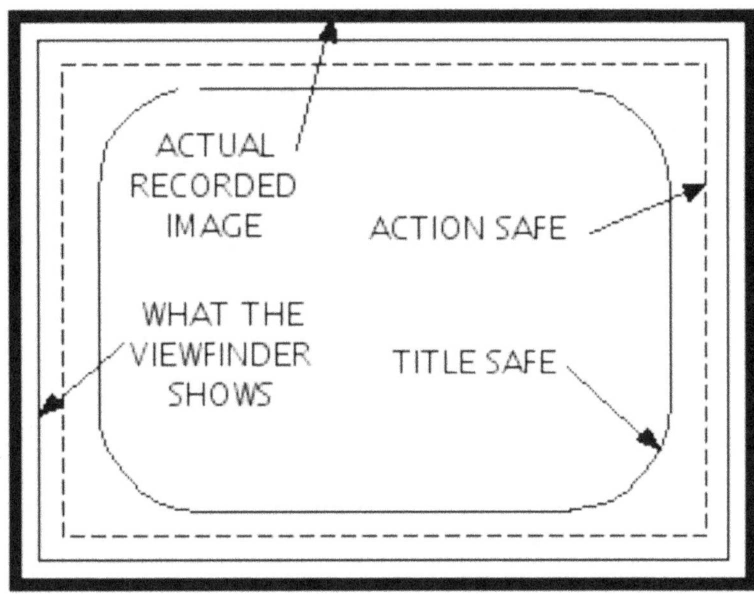

The sketch shows what happens. The actual recorded image is represented by the large rectangle. Inside is what you see on the camera viewfinder. (Note that professional cameras show the entire recorded image in the viewfinder.) The dotted line inside this is called *action safe,* meaning that any action displayed within this area is *likely* to be seen on any TV set. The area labeled *title safe* will be seen on any set, and thus is safe for titles.

While digital displays (such as LCD or plasma screens) could be built to always show 100% of the transmitted picture, they are not. There are two main reasons for this. First, a lot of older analog content may have slight variations in image size, and could show black edges on such a display. Second, many viewers still use VHS tape, which can create disturbances in the video near the bottom edge of the screen due to the way the video heads are switched between fields. Unfortunately, there is no standard among manufacturers as to the amount of overscan. So exactly where the so-called "safe" lines are is anybody's guess. A word to the wise: don't take anybody's "action safe" or "title safe" as being true – it's always an approximation. Just be sure anything you <u>don't</u> want to be seen is outside the recorded picture, and anything that <u>must</u> be seen is inside "title safe"!

To complicate things even more, some viewers will be watching 4 x 3 content on 16 x 9 displays – which means (depending on the display setup) that areas above and below "title safe" may be cropped away, while everything to the left and right of "title safe" may still be seen. Similarly, some 4 x 3 displays will crop away the left and right portions of 16 x 9 content. It sure will be nice when the day comes that everybody is watching 16 x 9 content on 16 x 9 screens! Until 16 x 9 displays become universal, it's best to observe a "shoot-and-protect" philosophy, so your film is OK for a viewer who sees the whole frame and also OK for those that only see what's inside "title safe".

Camera Bells and Whistles

Modern cameras, especially prosumer models, offer a bewildering array of features affecting the recorded images and allowing specialized uses. For the filmmaker, some of these features can be helpful, others become obstacles and create confusion. While there are too many of these "extras" to cover here, below is a rundown on the most important ones, beginning with features commonly found on high-end cameras.

Gain Adjustment

This feature allows the operator to control the sensitivity of the camera for various shooting conditions. It's similar to a cinematographer's ability to choose a fast (sensitive) or slow (higher quality but less sensitive) motion picture film stock. As a camera's gain is boosted (+ values of gain) its sensitivity increases, but so does the *noise*; the word "noise" is a holdover from the audio world – it's equivalent to the "hiss" you hear when you turn up the volume (gain) on an audio amplifier. In video, noise appears as *grain*, moving tiny dots in the picture, similar to the grain caused by silver particles in motion picture film. Gain settings are specified in *decibels* (db); an increase of 6 decibels is equivalent doubling the sensitivity. Changing the gain to +6 will create an image of equivalent brightness and contrast with 1/2 as much illumination on the subject. Another way of saying this is: 6 db of gain boost is equivalent to one *f*-stop. Obviously, it's best to use as little gain boost as necessary to get a normal exposure, keeping noise as low as possible. There are exceptions to this rule, too: you may want a grainy appearance to get a particular "look" for your film. Some cameras also have the ability to reduce the gain from normal, with a corresponding reduction in sensitivity and noise. Under adequate lighting conditions, gain reduction can produce a wonderfully noise-free image.

Shutter Speed Adjustment

A digital camera doesn't usually have physical shutter like a film camera, but it has the functional equivalent that allows the image sensor to accumulate light for a specific interval for each video frame. "Normal" shutter speed for 60-field video is 1/60 second, so that each image captured corresponds to one field. Higher shutter speeds (1/120, 1/500, 1/1000, etc.) reduce the sensitivity of the camera and create less *motion blur,* the natural "smearing" of images in which the subject moves during the exposure. Short shutter speeds can create a very crisp image. They are often used for subjects like fast moving sports action. Another use for the variable shutter is its ability to reduce the effective sensitivity of the camera, allowing more control in the use of the lens. For example, if it's desired to have foreground objects in sharp focus with an out-of-focus background, a fast shutter speed can give the correct exposure with the lens wide open, the setting that produces minimum depth-of-field. Keep in mind that doubling the shutter speed (from 1/60 to 1/120, for example) reduces the light sensitivity by the equivalent of one *f*-stop.

Cameras often include a 1/100 second exposure time to allow shooting under lighting powered by 50 Hz. power, common outside the US. With no compensation, shooting 30- or 24-frame video under 50 Hz. lighting can produce an undesirable pulsing effect.

Progressive Scan

Shutter speeds of longer than 1/60 second cause the CCD to accumulate its charge over a period longer than one field, thus increasing effective camera sensitivity. A shutter speed of 1/30 second creates the motion equivalent of a 30 frame per second progressively scanned image, minimizing interlace artifacts and creating more film-like motion. Longer shutter speeds (1/15, 1/10, etc.) produce a stop-motion effect. Unless you are working in extremely low light conditions, however, it's best to shoot footage normally and apply the effects during editing.

Some cameras also have a group of *clear-scan* shutter settings that are selected to match the scan rates of computer monitors. Since computer monitors operate at different scan rates than TV monitors, they will often appear to be flickering badly if shot with the normal 1/60 second exposure time. Clear-scan can minimize this effect. Note that scan rate differences usually aren't a problem when shooting LCD computer displays.

Skin Tone Enhancement

Some cameras offer a special setting for shooting people called *skin tone enhancement*. Since today's cameras are capable of producing extremely sharp images, they tend to bring out any defects in skin texture, certainly not flattering. This function works by identifying colors in the skin tone range and reducing the amount of detail only in those portions of the image. The effect, if used sparingly, can create the impression of near-perfect skin. Of course, it's not a substitute for good makeup, but its use, especially for close-ups, can improve the appearance of almost anyone. If it's overdone, however, people's skin begins to look like plastic.

In-Camera Special Effects

Manufacturers of consumer cameras throw in as many of these (usually tasteless) effects as they can, since they can do it very cheaply when they write the camera software. Such effects as "mosaic", "sepia", "posterize", "strobe" and others are best done after the fact, during editing, where you will have a great deal more control. Even if you want your film to be in black and white or sepia, it's better to shoot in color and create the effect during post-production, because you may change your mind or you may want to use your footage for another purpose. Avoid, too, the in-camera titles, fades and dissolves some cameras can do. The camera is not the right tool for these, either. The only reason they're there is for consumers who won't be editing their movies.

One possible exception to this rule is the "night vision" effect offered on a few cameras. This is one case where the manufacturers have added a legitimate feature that's good on some occasions. It takes advantage of the fact that CCD imagers are very sensitive to invisible infrared radiation, and they can have amazing sensitivity in this mode. Again, it's something to experiment with.

Some consumer cameras throw in a plethora of other features that are useless in serious filmmaking, and often can get in the way. They can take still images (though not as well as a good still camera), they can be a webcam, and some can even connect to the Internet and get email. Like other tools, if you need a chisel, you don't use a screwdriver even though you could.

Camera Audio

Don't forget to consider audio capabilities when choosing a camera. For serious work, there are two MUST-HAVE requirements: At least one microphone input and a headphone jack. Many otherwise excellent cameras omit these vital connections. An ALMOST-MUST-HAVE feature is manual audio level control. See Chapters 2.5 and 3.4 for more information on these important features.

"You need to learn to see and compose. The more time you waste worrying about your equipment the less time you'll have to put into creating great images. Worry about your images, not your equipment."

Ken Rockwell

2.4 Recording

"You can't make up anything anymore. The world itself is a satire. All you're doing is recording it."

Art Buchwald

Next, you'll need to choose how you're going to record your video and audio. The objective is to use the most *transparent* format you can. In this context, the word transparent means that what you get out of it is as close as possible to what you put in; the recording format shouldn't introduce distortions or artifacts into your images or sound. Of course, you choice of camera will also dictate your choice of recording format, since most cameras available today include the recorder – hence the name *camcorder.*

The ideal recorder would be able to hold all the digital data the camera generates without throwing away anything, but cameras generate prodigious amounts of data. For HD, the raw data rate is gigabits per second, a speed that can only be accommodated by very fast computer hard drives; it's beyond the capabilities of practical tape or optical disk systems. SD contains much less data, but no camcorder can accommodate its data rate, either.

Analog to Digital and Digital to Analog Conversion

In digital recording, analog signals are converted to numbers (hence the origin of the term "digital"), which come out as a stream of *bits* (binary digits). Each bit can have only two states: on or off, but combinations of bits can represent any number. The data stream leaving the camera will contain a series of bits corresponding to the color of each pixel in the scene.

Although the imaging chips in the camera are part of a digital system, they are actually analog devices that are digitally controlled. Similarly, microphones are analog devices, as are monitors and speakers. Before we can record images and sounds digitally, we must convert the analog signals to digital representations; before we can watch or listen to the output of a digital recorder, we must convert digital data to analog signals.

Analog to digital conversion is a three-step process: filtering, sampling and quantizing. When the imaging chip in a camera is “clocked out”, the result is a voltage that varies with time, with the actual voltage at any given instant corresponding to the amount of light falling on one pixel of the thousands or millions on the chip. You’ll remember that the number of pixels on the chip doesn’t necessarily correspond to the number of pixels in the image format – in fact, it usually doesn’t.

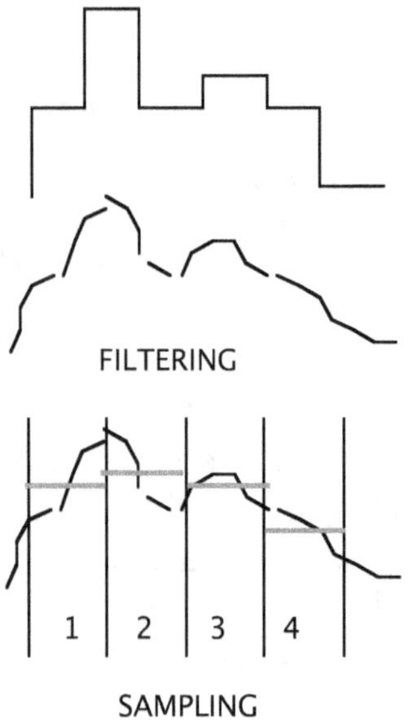

Displayed on an oscilloscope, the actual output of an imaging chip might look like the top line in the drawing. Each of the “steps” is a voltage value representing the amount of light falling on one of the thousands or millions of pixels on the chip, in this case we see six pixels. This signal is passed through a circuit called a low-pass filter, which causes the waveform to become a smooth curve. The curve is then “re-sliced” into pieces that correspond to the number of pixels in the desired output format. In the case of SD formats, there are 720 slices for each horizontal line of pixels.

In this closeup there are about four slices for six pixels on the imaging chip. An average value for each slice represents a single *sample* of the signal (gray lines). Since the number of samples is less than the number of pixels in the image, the signal is said to be *undersampled* or *subsampled*. Each sample is assigned a numeric value in digital form, in most cases with an 8-bit (a bit is a *binary digit*) representation (although some high-end cameras use up to 16 bits). Eight bits (or one *byte*) can represent 256 different discreet values; with 0 representing black (or no light) and 255 representing white (or maximum light). Ten bits can represent 1024 different values, twelve bits 4096. In a camera, conversion is done separately for each of the three primary colors, so 8-bit representation is called 24-bit color, capable of reproducing over 16 million different shades.

How Bits Work

Bits represent *binary* digits, and all computers use binary numbers. Unlike the decimal (base 10) numbers we normally work with, we don’t have ten digits to represent a number, we only have two: 0 and 1. Just as the decimal number 326 indicates three “hundreds” plus two “tens”, plus 6 “ones” (300+20+6), the binary number 101 represents one “four” plus zero “twos” plus 1 (which converts to decimal 5: 4+0+1). It’s easy to figure out how the maximum value for eight bits is binary 11111111 (all ones) or decimal 255. Of course, 00000000 (all zeros) is zero, and including zero gives 256 possible values for an 8-bit byte. 8-bit representation (*byte*) is the usual length of a digital *word* in computers. If a camera uses 10- or 12-bit representation, 10 or 12 becomes the length of a word in that particular system.

Binary numbers are very hard for humans to read, but they're perfect for computers since they can be represented by only two states: off (0) and on (1). Each off or on signal is a single bit.

This process of measuring a signal and converting it to a digital number is called *quantization*, and the number of bits used is called the *quantization resolution* or *bit depth*. At the end of the quantization process, we have a string of bits that represents our picture, and there are a lot of bits!

Quantization works just like a digital voltmeter or digital thermometer – it simply converts an analog value to a number. The same process is used for the audio signals, except their sampling rates are much lower – usually 48,000 or 44,100 samples per second. The resolution for audio, however, is 16 (or sometimes 24) bits, because the ear is considered more sensitive than the eye when it comes to accuracy of reproduction.

Remember that once an analog signal, (audio, video, temperature, voltage, whatever) is converted to digital, it becomes essentially identical to any other kind of data. Computer hardware handles all data the same way, whether it's your film, your favorite song, or your bank account records. The data can be transmitted, recorded, stored and copied. Data is data, it's just a "bucket of bits" that can be moved around and manipulated by computers. In the case of your camcorder, the defined format simply creates a stream of bits, the data that represents your audio and video. There are a few extra housekeeping bits, too, representing things like the beginning of each frame or field, and timecode.

Digital-to-analog conversion simply takes a particular stream of bits and reverses the process. Each sample value is given a voltage equivalent for an analog signal output. For example, a digital value of 255 might represent one volt of analog signal, a value of 0 would create zero volts.

Compression and Data Reduction

To be able to economically record digital video, *data rate reduction* and *compression* are required because (as we say in the South) there's a whole bunch of bits coming out of the camera. In digital video recording and transmission, mathematical techniques are used to discard as much information as possible, while retaining enough to reconstruct the picture with pristine or at least adequate quality.

Some data reduction is possible because the human eye cannot perceive certain shortcomings in the reproduced image. It turns out, for example, that we see fine detail only as variations in brightness (contrast), not as variations in color. This is because the eye has a lot more "rod" cells (which respond to light intensity) compared to the number of "cone" cells (responsible for the perception of colors). To help you understand one way we can take advantage of this fact, here is a simplified explanation:

Instead of recording the direct output from the red, blue and green chips in the camera (RGB), these three signals can be mathematically combined (added) in certain proportions to form a single *luminance* (or *"Y"*) signal, which becomes essentially a black-and-white version of the color image. We can now take the original signal from the red chip and subtract the Y signal from it, creating a new signal we call *red difference* (R minus Y or R–Y, also called C_r or *U*). If we do the same for the blue chip, we can create *blue difference* (B minus Y or B–Y, also called C_b or *V*). (Note: Analog broadcast television standards define a slightly different trio of signals called *YIQ*, but they function similarly.)

These two difference signals together are called *chrominance*. So now, we still have three signals, but instead of red, blue and green, we have three other signals: *Y, R–Y* and *B–Y* (also called *Y*, C_r, C_b or *YUV*). Without specifically trying, we also have a *G–Y* (*green difference*) signal buried in the combination and it can easily be derived. Reversing the math, we can re-create the original R, G and B signals. Interestingly, with black and white video, the R-Y and B-Y signals become zero and essentially disappear. Thus, a color camera shooting a black-and-white image creates an output essentially the same as a black-and-white camera shooting the same image. Conversely, turning off the chrominance information turns a color camera into a black-and-white one. (Since the chrominance signals aren't required, black and white digital video automatically requires fewer bits than color.)

The question presents itself: why bother? Remember, we said the human eye can't perceive color information in the fine details of an image? Well, it turns out that we can record the R–Y and B–Y signals with half the resolution of the Y signal (or less) without visibly impairing the picture. In fact, every color television system in use today, digital and analog, embodies this technique. By using half resolution in the chrominance signals, we can reduce the required amount of data we need to transmit or record by one third – some of the data rate reduction we're looking for. One such method is called *4:2:2*, meaning that there are four samples of luminance information (Y) for every two samples of each color signal (R–Y, B–Y).

Actually, cutting the R–Y and B–Y resolution to 1/4 is common (as in the popular DV, DVCam and DVCPro formats, described in more detail later), and on most material, it's very hard to see the difference. In fact, analog broadcasts, analog video recorders and TV monitors (except the most expensive professional ones) function with greatly reduced chrominance resolution for this reason. This 1/4-

bandwidth color encoding is called *4:1:1* or *4:2:0*. (There are subtle differences between 4:1:1 and 4:2:0, but they provide essentially the same visual quality.)

The combination of luminance and chrominance signals instead of RGB is sometimes called *matrix color*, and is used in both analog and digital video to reduce bandwidth.

In the previous chapter, we talked about lines of resolution. Suppose, for example, we need to transmit a signal with 300 lines of resolution. Neglecting the synchronizing and other information, the video system needs to be able to send a signal that varies 300 times within each horizontal line. Since (in NTSC, for the purposes of this discussion) there are 480 active scanlines transmitted 30 times per second, we need to be able to transmit 300 x 480 x 30, or 4,320,000 variations per second. Thus, the bandwidth required is 4.32 MegaHertz (1 MegaHertz = 1 million cycles per second). To accommodate this bandwidth plus the audio and some other signals, the standard NTSC analog broadcast channels were designed to have a 6 MHz bandwidth; for example, US television channel 2 extends over the broadcast frequency range of 54 to 60 MHz. The original signal from the camera contains frequencies up to roughly 4.5 MHz. In effect, a television transmitter converts those frequencies up and greatly intensifies them, a process that doesn't change the required bandwidth. Note that we've been talking only about black-and-white (*monochrome*) video. When the NTSC worked out the color system in the 1950s, they figured out a way to transmit reduced bandwidth color information in the same channel designated for black-and-white transmission. While the arcane details of this process are beyond the scope of this book, the process they developed was a form of bandwidth reduction, or compression, that has worked well for over fifty years.

Looking again at digital video and applying some of the same calculations, let's consider an SD 480i digital video signal. Remember there are 720 pixels per line, 480 lines per frame and 30 frames per second, so 720 x 480 x 30 = 10,368,000 pixels per second. Since each pixel effectively has 8 bits for luminance and 8 bits for chrominance (16 bits), the total data rate is 720 x 480 x 30 x 16 = 165,888,000 bits per second, or over 165 MHz of bandwidth – much greater than the 6 MHz used for analog television. Recording or transmitting 6 MHz is difficult enough, but handling 165 MHz bandwidth is extremely daunting. We need to do something to reduce the data or compress this bandwidth.

A digital compression method is often called a *codec*, a shortened form of *coder-decoder*. Compression is possible, fortunately, because moving images contain a great deal of redundancy – duplicated information. Suppose, for example, that the color of a particular pixel in an image is represented by a numerical value of 72. Further, suppose that pixel is located in a part of an image that represents the sky. If the sky is uniform in color, the camera may send out a string of numbers indicating the color of adjacent pixels, like, "72, 72, 72, 72, 72, 72, 72, 72, 72". Remembering that the camera is really a computer in disguise, instead of sending the same number over and over again, we could incorporate an *algorithm* that is smart enough to send data that effectively says, "the next 9 pixels have a value of 72." Maybe we could do that by creating a rule that says something like, "If you encounter a zero, the next number indicates the number of repetitions of the value that follows it." Incorporating this rule, the data the camera would send to the recorder would be: "0,9,72", instead of the long string of numbers above. For this particular section of the scene, we have replaced nine numbers with three, creating a *compression ratio* of 3:1 without damaging the quality of the data in any way – the compression is *lossless*. Since real-world images often contain areas of uniform color, actual compression ratios achieved can be considerably higher.

For many applications, a compression ratio of 3:1 helps, but is not enough – there may still be too much data to handle in an inexpensive recording or broadcasting system. To help solve this problem, let's think about adding another rule that goes like this: "If there's a string of numbers with values that are within ±1 of being the same value, average them to the same value." This could turn our "0,9,72" example into something like "0,23,72", since it's quite likely 23 pixels could have *similar* values, even though they're not *exactly* the same. This rule will greatly increase the compression ratio (in this case, 20:1), but at a cost: the compression is now *lossy* – we have lost some of the information, and we're not able to exactly reproduce the original picture. Hopefully, our compression has worked in a manner that it won't be *visible* in the image.

This is a very simplified explanation of just one of many ways that image data within a single frame can be compressed. Any scheme that is applied to frames on a one-by-one basis is called *intraframe* or *spatial* compression. A common standard of this type is the popular *JPEG* file format for still pictures, standardized by the Joint Photographic Experts Group. A variation of this is *Motion JPEG*, used in some video editing systems.

More advanced (but still lossy) compression, such as the various flavors of *MPEG* (Moving Pictures Experts Group), can achieve much higher ratios. For example, the MPEG-2 compression schemes used for HD broadcasting, DVDs and satellite TV are able to produce high quality images with compression ratios of 30:1 or greater, producing bandwidths comparable to analog video. They are able to do this because they take advantage of another form of redundancy in a video signal: *temporal* redundancy. Most of the time, the information in one frame is very similar to the information in previous or subsequent frames. Processes that take advantage of this redundancy are called *interframe* or *temporal* compression. It's also sometimes called *long GOP* (group of pictures) and it's computationally very complex. It's done by recording all the information for one frame and then, for a number of adjacent frames, recording only the *differences* between frames. After this process occurs, there is a lot less data to record. Suffice it to say interframe compression dramatically enhances the efficiency and produces large reductions in data rate for equivalent visual quality.

Although this explanation is greatly oversimplified, these approaches form the basic concepts behind the compression schemes used in camcorders, recording and digital broadcasting. While many codecs can produce very high quality pictures, keep in mind that during post-production, you will sometimes be decoding and re-encoding, so it's important that the codec you're using be as near lossless as possible. Repeatedly putting your images through lossy codecs will always degrade them to some degree, creating visible artifacts.

Recording Media

Digital camcorders are supplied with tape, disk or flash memory cards as recording media, though at this writing the majority use 1/2-inch (12.5 mm) or 1/4-inch (6.25mm) magnetic tape. Without exception, digital videotape recorders use a process called *helical scanning*. Analog audiotape recorders use a mechanism to physically pull the tape past fixed recording *heads* at a constant speed, each audio channel occupying a *track* of a certain width. Such recordings are called *longitudinal tracks*. Video recorders use *helical scanning*, which means the tape goes in a partial spiral (helix) around a spinning *scanner* or *headwheel* – the heart of any video recorder. Usually turning at one revolution per video frame, the scanner lays down tracks that are diagonal on the tape, instead of parallel to the edges; these are called helical tracks. Some video recorders use longitudinal tracks for timecode and control signals; others (such as DV) use only helical tracks to record all data.

Digital Recording Formats

All of digital camcorder formats, whether HD or SD, use compression in some form to reduce the amount of data that needs to be recorded. Here, we'll look at some of the popular digital formats used in camcorders, ranked in the order of their amounts of compression.

SD Formats

Digital Betacam

Developed by Sony and tracing its heritage to the original analog Betamax of the 1970s, Digital Betacam (commonly called *DigiBeta*) was the first digital camcorder format. It is still considered the highest quality, using 4:2:2 sampling and very mild compression, just over 2:1, claimed to be "essentially lossless". Tape costs are relatively high.

D-9

Developed by JVC and also called *Digital S*, D-9 also uses 1/2-inch (12.5 mm) tape and 4:2:2 sampling, but in a different cassette. Compression is somewhat greater than DigiBeta, at about 3:1, described as "virtually lossless". Tape costs are somewhat less than DigiBeta.

DVCPro 50

Panasonic's top SD camcorder format, DVCPro 50 has essentially the same characteristics as D-9, but uses 1/4-inch (6.25mm) tape. The 50 in the name comes from the data rate, 50 Megabits per second, and the format is an improved version of DVCPro (see below).

DV

Supported by multiple manufacturers, the basic DV format is used in the professional versions, *DVCam* (Sony) and *DVCPro* (Panasonic, also called D7), and in the "standard" DV format supported by most manufacturers. These formats are by far the most popular for digital filmmaking and are used universally by major network broadcasters. I've grouped them together because they all use the same signal specification, called *DV25*. The data rate is 25 Megabits per second, 4:1:1 sampling (4:2:0 in the PAL version), with two 48 kHz 16-bit audio channels. Alternatively, the signal format supports four 32 kHz 12-bit audio channels. Compression in all DV formats is intraframe and about 5:1, not lossless, but easy to edit in its native format and under most circumstances it is "visually lossless". In other words, you are not likely to see any compression artifacts in any DV format. You should be aware, however, that the 4:1:1 sampling can cause problems for blue- or green-screen work because of the reduced color resolution. (More about this in the section on editing).

All these formats use 1/4-inch (6.25 mm) tape, with the cassettes being available in two sizes, although most camcorders only allow the use of the smaller (Mini) size. Of the three, DV is considered the prosumer format. Mini DV tapes can hold one hour, although some camcorders have an extended play (EP) mode that allows 90 minutes per tape; also, at least one manufacturer makes an 80-minute nominal Mini DV tape. DVCam and DVCPro have identical tape dimensions, but use what is described as a "more robust" recording method. Both run the tape at a faster speed for better reliability of data recovery, resulting in a maximum recording time on a mini cassette of about 40 minutes. The DVCam and DVCPro formats' higher tape speed also makes them more immune to *dropouts*, momentary losses of signal caused by dirt on the tape or tape damage.

A word of caution: beware of using the extended play mode of DV. While there is no loss of picture quality in this mode, the playback process becomes extremely sensitive to any variation in tape positioning or tension, to the point that tapes made in EP mode often may only be playable on the same machine that recorded them. They are also much more susceptible to dropouts. If you must use the EP mode, you should copy your tapes to a standard speed tape as soon as possible.

Many DV, DVCPro and DVCam recorders will play all three formats, but most will only record in one of them. (DVCPro and DVCam machines will not play DV tapes recorded in extended play mode.) A few recorders are equipped with dual heads and will record in either DVCam and DV formats, but subtle differences in recording methods generally confine recording to only one of the formats.

Betacam SX

This is another Sony format with similar characteristics to the DV25 specification, but uses the larger 1/2-inch cassettes. It is an older format than DV and was intended to be a lower-cost alternative to Digital Betacam. The signals are incompatible with DV.

MPEG IMX

This Sony-originated format actually uses somewhat more compression than DV25, but is claimed to have higher picture quality because it uses 4:2:2 color sampling and MPEG interframe coding. This combination approximates the quality of D-9 or DVCPro 50 with twice the compression, and is considered an alternative to Digital Betacam. MPEG IMX is used on tape and also on Sony's XDCAM and XDCAM HD disk and memory-based recording (see below).

Disk-Based Formats

Several manufacturers offer camcorders using optical disks instead of tape for recording (Sony calls theirs XDCAM). The professional camcorders use optical disks similar to DVDs but with higher data capacity. The signal format for these disks is usually DV25, although MPEG IMX is also offered as a disk recording option. The quality of these disks is in every way equal to the same format recorded on tape, but they have the advantages of quick media change, the ability to instantly erase "bad takes", and faster transfer of data to editing systems. The disadvantages are increased media cost, shorter recording times, and limited compatibility with editing systems.

Some manufacturers are offering hard disk recorders that are compatible with *Firewire* (*IEEE-1394*, also called *iLink*) equipped camcorders, allowing recording from the camera direct to the hard drive. For post-production, the drive can be connected directly to the editing system, eliminating the step of transferring the video to the computer. The main disadvantage of these recorders is the need for separate wiring and power source for an additional unit.

There are also consumer-level SD camcorders that record on consumer-standard DVD instead of tape. Because these units generally use much higher compression ratios than other disk or tape-based systems and are not directly compatible with professional editing systems, they should be avoided for serious filmmaking.

HD Formats

HDCAM

Sony's tape system for their high-end HD camcorders is called HDCAM, and it works in the 1080i 60, 1080i 50, and 1080p 24 formats. It is a derivative of Digital Betacam (described above) with the data rate, tapes and transport mechanisms being nearly identical. The main difference is in the signal format. It uses intraframe compression with an effective ratio of around 6:1. One unusual aspect of HDCAM is that it undersamples the number of horizontal pixels from 1920 to 1440 during recording, reconstructing them during playback. Also, unlike other formats, it does not use 4:2:2 sampling. Instead, it uses approximately 3:1:1, resulting in slightly reduced color resolution (somewhere between 4:2:2 and the 4:1:1 sampling used in the DV25 formats). The format is robust and there are virtually no visible artifacts from these compromises; the picture quality is superb.

DVCPro HD

Panasonic's HD camcorder offering, DVCPro HD is based on DVCPro 50, and is capable of handling all primary HD formats. It uses intraframe compression of about 10:1, but unlike HDCAM, it does not sub-sample the horizontal pixels, and uses 4:2:2 color sampling. Its quality is comparable to HDCAM. (Panasonic also offers a 1/2-inch format called D5 HD, providing lower compression and somewhat higher quality, but its use is confined to studio recorders, not camcorders.)

D9 HD

JVC's HD camcorder format, D9 HD, is similar to DVCPro HD in data rate and compression, using the D9 1/2-inch (12.5mm) tape.

HDV

This is the HD version of DV, originally offered by JVC but now a standard for many manufacturers. Unlike the other HD formats, HDV uses MPEG-2 interframe compression and creates a data stream similar to that used in HDTV broadcasting. This results in picture quality approaching the other HD formats. Most editing systems support it natively, and current computers can handle it with relative ease. HDV is a breakthrough format, making it possible to shoot HD on a DV budget. It uses essentially the same tape as DV and the MPEG-2 compression makes it possible to use the same data rate, about 25 Mbps.

Some HDV cameras are priced under US$500, and some allow shooting either HDV or DV. Most can also *down-convert* the HD signal to SD for viewing on an NTSC monitor, or for editing in SD. HDV is an excellent choice for low-budget HD production.

While HDV uses tape cassettes that are identical to the standard DV, manufacturers recommend special, more expensive HDV tapes. The difference is that HDV tapes are formulated to minimize dropouts (short-term loss of signal due to tape imperfections). The DV format uses error concealment techniques to allow masking these defects, and even if these concealment efforts fail, errors rarely affect more than one or two frames of video. Because HDV uses MPEG encoding, a dropout can affect a much larger number of frames and can be very objectionable, possibly ruining a scene. If you're shooting HDV, use the best tape possible!

Disk-Based Formats

Some of high end HD systems, notably Thompson's *Viper*, can record directly to computer disk arrays, allowing very high data rates and/or uncompressed recording. While very expensive, these systems can record all the data the camera provides, and are being used in feature film production. They show their value most for films with intensive special effects, where every pixel is important.

Using optical recording, Sony has their disk-based XDCAM HD camcorders with matching studio disk drives for retrieving the data.

Also disk based, several manufacturers are supporting a new and highly efficient codec called *AVCHD*. This codec is very bandwidth-efficient and allows hours of storage in camcorders using either optical disks or with built-in hard drives. AVCHD offers several data rates and (like DV) uses 4:1:1 sampling. It's based on the H.264 compression standard and delivers excellent quality at low bit rates.

Memory-Based Recording

Some camcorders (and still cameras, and even cell phones) allow the acquisition of video directly to flash memory cards, similar to those used in digital still cameras. While many consumer cameras offer video recording to flash memory, the first system offering professional quality HD video was the Panasonic P2 system, using the DVCPro HD codec. Sony's similar system called XDCAM EX. Many memory recorders also use AVCHD or one of its variants. While these have many advantages, they are costly per minute of storage than tape or disk.

Some of the advantages of memory recording for professional filmmaking include:

- Extremely rugged recording hardware
- No moving parts, no noise
- Very high reliability, complete freedom from tape problems
- Unlimited re-usability
- Ability to record at many different formats and frame rates
- Hot-swappable media provides the ability to record continuously
- Allows simple in-camera editing, such as elimination of bad takes
- Faster than real-time transfer to cheaper storage on a computer or external hard drive
- Easier management of recorded media

While memory recording will be more expensive than tape or disk for awhile, its reusability and other advantages make it a viable choice. As cost of memory drops (which it certainly will), it will probably become the dominant recording medium for video.

Format Summary

The formats above are the most common ones used as of this writing; others will surely be developed in the future. For low-budget projects, the DV-based formats (DV, DVCam, DVCPro, or HDV) are most popular. These formats offer a high degree of compatibility, and the support of several manufacturers. The SD versions use the same signal format and can be used freely with most currently available editing systems. Another advantage of these formats is that their data rate is within a range that can be easily handled by inexpensive computer disk drives. The newer disk and memory-based HD formats have similar advantages.

Advice: To "future-proof" your film, you should certainly shoot in HD, even if you are going to release in SD. And go "tapeless" if you can..

The Camera or the Recording Format?

It's appropriate here to address a very common misunderstanding about recording formats and cameras. You'll hear people say things like, "DVCam looks sooooo much better than DV." In fact, the digital signals recorded are identical, though their physical placement on the tape is slightly different. If the same material were recorded on both formats, it would be impossible to determine which format is being used just by looking at the picture, or even by using test equipment to measure the signals. The difference people are seeing is in the camera, <u>not</u> in the recording format. Cameras containing DVCam (or DVCPro) recorders are usually of higher quality than those sold with only DV recording capability – professional tape formats for professional cameras. The same applied with analog formats – cameras with Betacam recorders are also often much better than those with DV recorders, and so look better, even though Betacam (as an analog format) is inferior in virtually every respect to DV. (Have you heard: "Betacam looks sooooo much better than DV"?)

Just remember: when comparing formats, be sure you are really comparing formats, not cameras!

Timecode

All digital camcorders create *timecode* data along with the sound and picture. In principle, timecode is a simple idea. Every frame of video is digitally marked with a number in the format HH:MM:SS:FF – two digits each for hours, minutes, seconds and frames, up to 24 hours. For example, 13:26:15:10 would be the tenth frame following 13 hours, 26 minutes and 15 seconds. The highest number for hours is 23, for minutes 59, for seconds 59 and frames 29 (or 24 in non-NTSC countries; 23 for 24-p recording). The use of timecode is essential for editing operations; in fact, even if the original source material doesn't contain timecode, every editing system will create it. This even applies to still images, because in the context of a film still images have duration – a dimension of time.

While all digital cameras generate and record timecode, consumer camcorders do it in a "bare-bones" fashion. Each time you insert a new tape (and in some units, every time you turn the camera off), the timecode is reset to 00:00:00:00. This is a distinct disadvantage because it allows different tapes (or even scenes on the same tape) to have duplicate timecode numbers. Since editing systems can only locate scenes by these all-important numbers, finding scenes on tapes with duplicate numbers can be a nightmare.

Professional recorders permit you to set the timecode to any value you want, and retain their timecode even when they're turned off or a tape is changed. They also have timecode inputs and outputs. This is important in many applications. For example, you may want the timecode to be set to "time of day" so that you know when a particular scene was shot. You may also want to synchronize the timecodes for multiple cameras so it will be easy to match the resulting shots in time. To do this on professional cameras, you can connect a cable from the timecode out of one to the timecode in on the other, then set the timecode generator to "slave" or "jam" the code – that is, match to the external timecode. Importantly, the generators are accurate to within a few parts per million, so if the timecode is allowed to "free run", multiple cameras can stay together for a full day's shoot even if the cables are disconnected after synchronization.

Some videographers like to use the first two digits of the timecode to represent the reel number of the original tape, definitely a convenience for the editor. Depending on the importance of these features to your project, you'll want to check out the timecode recording capabilities when choosing a camera.

Some Timecode Intricacies

In non-NTSC countries, timecode is pretty straight forward, but in NTSC countries (like the US, Canada, Mexico and Japan), it gets a bit more complicated. It turns out that when the NTSC color specifications were established in 1953, the engineers who designed the system slightly shifted the frame rate from the nominal 30 frames per second to 29.97. The reasons for this change are a bit arcane, but they had to do with interference issues between the color signals that were being added to the then black-and-white broadcasts interfering with the sound transmission. While nobody can notice the difference between 30 fps and 29.97 fps, timecode certainly can. At 30 fps, there are 108,000 frames in an hour; at 29.97 there are 107,892. The results is that if you go by the timecode for what appears to be a one hour show, it will actually play several seconds longer than one hour. With broadcasters' to-the-second timings, this is intolerable; it could accumulate to more than a minute over a broadcast day.

To compensate for this discrepancy, *the Society of Motion Picture and Television Engineers (SMPTE)* came up with a solution: NTSC timecode comes in two varieties: *dropframe* and *non-dropframe.* Both are widely used, but dropframe is probably more common; professional cameras and recorders give you a choice.

Here's the difference between the two: Non-dropframe simply counts each frame consecutively, but is inaccurate when compared to "real" time. Dropframe corrects the problem by "dropping" two frame numbers at the beginning of each minute except for the tenth minute. Thus, for example, 10:14:00:01 is not a valid dropframe timecode (though it is valid in non-dropframe) because it is not the tenth minute (it is the 4th minute after the 10th minute). In dropframe, 10:13:59:29 would be followed by 10:14:00:02. (:00 and :01 are dropped).

In the real world, it's probably safest to just use dropframe timecode. An exception is in doing short pieces, such as commercials. In this case, non-dropframe is often more convenient because it relates directly to the frame count, and animation is done by the frame.

If you work in a non-NTSC country, dropframe isn't an issue, but in the US, it applies to everything. All the US HD formats use 29.97 as the frame rate, and it even carries over to 24p and 24 fps film (which becomes 23.98) because it will probably be transferred to a broadcast video format at some point.

Timecode can also include some potentially useful information in what are called *user bits.* On some professional cameras, user bits can be set just as you would set timecode. Some shooters encode the date or the reel number in the user bits. They can also be used as a secondary timing reference, such as time of day. Disk and memory-based camcorders have their equivalent of user bits in the form of metadata included with each of the video files recorded. This can include a wide variety of information including date and time and even "thumbnail" images of the scenes shot.

While disk- and memory-based systems use timecode, it's less important because it isn't needed for finding scenes. With tape-based systems, the only way to find the original footage for a scene is by its timecode and reel number. Disk and memory-based systems work instead with files. Each time you pull the trigger on the camera, a new file is created in the digital media, and each file has a unique name. A default name (often just a consecutive number) is assigned, but those can be changed once the files are on a computer. Remember that tape-based formats must be "captured" into a computer in real-time for editing; disk- or memory-based files are merely transferred, at the fastest rate the hardware will allow.

Video Interfacing

Surprisingly, prosumer and consumer camcorders often have more flexible ways of getting video and audio in and out than professional units. All camcorders have video and audio outputs for monitoring purposes, and all have audio inputs. Prosumer and consumer camcorders may also have video inputs, allowing them to function as full-function VCRs in addition to normal camcorder operation; professional camcorder manufacturers assume you'll be using a studio VCR or media player for these functions and therefore omit them from their designs. If you're working with a low budget, you may want to use your camcorder to interface with your editing system, thus avoiding the cost of a free-standing player.

When working with DV, HDV and their derivatives, the de facto standard for interconnection is *Firewire*, also called *iLink* or *IEEE 1394*. It is commonly used to connect peripherals (including disk drives and cameras) to computers. In working with digital video, Firewire is a very convenient way of getting video, audio and control information into and out of your computer editing software. Some camcorders, particularly disk and memory-based units, use the USB-2 connection protocol instead of (or in addition to) Firewire for similar functionality.

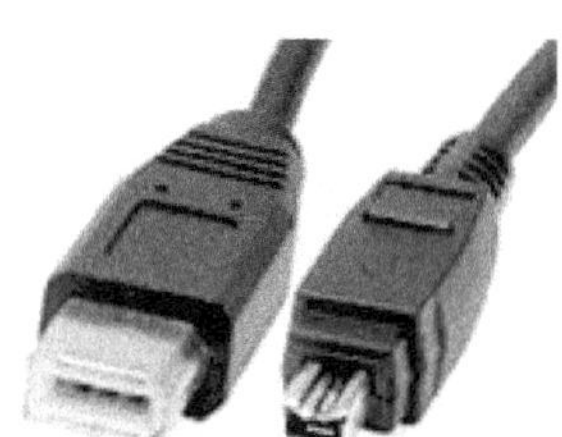

Another important use of Firewire is for making *lossless* copies of your footage. A single Firewire cable can connect two DV recorders (or camcorders) and allow an exact copy of digital data from one to the other. With some cameras, it is possible to use a Firewire connection to allow recording of your audio and video on an external computer or hard disk drive instead of (or in addition to) recording it in the camcorder.

For analog video connectivity, consumer and prosumer equipment will use RCA connectors for audio and video

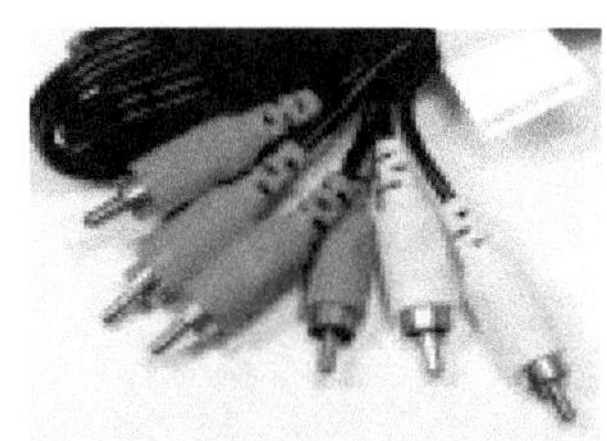

signals, the same kind used on stereo equipment and TV sets.

Professional level equipment will likely use the more robust BNC connectors. These have a locking barrel around the outside, providing a more secure connection. It's important to realize, however, that RCA and BNC connectors are electrically identical.

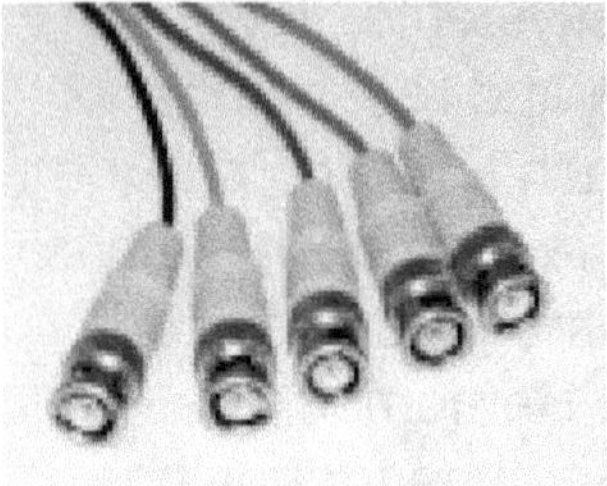

You'll often want to get video signals out of your camera for display on a monitor or for connection to an external recorder. Camcorders offer one or more outputs for this purpose, and they provide different signal formats of varying quality. Often, camcorders use proprietary connectors on one end of the provided output cables, but will have RCA or S-Video connectors on the other end.

The simplest way to get a picture from your camera is to use a simple composite video cable (either RCA or BNC), but this is the lowest quality signal. It's generally fine for using an ordinary TV set as a monitor, and HD cameras often have a SD output for this purpose. A better connection is S-video, which uses a special cable with two wires inside, carrying luminance and chrominance signals separately, thus offering improved quality. Remember, though, that these connections carry only an SD signal.

HD camcorders will have component video outputs with a triple cable carrying YUV signals, offering better quality. Another popular interconnect is HDMI (High Definition Multimedia Interface) which can connect to suitably equipped monitors. This is a pure digital interface and has the convenience of carrying both audio and video in a single cable.

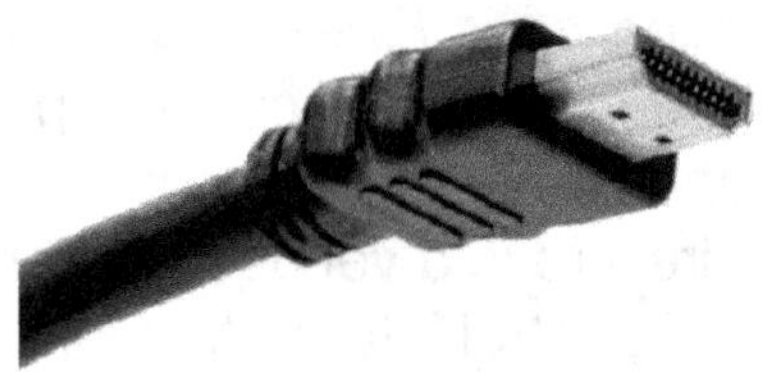

Pro cameras may also have and SDI (Serial Digital Interface) or HD-SDI output. Though rarely used in field shooting, SDI is often used in the studio environment for interconnecting equipment such as high-end monitors, studio recorders and monitoring equipment. Depending on the variety of SDI, it may also carry multiple channels of "embedded" audio along with the video.

2.5 Audio Technology

"We have also sound-houses, where we practise and demonstrate all sounds, and their generation. We have harmonies which you have not, of quarter-sounds, and lesser slides of sounds. Divers instruments of music likewise to you unknown, some sweeter than any you have, together with bells and rings that are dainty and sweet. We represent small sounds as great and deep; likewise great sounds extenuate and sharp; we make divers tremblings and warblings of sounds, which in their original are entire. We represent and imitate all articulate sounds and letters, and the voices and notes of beasts and birds. We have certain helps which set to the ear do further the hearing greatly. We have also divers strange and artificial echoes, reflecting the voice many times, and as it were tossing it: and some that give back the voice louder than it came, some shriller, and some deeper; yea, some rendering the voice differing in the letters or articulate sound from that they receive. We have also means to convey sounds in trunks and pipes, in strange lines and distances."

Sir Francis Bacon
The New Atlantis

The one factor that can most quickly make a film seem amateurish or non-professional is bad sound. Grainy images or shaky cameras are sometimes used for artistic effect; bad sound is never intentional, but it happens all the time. In the Digital Age, there's no excuse for bad sound, but it's still easy for sound to become an afterthought.

What is Sound, Anyway?

A dictionary definition of sound is: "vibrations traveling through air, water, or some other medium, especially those within the range of frequencies that can be perceived by the human ear." For the most part, we're concerned about sounds traveling in air. The frequencies we're interested in fall in a range from about 20 Hz (cycles per second) up to about 20,000 Hz, representing all the sounds a person with excellent hearing can perceive. In filmmaking, we intercept sound with a microphone, which turns the vibrations into electrical signals with corresponding frequencies. We amplify and record those electrical signals, manipulate them, and then play them back through a loudspeaker, which turns the signals back into vibrations of the air, creating a reproduction of the sound.

Sounds have several important characteristics:

- Frequency – the number of per second the air is compressed and rarefied by the vibration traveling through it, measured in Hertz (Hz) or cycles per second.
- Wavelength – this is related to the frequency and the speed of sound through air. Mathematically, it is frequency divided by velocity. For example, a sound of 100 Hz traveling in air with a velocity of about 1,100 feet per second has a wavelength of 9 feet.
- Amplitude – the strength of the sound wave. Sounds have an enormous range of amplitudes, from the softest rustle of a breeze through grass to the roar of a jet airplane taking off. The loudest sounds we hear are millions of times more intense than the quietest.
- Phase – the time relationship between identical or near-identical sounds. Sounds that are in-phase add together and get louder; out-of-phase sounds tend to cancel each other out. (Use of out-of-phase sound is the principle behind the popular behind noise-canceling headphones.)

Recording Sound

For most digital films, the camera will also be the sound recorder. Although high-end productions often use a separate sound recorder (*double system*), digital camcorders are capable of high-quality sound recording on at least two channels. Since sound and video are recorded on the same medium, this approach is called *single system,* and it has many operational advantages, not the least of which is the elimination of the task of *synching* the sound during post-production. When double system is used, audio can be recorded on *DAT* (digital audio tape) with timecode, on a free-standing digital recorder, a digital audio workstation (DAW), or even on a laptop computer.

Most cameras come with some kind of built-in or on-camera microphones, usually of questionable quality. Though it seems convenient and logical, this rarely a good place to put a microphone. It's usually not close enough to your subject, and camcorders (and camcorder operators), though reasonably quiet, can make some noise when they're running. So make a rule for yourself:

Try to avoid using camera's built-in microphone.

You'll need a small selection of external microphones to do a good job of sound recording while you're shooting your film. And, of course, you'll need a camcorder with a jack for an external microphone. Many of the otherwise excellent low-cost cameras, unfortunately, don't have this simple feature, which rules them out for serious filmmaking.

Microphone Types

Microphone design, like the motion picture itself, is a mature science. Extremely high quality microphones have been available for at least seventy-five years. Personally, I own a pair of Telefunken (Neumann) U-47s built in the 1950s. While they have been well maintained and updated, they are unchanged from their original specifications and can hold their own with the finest current units. A microphone is one item in your equipment kit that won't quickly become obsolete.

A microphone catalog will contain a bewildering array of types and designs for a wide range of applications, but only a few are commonly used in filmmaking. The mics you'll be using most frequently are the *shotgun, cardioid* and *lavalier*, but you should be familiar with all the basic types. The drawings below are polar plots of various microphones' directional characteristics, indicating the shape of their directional patterns.

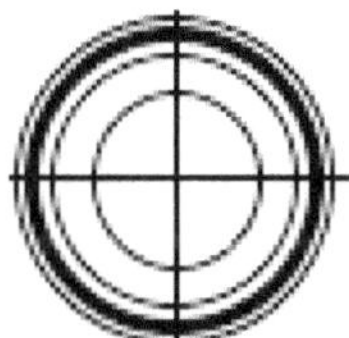

Omnidirectional microphones pick up sounds from all directions. They are relatively inexpensive and are sometimes used for ambient sound. *Omnis* are the mics of choice for hand-held use, where the talent is holding the microphone while doing a stand-up, as in a newscast. They are very rugged and are not generally as vulnerable to wind noise as other types.

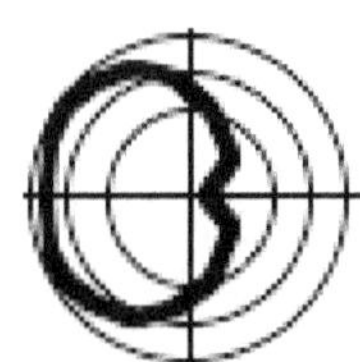

Cardioid mics have a roughly heart-shaped pickup pattern, favoring sounds arriving at them head-on with signals from the sides somewhat attenuated. Sounds approaching from the back are strongly reduced. You can think of cardioids as being capable of picking up their best sound over roughly a 120-degree angle. They are usually stand-mounted and are popular for studio use or sound reinforcement systems. One reason they are favored for recording vocalists or voice-over tracks is that they exhibit a phenomenon called *proximity effect*. This creates an effective boost of the lower frequencies for sounds originating close to the microphone – the classic booming announcer.

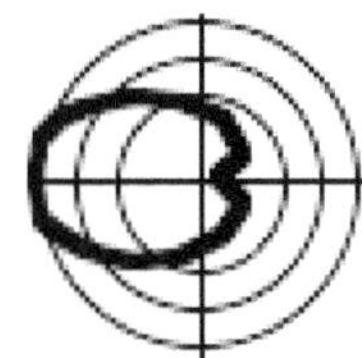

Shotgun (or *hypercardioid*) microphones behave similarly to cardioid mics, but are more directional. They come in *short shot* and *long shot* versions, with varying directivity. A short-shot mic is useful over about a 60-degree angle; a long shot covers about a 45-degree angle. These mics are mostly used for recording dialog during field shooting, and are usually mounted on booms or used with pistol grips. Long shots are most useful outdoors, short-shots for interiors. With any shotgun mic, it's important that shock mounting be provided to insure that vibrations resulting from motion are not transmitted to the microphone itself. A means should also be provided to be sure that microphone cable has a loop of slack near the connector, also to avoid vibration and handling noise. For outdoor use, it's essential that your mic be equipped with a windscreen.

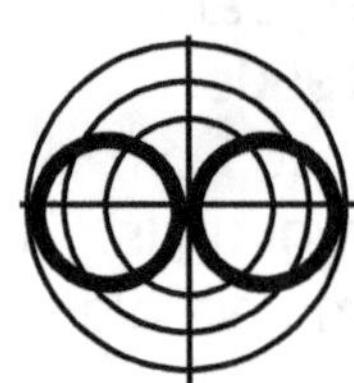

Bi-Directional mics have a *figure-8* pickup pattern. Very few mics sold today are bi-directional, but some studio mics offer switched patterns, including figure-8. A mic like this can be valuable in certain situations, because it has virtually zero sensitivity at right angles to the axis, very useful when you need to reject a single source of noise. Before the development of the shotgun mic, bi-directional mics were frequently used in studio shooting because they had longer "reach" than other types.

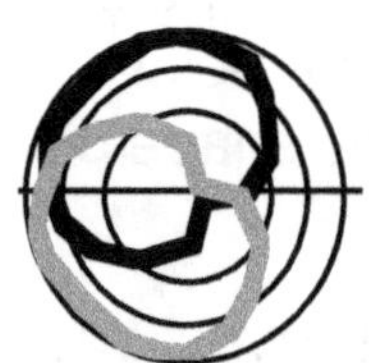

Stereo mics are a special case where two matched cardioid mics are mounted together. Properly used, they can produce an exceptionally realistic stereo recording, with sounds seeming to come from the right direction. Of course, they require the additional precaution of keeping them "right side up", so the left side of the mic corresponds to the left side of the scene you're shooting. Interestingly, if the two channels of a stereo mic are mixed together (in a mixer while shooting or during sound editing), the directional patterns of the two microphone elements will effectively add, creating a "virtual short shot", so a stereo mic can do double duty.

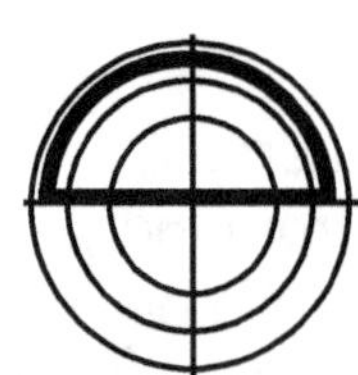

Pressure Zone Microphones (PZM or PZ) are designed to be placed on flat surfaces, such as tabletops or lecterns. Also called *boundary effect* microphones, they take advantage of the fact that hard, flat surfaces can reflect sound waves and thus increase the amount of signal the microphone receives. The surface reflects sound back into the mic, and blocks sound from the opposite side, thus creating directionality. PZMs can be thought of as covering a 180-degree angle, and are useful for recording dialog between people seated at a table or counter. Most are small, inconspicuous and easily hidden in a scene. A PZM can be simulated by placing an omnidirectional (or cardioid) microphone as close as possible to a flat surface. Some *lavalier* mics are available with a flat-plate mount for using them in "PZM mode".

Lavalier mics (also called *lapel* mics) are designed to be clipped to a lapel, shirt or necktie, though they are often hidden under clothing. The come in omnidirectional and cardioid varieties, some are amazingly small but can produce very high quality voice recordings. They are popular for both field and studio shooting, and are often used with wireless transmitter-receiver combinations.

It's important to remember that the directional characteristics of all microphones are somewhat frequency dependent – they are more directional (cover a narrower angle) at the higher frequencies. Even a so-called omnidirectional microphone will exhibit a "sweet spot" for high frequencies; there will be some difference in the sound depending on whether the microphone is aimed at the sound source. The uniformity of a microphone's directional pattern with frequency has a lot to do with its perceived sound quality in practical use, and accounts for a major difference between cheaper and more expensive mics.

The microphone types are commonly available with two different types of *transducers,* the heart of the system that actually converts the sound into electrical signals: *dynamic* and *condenser* (or capacitor).

Dynamic microphone elements are similar in construction to a small loudspeaker. They consist of a *diaphragm* (usually about one inch in diameter or smaller) attached to a coil of wire, which is suspended in a magnetic field. When the diaphragm is vibrated by an incoming sound wave, the coil moves in the magnetic field, generating a small electric current that is proportional to the intensity of the sound wave at any given instant. (Electrical generators work by moving coils of wire through magnetic fields.) This current is an electrical *analog* of the sound wave, and can be amplified and ultimately converted into a digital representation. Dynamic microphones create their signals directly, without an external source of power.

Condenser microphone elements are made up of a stretched, flexible diaphragm that is positioned very close to a fixed metal back plate. The diaphragm is made of a plastic film that is coated with a very thin, electrically conductive metal layer. The diaphragm and back plate form the two surfaces of a *capacitor* (also called a *condenser*), a device capable of holding an electric charge. The charge (or *polarizing voltage*) may be supplied by a battery or an external source (often referred to as *phantom power*, usually 48 volts), or the diaphragm may be made of a plastic material capable of holding an electric charge for a long period of time: an *electret*. (An electret is similar to a magnet; it holds an electric charge the way a magnet holds a magnetic charge.)

When an incoming sound wave causes the diaphragm to vibrate, the physical distance between the diaphragm and the back plate changes, thus changing the *capacitance* of the microphone element. When the plates are closer together, the capacitor is capable of holding a larger charge, so current can flow into it. Conversely, when the plates are farther apart, current must flow out of the capacitor because it can no longer hold the charge. These changing currents are an analog of the incoming sound wave, but because they are extremely weak, condenser microphones always include a built-in amplifier to increase the tiny signals to useable levels. Since the amplifier requires power, condenser microphones either use a small battery or get their energy from a source of phantom power, provided by most audio mixers or preamplifiers.

It's generally accepted that condenser microphones provide the best quality. Dynamics can also sound very good, are generally more rugged, and have the advantage of not requiring a power source.

For outdoor use in particular, it's essential that your mic be equipped with a *windscreen*. Most mics are supplied with a foam windscreen that completely encloses the active element. Foam windscreens are adequate except under windy outdoor conditions, for which you might need something more effective such as the "fuzzy bunny" or "zeppelin" styles. Manufacturers also offer combination shock mounts and windscreens.

Another needed accessory is a collapsible boom fitted with the right hardware to attach your mic. Your boom must include a shock mount to isolate the microphone from vibration. Low-budget filmmakers have found that extension paint-roller handles work great as mic booms with a bit of mechanical ingenuity to get the mic, shock mount and cable attached. They are far less expensive than purpose-built mic booms, but can be functionally equivalent.

Wireless Microphones

A wireless mic is simply a microphone with a small radio transmitter added. These operate in the VHS (very high frequency) or UHF (ultra high frequency) ranges and come in both analog and digital versions. They use very low power FM or digital transmitters, usually in the form of a small belt pack to which a lavalier mic is attached. Alternatively, the transmitter is built into a hand-held mic, although this type is rarely used for film work. Wireless systems are usually sold as matched sets of transmitters and receivers; a receiver for one manufacturer's mic will rarely work properly (if at all) with another manufacturer's receiver.

Digital wireless mics are more expensive than their analog counterparts, and usually provide better performance. For covering short distances, however, analog systems are adequate and won't noticeably degrade the sound quality. VHF analog systems can have better range than UHF models, but they are also more likely to have problems with interference. With any wireless system, greater distance between transmitter and receiver will bring with it an increase in possible interference and a phenomenon called *dropout*, where the signal momentarily disappears. Certain wireless receivers use a process called *diversity reception,* incorporating two receiving antennas to minimize this problem. The difference in cost between the cheapest and most expensive systems is likely to be reflected in the maximum distance over which the transmitter-receiver link can maintain acceptable quality, not in the sound quality under ideal conditions.

Inexpensive wireless systems can perform beautifully if the receiver can be kept close to the transmitter (mounted on the camera, for example), and if you're not in a location where you might receive outside interference. To avoid such interference, particularly in urban areas, it's a good idea to choose a wireless system that can be switched to two or more frequencies or channels. Frequency switching is also essential if you're using multiple wireless mics, since they will interfere with each other if used on the same frequency.

About Microphone Specifications

A spec sheet for a microphone is a difficult document to understand or interpret, and there seem to be no real standards for how the information is presented. For example, the spec for frequency response might say 20-20,000 Hz or 70-12,000 Hz, but often won't have a tolerance listed, like ±3 db. So, both of these specs could be applied to the same microphone – it could be 20-20,000 Hz ±6 db, or it could be 70-12,000 Hz. ±3 db. Fortunately for the filmmaker, the frequencies present in dialog (the speaking voice) extend from about 100 Hz to perhaps 8-10,000 Hz, so wide frequency response is not a primary consideration. What is important is the uniformity of frequency response over the speech range, so you could be relatively sure that the mic with the spec of 70-12,000 Hz. ±3 db would sound good on dialog. You couldn't necessarily say the same for the mic with the spec of 20-20,000 Hz ±6 db because that 6 db variation could be right in the middle of the speech range, adversely affecting the sound.

The directional characteristics of the mic are equally important and difficult to read from the spec sheets, though the better manufacturers publish polar plots of the microphone's directional performance at various frequencies. What you're looking for here is a mic with similar performance over the speech range – the polar plots for 100 Hz, for example, should be similar to the one for 5000 Hz.

Since dialog recorded at a distance from the mic will be lower in level than a loud lounge singer with her lips against the windscreen, it's best to choose a mic with high sensitivity and a low noise level.

Audio Interfacing

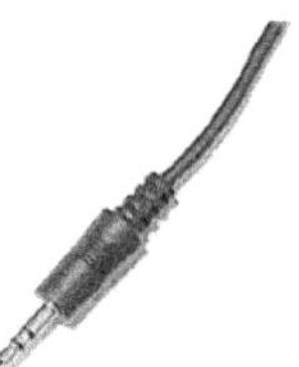

Consumer microphones and camcorders most often use 1/8-inch *mini* phone connectors.

Professional equipment normally uses the popular *XLR* connector, a 3-pin round plug about 3/4-inch in diameter.

In addition to being physically stronger and more robust, the XLR connector supports a *balanced* line configuration, using two wires to transmit the audio signal instead of one. A third connection is used for a shield, a metal foil or braid that completely covers the two signal-carrying conductors. The two conductors inside a balanced microphone cable actually carry the same signal in two versions; one is *out of phase* with the other. In the audio mixer or preamplifier, these two signals are combined through a transformer or differential input amplifier to create a single signal. The advantage of a balanced connection is that any interference that may be induced into the microphone cable by external fields (such as nearby power cables) will be *in-phase* in the two conductors. Since the desired audio signals are out of phase, these in-phase signals cancel each other out, so the interfering signal is not heard. Using balanced wiring to microphones can be good insurance against picking up stray noise. Obviously, however, the balanced configuration is more expensive to implement.

In an unbalanced hookup, the audio signal is carried by a single wire inside a surrounding shield. While the shield provides some protection against picking up interference, there is no mechanism for canceling out induced signals. Contrary to popular belief, however, there is no inherent quality difference between balanced and unbalanced connections, provided no noise is being picked up by the cables. Obviously, the longer the cable the more likely it is that noise will be a problem, but since the cable from the microphone to your camcorder is likely to be short and can be kept away from power lines, using unbalanced lines can be perfectly ok.

If you're using a camcorder with unbalanced 1/8-inch microphone inputs, you can still use professional XLR-equipped microphones in a couple of different ways. XLR adapters are available that use transformers or differential amplifiers to convert the balanced signals to unbalanced while maintaining all the advantages of the balanced microphone outputs and cabling. These adapters usually have two XLR connectors, one for each of the two stereo channels. Their output feeds a single 1/8-inch stereo connector that carries both audio channels, one on the tip of the plug and the other on an insulated sleeve just below the tip. Such an adapter is a highly recommended addition to your tool kit.

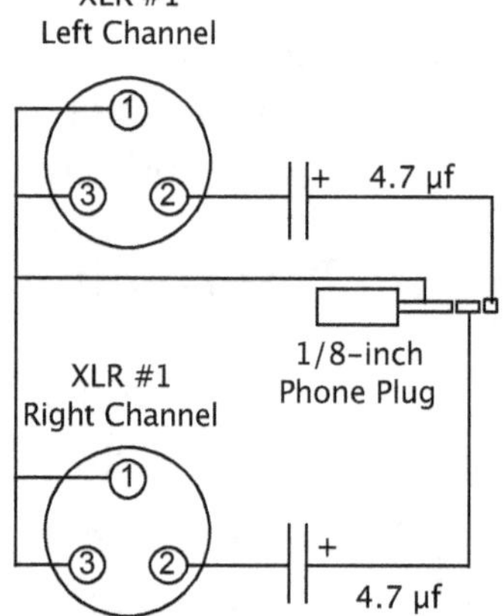

If you will be using relatively short microphone lines and are adept at soldering, a simple mic-to-camcorder cable adapter can be constructed from parts available at your local electronics parts store, as shown here.

Note that this adapter cable is not suitable for professional microphones requiring phantom power – these require an external power source. Also, it effectively converts balanced microphones to unbalanced, removing the ability to reject induced noise. The 4.7 μf capacitors isolate the microphones from the low-voltage microphone power supplied by some camcorders, and their value is very non-critical; any value from 3 to 100 μf should work just fine. They should be tantalum electrolytic types rated for at least 10 volts. Be sure to observe the polarity as marked on the capacitors when you wire them up. If you choose physically small capacitors, you should be able to put them inside the XLR connectors for a neat and adapter cable.

Again, there is no quality penalty for using a simple adapter like this, as long as you can keep your microphone cables well away from noise sources, such as power cables.

Using an Audio Mixer

On many shoots, it's common practice to use an audio mixer to get the audio from the microphone(s) to the camcorder. In using a mixer, the sound recordist will confirm that the audio levels being sent to the camcorder are correct and will often use headphones connected to the camcorder output in order to monitor sound quality.

Mixers also can include other features which are helpful during production. Some features available include:

- Low-cut filters (sometimes called high-pass filters) that eliminate very low frequencies such as air conditioner rumble.
- Equalizers that allow adjustment of the relative proportions of low, medium and high-frequency energy in the audio.
- Monitoring systems that allow adjustment of headphone volume or to connect external speakers.
- Solo buttons that allow individual microphones to be monitored without affecting the feed to the recording system.
- Multiple outputs for feeding a camcorder and additional audio recording devices.

Higher end mixers may also include their own analog-to-digital converters, and have the ability to control the audio in the digital domain and output to a recorder in a digital format.

Mixers generally provide four or more microphone inputs and stereo (2-channel) output, and are required when more than two microphones are being used on the set. Most mixers also provide phantom power as required for some condenser microphones. They have the advantage of balanced inputs and most have both balanced and unbalanced outputs, using XLR, phone plugs, and/or *RCA* connectors. RCA connectors are the common variety used to interconnect most home stereo equipment. They are not used for microphones, but are primarily used for *line-level* signals. RCA cables are also used for video signals on prosumer and consumer devices.

In using a mixer, the sound recordist will confirm that the audio levels being sent to the camcorder are correct and will often use headphones connected to the camcorder output in order to monitor sound quality. You probably want to include a headphone splitter in your tool kit, along with some headphone extension cords. You can't have too many ears listening to your sound.

About Decibels, Line and Mic Levels

Mixers and other audio devices commonly use two (or sometimes three) different signal levels (voltages) to connect with the outside world. These are known as mic and line levels. It's important to understand the difference, and why it's necessary to use more than one level of audio signal. For many people, this is one of the most confusing aspects of sound recording, but it's important.

Warning: Math ahead, but I'll try to keep it to a minimum!

Sounds levels and audio signals are measured in *Bels (*abbreviated *B),* named after Alexander Graham Bell, the inventor of the telephone. (Why there's only one *l* in Bel, I don't know.) More accurately, the relationship between audio signals can be measured in Bels. A difference of one Bel between one signal and another represents a power ratio of 10, but to the ear, it's often said that a difference of one Bel sounds twice as loud. Mathematically, a Bel is ratio of power levels expressed as a logarithm: (Don't worry, there's not going to be a lot of math!)

$$B = \log \frac{P1}{P2}$$

(Where *P* is power.)

Bels can also be used to express differences in voltage levels in a circuit:

$$B = 2\log \frac{V1}{V2}$$

(Where *V* is voltage.)

A *decibel* (*dB*, or more commonly *db*) is 1/10 of a Bel, and is a more common and more precise measurement, thus:

$$dB = 10\log \frac{P1}{P2}$$

$$dB = 20\log \frac{V1}{V2}$$

Since decibels are a measure of power ratios, in audio equipment they are calculated based on a standard level. In the early days of telephone and radio equipment, a standard level was defined as one milliwatt (1/1000 watt) in 600 ohms. This level is called *zero dbm*, or zero decibels above (or below) one milliwatt. Under these circumstances, 0 dbm produces 0.775 volts. Traditionally, dbm is the unit used for balanced audio circuits, but more recently, the term *dbu* (decibels unloaded) has come into common use. It is essentially the same as dbm, but is a reference to 0.775 volts instead of one milliwatt. For practical purposes, either term may be used. Another term, *dbv* (decibels relative to one volt) has also been used. Since 0.775 volts (0 dbu) is fairly close to one volt, these terms also frequently used interchangeably, if incorrectly. You'll also often hear people refer simply to *zero db.*

One other reference you'll see is *dbFS,* for decibels relative to full scale. This measurement refers only to digital audio, and full scale means a digital system will create "all ones" at that level; zero dbFS is the maximum level the system can record. Any signals above 0 dbFS (any positive number) will be clipped, resulting in severe distortion.

You'll also come across the term *VU* (Volume Units), which is equivalent to dbu with some caveats applied. A *VU meter* is a special mechanical instrument designed to measure the relative *volume* of typical audio signals. It has special characteristics related to its response speed and takes into account psycho-acoustic characteristics related to how the ear perceives loudness. More recently, a variety of *loudness meters* has become available.

There are actually several kinds of meters commonly found on audio equipment. The one you'll see most often is the *peak- reading meter* (or just a *peak meter),* sometimes referred to as a *PPI* (program peak indicator). The other common one is the VU meter, or something similar. The difference is that a peak-reading meter indicates the instantaneous maximum value of an audio signal while a VU meter indicates the average value over a short period of time – like 1/10 second or so. If you connect an audio tone generator to both meters and they're correctly calibrated, they'll read the same. On the other hand, if you feed a typical audio signal (such as speech or music) to both of them, the peak meter will read much higher. That's because the tone is continuously at its maximum value, while typical audio has a few peaks that are at maximum value, but most of the time it's much lower. In short, a VU meter (or any averaging meter) gives an indication of perceived volume while a peak meter indicates the maximum instantaneous electrical value of an audio signal.

Here's how all this applies to your audio equipment. Audio meters have a scale that goes both above (+ numbers) and below (– numbers). When we talk about "zero" level, we mean zero as indicated by the output meter on your mixer when looking at a steady tone.

For some obscure and arcane reasons I won't bore you with, the balanced line "zero" output level of your mixer is almost never 0 dbm or 0 dbv. It is actually +4 dbm, which means 4 decibels *above* 1 milliwatt (or 0.775 volt). There are some arcane reasons for this, and you'll be glad I won't bore you with them.

The unbalanced line "zero" output level of your mixer is (usually) -10 dbv, which means 10 decibels *below* one volt (about 14 db below the balanced line level).

The output of a typical microphone recording a normal speaking voice is around -60 dbm (or about -60 dbv, depending on how you measure). From this, you'll quickly realize that microphone level is very much lower than line level – if you do the math, you'll see it could be 1/1,000,000 as strong. At such low signal levels, it's easy to see how interference (hum, induced signals, crosstalk, etc.) could be more serious than with higher signal levels. For this reason, wiring carrying mic level signals should be minimized, and the first thing mic level signals see in your mixer or camcorder is a *preamplifier (preamp)*, which provides up to 60 decibels of *gain* (amplification), to bring the extremely weak microphone signal up to approximately line level for further processing.

Some camcorders have inputs to connect line-level signals (as from a mixer) for recording, but consumer types have only microphone-level inputs. Some mixers have microphone level outputs that can go directly to the mic inputs on your camcorder, but often it's necessary to use an *attenuator* (sometimes called a *pad*), which uses resistors to reduce the signal from line to mic level. Without a pad, a line-level output connected to a microphone input will give you very loud and very distorted audio.

A simple pad for use between a mixer and a camcorder microphone input can be assembled according to the diagram. This one provides about 45 db of attenuation. (Such pads have attenuation that can be approximately calculated by the formula: *db = 20 log R1/R2*)

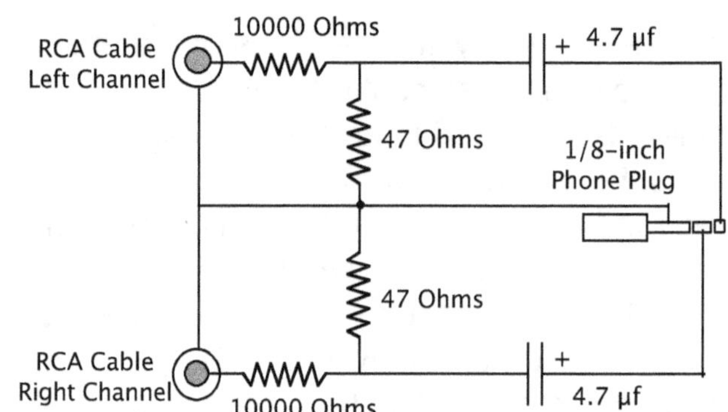

I have assembled attenuators like this inside a short length or plastic tubing, or merely on a cable, securely taped with plastic electrical tape. The resistors should be 1/4-watt 5%. The two capacitors, again, isolate the pad from the microphone power supplied by the camcorder – be sure to observe the polarity. They may not be necessary for your camcorder, but won't do any harm to your sound quality if you put them in. Pads for this purpose are also commercially available.

Working Without a Mixer

On many (if not most) shoots, only one or two microphones are used. In these situations, it is often easiest to connect the microphones directly to the camera.

All camcorders have *automatic gain control* (AGC) for the microphone inputs, but on higher-end cameras, the AGC can be disabled. In analog camcorders, AGC systems were notorious for causing the audio levels to go up and down in response to ambient noise, creating an undesirable effect sometime called *pumping* as the gain varied. During periods of silence or quiet sound, they would raise the system gain, bringing up undesired background noise, sometimes to booming levels. Because significant audible noise is inherent in the analog recording process, these systems used a high level of audio compression (not to be confused with digital compression or bitrate reduction). In digital camcorders, however, the AGC system can be much more gentle and sophisticated because the digital recording process doesn't introduce significant noise into the audio signal. Unlike the older analog systems, digital camcorders are often better at "riding gain" than a human operator and don't cause serious or audible side-effects, they simply avoid excessive levels. I have had great success recording high quality dialog with digital camcorders using the AGC system and with microphones connected directly to the camera, though many seasoned filmmakers and sound recordists will naturally be skeptical of this approach.

If you find that the AGC on your particular camcorder produces undesirable degradation of the sound (and some certainly do!), there are two simple ways to eliminate the problem: either disable it and set levels manually or use an attenuator (and/or outboard mixer) to reduce the audio levels so that the AGC's operation isn't apparent. It's important to remember that digital audio recording systems have a very high signal to noise ratio – very little noise is introduced by the recording process. The most important consideration is making sure that audio levels are not too high. Digital recording systems produce very high levels of distortion when overdriven or overloaded, so recording low is preferable to recording high.

About Recording Levels

Like the audio levels on a mixer, digital recording levels are specified in decibels (db), with maximum recording level defined as zero dbFS. Any audio above zero level will overload the system, causing overload or clipping – the system simply clips off everything above this level, resulting in severe distortion. Prosumer equipment (such as DV camcorders) often uses a reference level of –12 db, which means 12 decibels less than maximum. Professional equipment (such as HDCAM) uses a reference level of –20 db, giving a bit more *headroom* to the recordings. In other words, signals can go above reference with less risk of clipping or distortion, but for either reference, audio should <u>never</u> go above the maximum level (*0 dbFS*). Be aware of the disorienting fact that these levels have nothing to do with dbm, dbu or dbv.

The difference between the recorder's reference level and "zero" level coming out of your mixer has created a lot of confusion, but it's relatively simple to understand. For everything to operate correctly, when the meter on your mixer is indicating "zero", the meter on your digital recorder or camcorder should indicate its appropriate reference level (–12 dbFS or –20 dbFS). For accuracy, these levels should be set with an audio tone instead of music or speech. Some mixers have a built-in tone generator for this purpose (usually 400 or 1000 Hz). Simple freestanding tone generators are also available.

Standard practice throughout the history of analog recording has been to set the set the level as high as possible without exceeding zero db, thus attaining the highest possible *signal to noise ratio.* The objective is to make the recording as loud as possible, overriding the noise. A measure of the difference between the loudest and quietest usable recording is called the *dynamic range*, also measured in decibels. Digital recording systems have a dynamic range of at least 90 db, compared to about 60 db at best for analog systems, so if you digitally record 30 db below normal level, you'll still have a signal that's at least as good as analog recording. (A signal-to-noise ratio of 90 db simply means that the loudest signal that can be recorded is 90 db louder than the noise created in the recording channel.)

Levels can be increased during post-production, so "riding gain" during recording is not nearly as important as it once was. In fact, it's often preferable to postpone riding levels until the editing phase, an idea that would have been crazy in the analog world.

This opens up some important considerations in digital shooting. For many situations, it's fine to simply connect one or two microphones directly to the camera and simply record what you get. Of course, someone should always be monitoring the audio on headphones to be sure there's no distortion, microphone handling noise or wind blasts. This can be a real time-saver, and can reduce your crew size. If you try this approach, your editor might complain because he'll have a bit more work to do keeping the audio levels consistent. Just remember that his time is probably cheaper than your whole crew's time on the shoot.

Audio Quality Considerations

While shooting your film, you'll be most interested in recording dialog, and, to a lesser degree, sound effects. Capturing high quality, clean, consistent dialog can be the biggest challenge in creating your soundtrack, and this process involves skill as much as equipment. It's particularly daunting in noisy locations; it's utterly impossible in some of them.

Sometimes you just can't eliminate background noise, such as the rumble created by air conditioning systems. This and other low-frequency noise can often be minimized by using a high-pass (or low-cut) filter, available on some mics and/or mixers. As long as the noise doesn't create excessive levels (overload), low-frequency rumble can also be minimized during editing. Special purpose audio software programs can be useful and amazingly effective for solving noise problems. It's a good idea for your sound recordist to be familiar with their capabilities and limitations. (Much more on this in Chapter 3.4.)

About Double-System Sound

In most low-budget productions, the camcorder will also be the sound recorder. Higher-end productions (and all film productions) use *double-system* sound (also called *separate sound*). This means that the sound recording system is totally independent of the camera, but there's a mechanism in place to be sure sound and picture can be maintained "in-sync". The primary reasons for using double-system recording are: 1) It allows more channels to be recorded simultaneously, 2) the recording can be of higher quality than camcorders offer, and 3) wiring of sound equipment to the camera can be eliminated. In spite of these advantages, double-system sound introduces a lot of complexity into the production process. First, the camera an sound system must be synchronized, usually using timecode. Either the sound recording system is *slaved* to the camera timecode, or a single external timecode signal is used for both. Often, camera and sound recording timecode is set to "time-of-day" at the beginning of the shoot, and the accuracy of the timecode is sufficient to maintain sync within one frame for an entire shooting day. Editing and audio post-production software is able to synchronize audio and video through timecode, though it's possible to use the tried-and-true "slate" as the primary synchronization system (See Chapter 3.1).

The sound recording system may use a free-standing multi-track recorder, a digital audio workstation (DAW), or a computer equipped with suitable audio input-output hardware. Using such a system is similar to using a mixer during recording, except each microphone can have its own channel (track), so the recordist is not really mixing, but simply assigning tracks and being sure recording levels are correct.

During post-production, it's necessary to "sync up" the sound, and have a flexible workflow designed to handle multiple tracks. In complex productions, an assistant sound editor will do the synching and will arrange the tracks so they are conveniently available to the editor.

About Stereo and Surround Sound

You've probably noticed that most of what's been discussed in this chapter has been about a single channel of audio – one microphone at a time. In the real world, however, except for AM radio and the telephone, most of our listening to media involves more than one channel – two for stereo and up to eight for the several breeds of *surround sound* available in theaters, on HD broadcasts, and on movie DVDs. A few special systems have even more channels. These multi-channel systems have one thing in common: they are groups of single-channel (monaural) recordings. Sometimes all the channels are recorded at the same time, but more often they are recorded separately, one or two at a time.
Just as there are stereo microphones that allow recording of two channels at a time, there are also a few "surround" microphones available that output up to

eight simultaneous channels. Such hybrid mics are often used for surround sound broadcasting of live events (like the Super Bowl) allowing very realistic ambience effects.

In reality, surround sound is created in the “mix”, when the final soundtrack is assembled from a variety of recorded sources. When multiple mics and multiple tracks are used during shooting, the sound designer has a lot more to work with. (More in Chapter 4.4.)

2.6 Lighting Technology

"Darkness is cheap."

Charles Dickens

I'm continually surprised by the blatant lack of concern for lighting in discussions of digital filmmaking, particularly for the amateur or beginner. Electronics stores carry a wide variety of cameras, monitors and accessories, but their lighting offerings usually consist of nothing more than a few "video lights" you can mount on your camcorder. Even Internet discussion boards, blogs and groups offer very little emphasis on lighting, and otherwise good books on filmmaking often gloss over this important topic. Yet, good lighting can have more impact on the visual quality and "look" of your film than any other single factor. With good lighting, even an inexpensive single-chip DV camera can produce professional quality pictures, although you have to work harder with such equipment. Undoubtedly, good lighting is an important index of the professional quality of your work. In this chapter, we'll talk about the technology of lighting; we'll go into more detail about lighting technique in the Production section (Chapter 3.2.)

The Digital Age has not affected lighting equipment very much. In fact, lighting instruments are little changed over the past few decades, though some manufacturers have introduced innovative lightweight units that are easier to handle and move. Also, a wider selection of smaller instruments (under 1000 watts) is available, and lower-wattage lamps are available for larger units. Lower wattage means you can use smaller, lighter cables, too. For small lights, extension cords from your local hardware store will work just fine, and you can operate several of them from a single household circuit if necessary.

You often hear the argument that digital camcorders work so well in low light that you'll rarely need any lighting equipment. It's true that they work very well under remarkably little illumination, but good lighting is more about the quality of the light than the quantity. Compare, for example, the very flat fluorescent lighting of a factory floor with the controlled lighting on a theater stage. The factory lighting will be more even and probably brighter if measured with a light meter, but it does not create the ability to use both light and shadow for effect, it can't accent some areas and hide others. Factory lighting is very soft and virtually shadow free, it's excellent for seeing what you're doing, but it certainly isn't flattering to people.

Household lighting brings another set of problems. While office and industrial lighting levels are around fifty foot-candles (500 lux), residential settings are more like ten foot-candles (100 lux) or less, sometimes much less. In the daytime, much of the illumination will come from outdoors, from windows. At night, the light often comes from overhead fixtures or table lamps, neither of which are flattering to people. Also, the color of daylight is much bluer than yellowish incandescent lights, and mixing the two may be problematic.

Judicious lighting to the rescue! The extra sensitivity of modern cameras gives you one important advantage over earlier technologies: in many cases, you can use smaller lights to get the same effect.

Color Temperature

The color of light is specified by its *color temperature*, measured in degrees Kelvin (°K), equivalent to degrees Celsius above absolute zero (0° C = 255.37° K). Technically, the color temperature of a source is the temperature of a *black body* (an object that doesn't reflect light) emitting a particular combination of wavelengths of light through heating, just as the element of an electric stove glows when it's hot.

Some examples of the color temperatures of typical light sources are:

Afternoon daylight under a cloudless sky	5600° K
Mid-day daylight under a cloudy sky	6500° K
Standard household light bulb	2800° K
Tungsten halogen studio lighting	3200° K
Studio Halogen-Metal-Iodide (HMI) lighting	5600° K
Daylight fluorescent lighting	6000° K

While photographers have traditionally tried to avoid mixing color temperatures, many cinematographers like to use mixed lighting for artistic reasons.

Character of Light

Various sources of light also differ in their *hardness* or *softness*. Think of hard light as being like direct sunlight, coming from a point source. It casts hard, sharp-edged shadows, and there is high contrast between highlight and shadow areas. Soft light is more like an overcast day, with virtually no shadows. The illumination is very even and the contrast is low. Hard light can be softened (or *diffused*) by using some kind of translucent material, such as lightweight fabric, or by bouncing the light off a white surface. The larger the light source, the softer the light. A mixture of hard and soft creates the most interesting lighting.

Strangely, scenes lit with hard, contrasty light are called low-key; scenes using predominately soft light are called high-key. These expressions came from movies; dark nighttime scenes shot with a single key light, creating heavy shadows, are low-key. Bright scenes with minimal shadows are high key.

The Inverse Square Law

Light loses intensity the farther you get from the source, it's intensity dropping in inverse proportion to the square of the distance – what is called the *Inverse Square Law:*

$$\textbf{Light intensity} = 1 / \textbf{distance}^2$$

Uh oh! More math! Relax. This simply means that if you double the distance between the light source and the subject you're lighting, the light intensity drops to one quarter of its original value ($2^2 = 4$, the inverse of 4 is 1/4.) Therefore, you can see that getting the light produced by a 250-watt lamp at 10 feet will require a 1000-watt lamp at 20 feet. For practical purposes, Inverse Square applies to all light sources, although sunlight appears to be an exception, since it produces very uniform light on the surface of the earth. With a little thought, it's easy to understand why: the vast distance to the sun means that we'd have to move out past the orbit of Mars before the light intensity will drop to one-fourth because of Inverse Square.

Note: Practically speaking, Inverse Square holds true for all production lighting equipment except focusable instruments. In effect, these lamps create a "virtual light source" some distance behind the actual instrument, so the light in close proximity to the fixture falls off somewhat slower than Inverse Square would predict.

The practical impact of Inverse Square is that it takes a lot more power to light large areas than small ones – a football stadium may require 250,000 watts (or more) of light to provide the same illumination on the field that you can get on your desktop from a tiny table lamp.

Tungsten Lighting

Lighting instruments (sometimes called *luminaires*) include a variety of types, light sources and beam shapes. Most instruments designed for film and video employ *quartz tungsten halogen* (or simply *quartz*) lamps. Much smaller for their wattage than ordinary light bulbs, these lamps are pressurized with halogen gas and have quartz (instead of ordinary glass) envelopes. They produce a whiter (technically, bluer) light than household lamps and are substantially more efficient. Because they run at a higher temperature than ordinary household lamps, they have a shorter life – as short as 50 hours instead of over 1000 hours.

The color temperature of these lamps is about 3200°K, much more yellow/orange than the 5600°K of daylight. 3200°K has become the de facto standard for interior lighting in the film industry; theatrical lighting is closer to 3000°K, lowering the temperature in order to gain longer life of the lamps (although this reduces the efficiency). To change the color to more nearly match daylight, filters can be used. The most efficient of these is the *dichroic* filter, made of glass with special coatings that reject the undesired radiation at the red end of the spectrum by reflecting it away. Acetate or polyester filters (called *gels* because they were originally made of gelatin) can also be used. Gels and filters are often specified by *Wratten* numbers. For example, a Wratten 80 (or 80A) filter converts 3200°K light sources to 5600°K; a Wratten 85 converts in the opposite direction. Unlike dichroic filters, gel filters absorb the excess red-light energy instead of reflecting it away, so they can get hot enough to melt if used close to a lamp. Other filters, such as *booster blue*, make partial corrections.

Because dichroic and color correction filters reduce the effective light output of tungsten sources by as much as 70%, they are primarily useful for balancing to match low levels of daylight, such as the light from a north-facing window. In direct sunlight, tungsten lighting with color correction filters is so inefficient that it's almost useless, so other sources (such as HMI instruments, discussed below) should be used in these situations.

A word of caution about correcting tungsten lighting to daylight: Some video cameras are quite sensitive to invisible radiation in the infrared part of the spectrum, which they render as red. For this reason, dichroic filters (which suppress infrared radiation from tungsten lamps) are preferable to gels. Since gel filters pass infrared, they can lead to unpredictable results or even make matters worse with some cameras, particularly those using a single chip with no beam splitting optics. Only tests will determine if a particular camera suffers from this shortcoming.

It's important to remember that the fragile tungsten filaments in quartz lamps are sensitive to shock, so they shouldn't be bumped or jarred when they're turned on. Also, you should never touch the lamp with your bare hands when you're installing or replacing it. Oils from your fingers can create hot-spots on the quartz envelope and cause it to shatter. Remember, too, that quartz instruments get very hot while in operation and can be a severe burn hazard, so safety is a vital consideration in their use.

Also, while quartz lamps can be used with inexpensive dimmers to adjust their intensity, color temperature changes radically toward the red (lower color temperature) when they are not run at rated voltage. For this reason, light intensity is more often controlled by using *scrims*, pieces of various density screen wire mounted in retainer rings that are attached to the instrument.

Traditionally, manufacturers have offered the greatest variety of instruments in the 600-1000 watt range, and lower-wattage lamps are available for most of them. Also, theatrical lamps are offered in many cases. Using them will reduce the light output slightly, but the expensive lamps will last much longer.

Focusable instruments come in two types: *reflector* (also called *open face*) and *Fresnel* (pronounced "Fruh-nell"). The first uses a polished reflector with a mechanism for moving the lamp forward or backward in the reflector to vary the beam width, from an intense spot to a width of up to 45 degrees. The Fresnel (named after 18th Century mathematician Augustin Fresnel) uses a flat lens molded with concentric circles to concentrate the light, a smaller version of the huge Fresnel lenses used in lighthouses.

Open-face instruments are smaller and lighter, but don't provide as much control of the beam. While they can create a concentrated spot of light, the reflectors cause the coverage to be less and less even as the beam is adjusted to a broader setting. Many instruments use a reflector that has a textured surface to minimize this problem, but at a sacrifice of efficiency and light output. Interchangeable reflectors are also available on some models. Most focusable instruments are fitted with *barn doors*, black metal "wings" used to restrict the light to a specific area and preventing "spill".

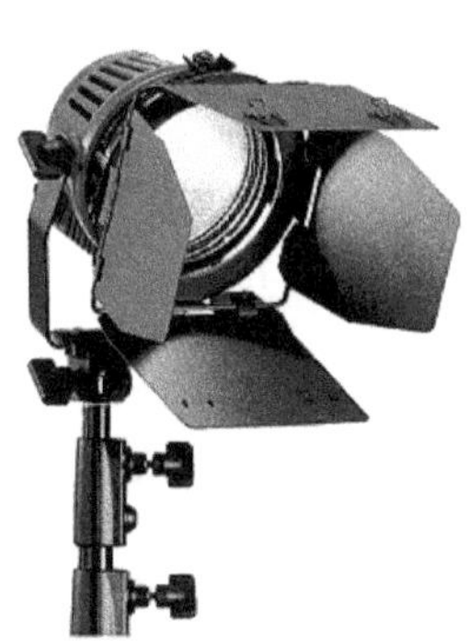

Focusable open-face instruments are available in wattages from 100 to 1,000 and are ideal for field shooting because of their light weight. The 650- and 1,000-watt models are the most popular, although with modern cameras the smaller, cooler-running versions have many advantages. Many are equipped with glass shields in front of the lamp, a worthwhile safety feature since quartz lamps can sometimes shatter unexpectedly, particularly if used outdoors. A sudden gust of wind or a single raindrop hitting the lamp can cause it to instantly disintegrate.

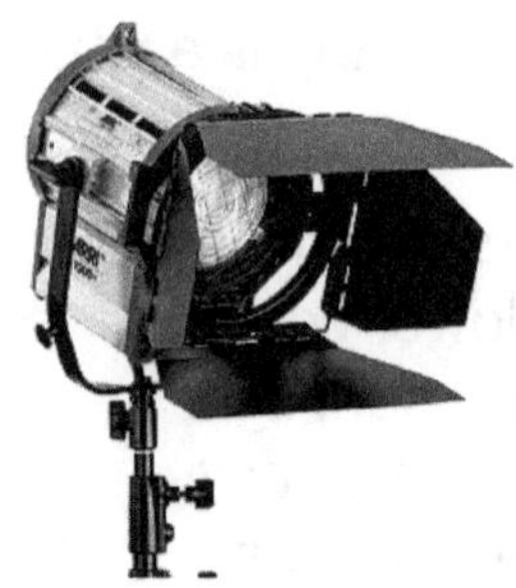

Fresnels run the range from under 100 to 10,000 watts, and are best for studio use, although the smaller ones (1,000 watts and under) are often used on-location. While larger, heaver and more expensive than their open-face counterparts, they provide more uniform beam coverage and the focusing lens provides protection for the fragile lamp.

Another type of instrument you may need is the on-camera light, sometimes called an *eye light* or *Obie* light. These lamps are designed to be mounted very close to the camera lens, providing a small light source that's especially helpful for close-ups. They soften skin texture and create attractive catch lights in the subject's eyes. Some Obie lights operate on low voltage and can obtain their power from the camera's onboard battery. They are very small, low-wattage units (25-100 watts), but are sometimes used as the only source of light – typically for news videography where quick mobility is an important consideration. A few manufacturers have introduced obies that uses white light emitting diodes (*LEDs*) instead of tungsten or HMI lamps (shown). These wonderful (and expensive!) little lights provide a relatively soft, compact source that is infinitely dimmable without affecting color temperature, making them perfect for "run-and-gun" shooting.

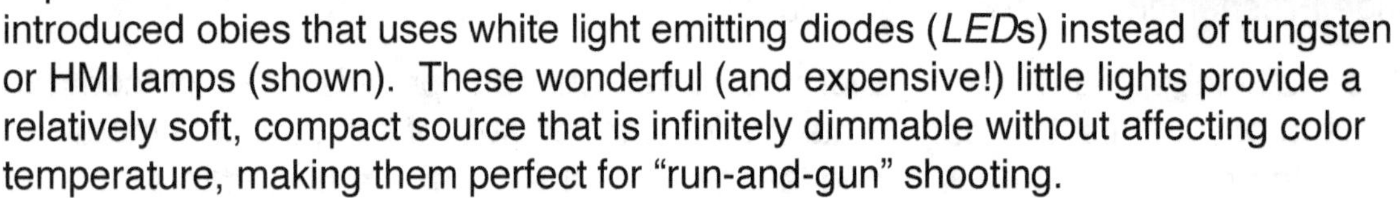

Broad lights are just what their name implies: they create a very broad beam of light, similar to a floodlight as opposed to a spotlight. They are used for lighting large areas or to provide fill light. Quartz broads usually have curved, fixed reflectors behind the lamp, providing a beam width of 90 to 120 degrees, and some are equipped with barn doors. Instead of the small, round lamps used by focusable instruments, broads often use tubular lamps with the power connections at the ends. Old TV studios often used *scoops*, which are broad lights using a more conventional lamps with a large round, matte-finish reflector.

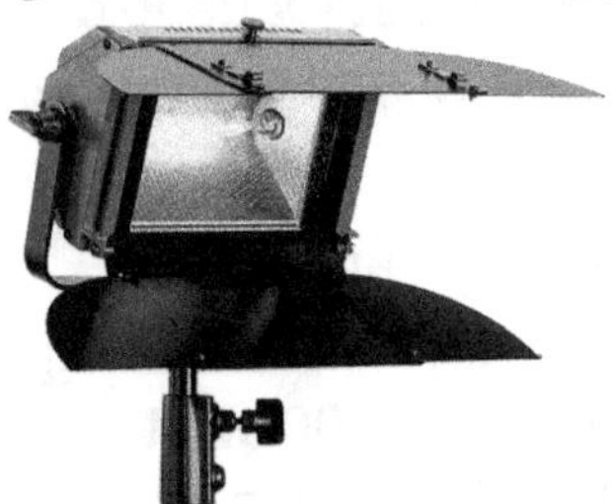

Many filmmakers have used quartz work lights, available at home improvement warehouses, as substitutes for more professional broad lights. Some are equipped with a cage covering the lamp, which must be removed for photographic use. These lamps are available in sizes from 150 to 750 watts and have a color temperature of about 3000°K, fairly close to the 3200°K commercial standard. They are very inexpensive, usually come with sturdy stands, and can be a great resource to have in your tool kit for those occasions when you need just a little more light. I've used a few of them to light the exterior of a Boeing

737 for a nighttime shot, with great results. Buying them was cheaper than renting enough professional lights to do the job, too.

PAR lights are sealed quartz (or HMI) units, similar in construction to sealed-beam automobile headlights. They are more efficient and provide more uniform beams than open face or Fresnel lamps, but have the disadvantage of having a fixed beam size. Also used for theatrical lighting, they come in a large variety of sizes, patterns and mountings, with and without barn doors. The floodlight types are a good substitute for open face broads, providing more light for the watt. A few quartz PARs are available with built-in dichroic filters and produce a close approximation to daylight color temperature with fair efficiency, although these lamps are notorious for having very short life. While the fixtures for PAR lamps are less expensive than other quartz instruments, the lamps themselves are more expensive since the lamp, reflector and lens assembly are built as a single, replaceable unit. PAR fixtures come in singles and in banks of three, six or nine lamps for lighting large areas.

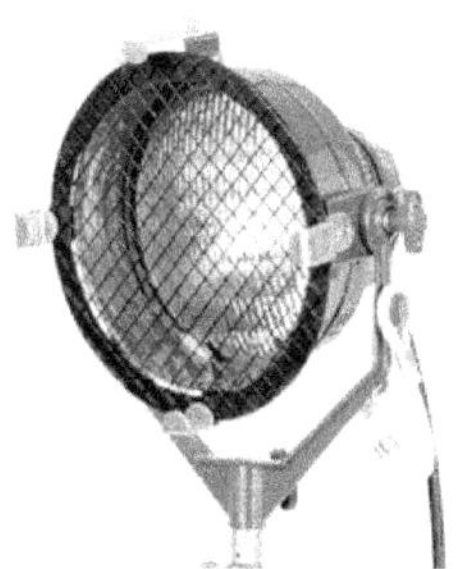

Ellipsoidal Spotlights are rarely used on location, but are common in a studio setting. They are similar in construction to Fresnel instruments, but use true focusing lenses to create well-defined pools of light, often using gels for color. They can also employ a metal stencil-like *cucalorus* to project a pattern, and are sometimes called *pattern projectors* or *Lekos (pronounced leak-oh).*

Quartz Soft Lights are built to provide a large source, minimizing the harsh shadows produced by a near point source, such as a Fresnel. The light is indirect, being bounced off of a white-painted or metalized surface, and/or diffused by a large translucent screen. Units designed for studio use are large, rigid boxes; soft lights for the field are collapsible for easier transport.

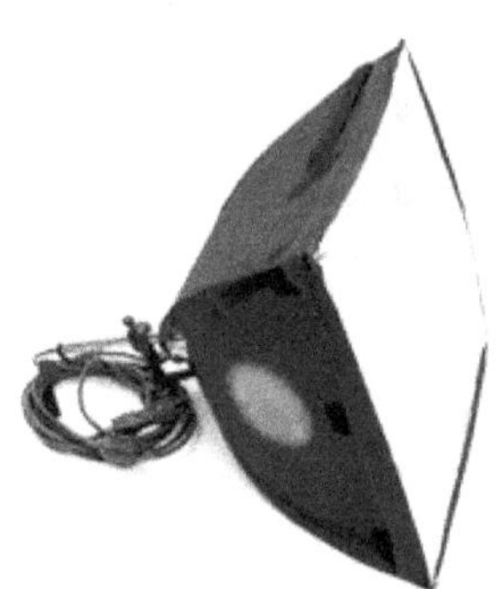

Low-budget filmmakers often use their other instruments to double for soft lights by bouncing them off large white cards or *space blankets,* metalized plastic blankets used for camping. Some instruments have special mounts for metalized umbrellas, allowing them to be used as convenient and versatile sources of soft light. Also, gel frames can be used either for adding color to the light or for holding a sheet of diffusion material, such as *tough-spun*, a virtually heatproof glass fabric made for this purpose.

Often, too, a very diffused source of soft light can be obtained by bouncing light off a white wall, or even a white bed sheet. Lights can also be made soft by beaming them through large sheets of translucent acetate or lightweight white fabric (often called *silk*).

For product shots and close-ups, a *light tent* is sometimes used. It's simply a frame holding up light-diffusing material; the object to be shot is placed under it and lights are put on the outside, creating a small area of near-shadowless light. In a studio environment, large light tents have been built using parachutes. Big sheets of diffusing fabric (sometimes called *butterflies*) and mounting frames for them are also available commercially.

HMI lighting instruments are physically similar to quartz fixtures, but use *halogen metal iodide* lamps (*HMI*). Like tungsten instruments, HMIs come in open-face, Fresnel, and PAR versions.

These lamps produce over three times as much output as quartz units of similar wattage and create 5600°K light that closely matches the color of sunlight. They can also be filtered to match 3200°K light with only about 30% loss. Given these advantages, they are the near-ideal instruments for any shoot. There are some downsides, though. First, both the instruments and the lamps are several times costlier than their tungsten equivalents. Secondly, they are heavier and bulkier than their quartz counterparts, largely because they require a current-limiting *ballast,* an external box that's required for each instrument. Another disadvantage is that they're not "instant-on" like a quartz lamp; they require warm-up time before they reach their normal output intensity and color. HMI lights cannot be dimmed using standard dimmers, either. In fact, they can be damaged if dimming is attempted. (Some use electronic ballasts that allow dimming.)

You should be aware that HMIs don't create continuous light output (except for a few units); they produce pulses of light, two for each cycle of the incoming alternating current (AC) power supply. This isn't a problem in most situations, since the incoming AC supply is 60 Hertz (cycles per second) and normal video is recorded at 60 fields per second. If, however, you're using a variable shutter on the camera or you must run the lighting on a generator, the pulsed-light nature of HMI lamps can cause serious problems. In the case of the variable shutter, you may be surprised to find that your exposure is varying. If a generator is not synchronized to the exact field rate of the video you're shooting, you can get severe brightness surges in the image from the camera.

Fluorescent lights have become increasingly popular in recent years, particularly in studio work, where they're often used in combination with quartz instruments. Much more efficient than quartz, fluorescent instruments are available in a variety of shapes and sizes and in color temperatures ranging from 3200°K to over 6000°K. Like HMI lamps, fluorescent instruments can flicker under some circumstances, and they require special dimmers. Their advantages include relatively low cost, very long lamp life, stable color temperature, and cool operation. They are an inherent source of soft light, since the banks of fluorescent tubes cover a much larger area than a typical quartz instrument of the same wattage. For this reason, the light output is not nearly as controllable as with conventional instruments, but directivity can be enhanced by using a plastic grid over the bank of tubes. This broad, even output is excellent for lighting a multi-camera setup in a studio, but not as convenient as other instruments for location use. Also available are instruments using compact fluorescent lamps, similar to an ordinary light bulb. These are cool-running equivalents to tungsten broads.

LED (light emitting diode) lighting instruments are also appearing on the market. While very expensive, LEDs have the advantages of very high efficiency, low power consumption, near-zero heat output, and they can be dimmed without flicker or changes in color temperature.

Light Meters

While most shooters judge their lighting by looking at the scene on a monitor, a light meter can be a very helpful addition to your toolkit. Good light metering was always essential for accurate exposures on film, but it can be important in digital cinematography, too, especially when you're lighting a scene in the absence of a camera and monitor. For video use, it's not important to have an especially accurate (and expensive) light meter because you only need it to establish relative amounts of light. When blocking action, for example, it's good to be able to know that the areas where actors may be moving are uniformly lit.

Light meters come in three basic types: *incident*, *reflected* and *spot*, though some combine the functions of two or all three of these. An incident light meter is used to measure the actual amount of light falling on your subject, and measures foot-candles or lux, and it is calibrated for film speeds and *f*-stops. The incident light meter is used at the location of the subject, not from the camera position. If you use an incident light meter consistently, colors appearing in one scene under one set of lighting conditions will look the same in other settings under different lights. For this reason, feature-film cinematographers depend very heavily on their incident meters.

A reflected light meter measures the amount of light reflected from the subject toward the camera, and is usually used at the camera position. It will read the same as an incident meter only if it is aimed at an object of a known color, usually a standard *gray card,* which provides a measured 18% reflectance, the standard for this use. If you measure a typical scene with a reflected meter, it will indicate an average amount of light for the entire scene. While less accurate than an incident meter, this average is often close enough for typical scenes. Usually, however, reflected light meters are only used in situations where you can't actually take readings at the subject position – shooting a mountain range, for example.

The third type, the spot meter, is a more refined version of the reflected light meter. It contains a viewfinder that indicates a very small area (the spot) that the meter actually measures. Looking through the spot meter, you can measure the brightness of a particular object within a scene – an area of an actor's face, for example. You can also look at highlight and shadow areas to determine if they are too bright or too dark to allow detail to be seen by the camera. By metering an object of known reflectance (I use the palm of my hand, which I've measured to have about 30% reflectance) under the subject lighting conditions, the spot meter can also effectively function as an incident meter. This makes the spot meter perhaps the most versatile of the three types, though it's also the most expensive.

Light meters are generally calibrated in terms of *ISO* (International Standards Organization) film speed (you may also see ASA, ANSI, IE or DIN specifications, which are very similar). Film speed is a measure of light sensitivity; the higher the speed (ISO number) the more sensitive the film. Common speeds for motion picture film are ISO 100, 200, 400, 800. Video camera sensitivity is not usually specified as ISO, but you can do some simple tests and establish an ISO number that is a reasonably accurate representation of your camera's sensitivity. You can do this anytime you're shooting a typical scene. Take note of the *f*-stop you're using to shoot the scene, then measure the light on the scene with your light meter. Using a 1/60 or 1/50-second shutter speed setting on the light meter, then change the ISO value until the *f*-stop is the same as the one being used on the camera. That ISO number is the equivalent sensitivity of your camera. Most cameras (without any gain boost) will be in the range of ISO 400 to 800.

Some light meters also offer an *exposure value* (EV) scale. Put simply, EV 1 is an exposure of 1 second with an *f*1.0 lens on ISO 100 film. Each EV unit is equal to a change of one *f*-stop, so if EV is 2, the exposure would be 1 second at *f*1.4 – one *f*-stop difference. Similarly, EV 3 would be *f*2, EV4 would be *f*2.8, and so on. The EV scale is most useful for comparing relative light levels within a scene, since each unit is equal to a ratio of 2:1. One EV unit more is twice as much light; one EV unit less is half as much light.

A special-purpose version of the light meter is the *color temperature meter*. This rather expensive instrument does what its name implies: measures the color temperature of a light source. Being able to accurately measure color temperature can be very important for photographers doing exacting work with transparency film, for high-end advertising photography, for example. For the videographer, such a meter is probably an unnecessary luxury, since the color correction capabilities of recent editing software are so powerful.

Lighting Accessories

There are literally thousands of accessories available for video and film lighting, and the sheer number makes the choices of what you will really need bewildering. Here, we'll cover the basic must-have items and a few that will be needed occasionally.

Light Stands are essential, and you'll probably want one for each lighting instrument. They range from small *pigeon* stands (for putting lights near the floor) all the way to very heavy crank-up *elevator* stands capable of holding 20,000 watt instruments 15 feet above the ground. For most instruments, you'll probably want collapsible stands that are adjustable from 2-3 ft. up 7-8 ft. height.

Lightweight aluminum (or magnesium or carbon-fiber) stands work well for small instruments, although the heavier steel stands have the advantage of being a bit more stable. Lightweight stands used with heavy instruments demand that sandbags be used for stabilization. The popular *C-stands* are excellent if weight is not a problem. They are study, convenient, and almost indestructible. They are fitted with industry-standard 5/8-inch mounting studs – different from the 1/4-inch studs sometimes used for equipment designed for still photography. Boom arms and extensions are available for mounting on most stands.

Flags and their cousins, cutters, nets, scrims, cuculoris (cookies), etc. are used for fine lighting control. They're usually mounted on stands using clamps designed for the purpose.

Reflectors are often used for providing fill under bright, sunny conditions. They range from commercial stand-mounted styles to homemade (but still effective) aluminum foil-covered cardboard. White *Foamcore,* available from art supply stores, is often used as a convenient reflector material. It is essentially a sheet of Styrofoam about 1/4-inch thick with heavy paper bonded to both sides, making it very lightweight and reasonably strong. It can be covered with aluminum foil to create a "harder" reflector.

Tie-in boxes are portable electrical distribution panels designed for use in locations where there is insufficient power available from the existing circuits. They allow an electrician to connect temporarily (tie in) to a building's incoming power service, and, through a long cable, extend this power to make multiple circuits available for lighting.

Generators are commonly used in locations where commercial power is unavailable or insufficient. While inexpensive household generators can be used for tungsten lighting, HMI or fluorescent instruments require a constant-frequency generator (often called a *crystal-controlled* generator because it uses an electronic crystal oscillator as a frequency reference). It's important that any generator used for film lighting be as stable as possible – that it's output voltage remains as close as possible to nominal at all times. This is because the color temperature of tungsten lights varies substantially with voltage. Also, tungsten lamps are very sensitive to over-voltage. A momentary surge in generator output can burn out expensive lamps in an instant. With poorly regulated generators (particularly when being used near maximum capacity), surges occur when the load changes. This can create a chain reaction – one lamp burns out, the generator surges to a higher voltage, burns out another one, surges again, and so on. On one occasion when I was using a small generator, a lamp failed in a PAR instrument. In a matter of seconds, three other similar lamps went out in a series of glorious flashes!

2.7 Monitors and Monitoring

While shooting in the field (and later, in post-production), it's desirable to be able to accurately monitor your pictures and sound. Your camera viewfinder will be your primary reference for shot composition but, unfortunately, the low-resolution pop-up monitors and color viewfinders on most cameras aren't good enough to assure pinpoint focus or for accurately judging exposure or color values. For most shoots, you'll want a reasonably good field monitor for quality control. The two most popular monitor types for field use are the venerable *CRT* (cathode ray tube) and the *LCD* (liquid crystal display). *Plasma* monitors are also used in studio environments.

A CRT is, of course, the display device that's been used in TV sets from the beginning, and in a pinch you can use any TV set with a video input as a reasonable monitor. The advantages of CRT monitors are good brightness, reasonable to excellent color fidelity, availability in a wide range of sizes, and moderate cost. Some also support HD display. Their main disadvantages are that they're heavy and bulky, and they are power hogs, especially in the larger sizes.

LCD displays have become increasingly popular and have been steadily improving in quality while decreasing in price. Their main advantages over CRTs are much lighter weight and lower power consumption. The smaller sizes have lower resolution than CRTs; they are similar to the pop-out LCD viewfinders on cameras. LCDs over about 7" have resolution capabilities on a par with CRTs, and many can accommodate HD. Depending on the particular display, LCDs image quality is to some extent dependent on the viewing angle; quality and color rendition are best when they are viewed head-on. For critical quality assessment, it's important to remember this limitation.

Monitor Features

Professional monitors (either CRT or LCD) provide high picture quality, rugged construction, and offer features you won't find in consumer TV sets. For one thing, they are likely to have a variety of inputs, probably using BNC connectors instead of the RCA connectors more common on consumer equipment. There may be a variety of input formats, too, including HDMI, composite, component and S-Video. Many also are multi-standard, supporting NTSC, PAL, SECAM, and various HD formats.

Other extra features offered on professional monitors include:

Pulse-Cross Display – This setting allows observation of the synchronizing (sync) and blanking signals present in the video by shifting the picture down by half the picture height and to the right by half the picture width. While not particularly useful during field shooting or for HD, a pulse-cross display can reveal problems in the sync, blanking, closed captioning and vertical interval timecode. It can also help spot problems in various outboard video hardware used in post-production and broadcasting, such as switchers, processing amplifiers and digital effects devices.

Underscan – Consumer TV sets (even LCD and Plasma monitors) display somewhat less than the whole transmitted picture, the displays are *overscanned.* Some of the image (usually about 5%) is cropped away at the top, bottom and sides, being hidden behind the mask on the front of the tube. An *underscanned* monitor allows the entire transmitted image to be seen. Video viewed on a computer screen usually has no overscan, so the entire transmitted image is seen.

Blue-Gun – This feature allows display of only the blue channel of the decoded RGB signals. It's useful for setting color rendition accurately.

Waveform Monitors

While expensive, having a waveform monitor in your field package can offer a way to accurately measure exposure and color values. Properly used, it can add an extra measure of quality control and assurance that your footage will be the best it can be. As free-standing instruments that can be easily used in the field, they range in cost from about $1,000 to well over $15,000, numbers that put them out of reach for many low-budget filmmakers. Fortunately, most editing systems have the equivalent of a waveform monitor built into the software.

Connecting Monitors

During shooting, it's helpful to have a picture monitor available, and you can simply connect a composite video output (NTSC or PAL) to the corresponding input on your monitor using a single cable. If your camera and monitor are so equipped, you can use an S-video cable for somewhat better quality. For HD output, you'll need a special cable for component video, HDMI, or HD-SDI connection to the monitor. (Most HD camcorders also have an NTSC down-converted output for use with SD monitors.)

When you want to use two or more monitors, there's a problem getting the signal to them. You can't simply use a "splitter" cable as you would for audio, because video monitors must have a standard 1-volt signal level, Using a splitter or "T" connector will reduce this voltage, producing a very dark, unusable picture.

Professional monitors (most of those using BNC connectors) allow "looping through" to a second monitor. Each input has two BNC connectors and a "termination" switch, sometimes labeled 75-ohms on-off. To connect two monitors, for example, connect the camera to one of the input jacks on the first monitor and turn the termination switch off. Connect a line to the second monitor from the second BNC jack, and so on. If the monitor is the last one in a chain of two or more, the switch should be on, terminating the line.

Consumer monitors (using RCA or S-Video connectors) are always terminated internally, so to feed multiple monitors you'll need a *distribution amplifier* (DA). These are available with either RCA, S-Video or BNC connectors, and usually have one input and four to eight outputs. (Radio Shack has a great one for about $50.) Using a DA is simple: just connect the camera to the DA's input and feed two or more monitors from the outputs. DAs can also be chained together for more outputs. For component video, a component DA is necessary. HDMI splitters are also available, and perform a similar function.

Audio Monitoring

When shooting in the field, the most important audio monitoring tool is a good set of headphones. By "good", I don't necessarily mean expensive, but you need a reliable, rugged set of phones that you can depend on. Over-the-ear fully enclosed phones are best, since the ear pads help keep out external noise. Don't use the popular noise-canceling active headphones, since their active circuitry sometimes cause distortion. It's a good idea to keep a spare set of headphones, too, as a backup and so that more than one person can monitor the audio. For this purpose, "earbud" or other lightweight phones are usually adequate. Inexpensive headphone splitters work just fine if the volume level from your camcorder is sufficient. If not, or you want to feed more than two sets of phones, consider an inexpensive headphone amplifier, available from audio equipment suppliers.

Choose headphones that sound good to you; it's best not to buy without listening. When you choose a set of phones, spend some time listening to known-good audio, like complete movies including dialog. When you're confident that you know how dialog is supposed to sound on your phones, you'll be able to tell if what you're getting during a shoot is what it should be. You should be able to tell instantly if your sound is not up to par.

When using a shotgun or boom-mounted microphone, it's always a good idea for the operator to wear headphones wired to the audio coming back from the camera. Sometimes, operators use phones connected to a microphone preamp or mixer, but this arrangement can't verify that good sound is actually being recorded. At least one person should *always* be listening critically to the actual camera headphone output. When working in noisy locations, an external headphone amplifier is very helpful, too.

In post-production and for screening your field footage, it's also important to have good audio monitoring. Don't depend on the tiny speakers in your monitor. They often won't reproduce low-frequency hum or rumble that can end up being very distracting when listening on a full-range speaker system. (More on audio monitoring in Chapter 4.4.)

2.8 Support Equipment

Here's a category of equipment that the Digital Age hasn't changed very much, except for the decreases in weight and bulk created by miniaturization. Regardless of the technology, camera support and supplementary equipment are as important as ever to digital filmmaking.

Tripods

The most important piece of support equipment is your tripod. Unless you're working toward a "shakycam" look, keeping the camera steady will go a long ways toward helping your film look professional. An ideal tripod will be sturdy enough to keep the camera steady yet lightweight enough to be quickly and easily moved and set up. It should be of appropriate size and weight for your camera and should be as rigid as possible. Most tripods are equipped with a *fluid head* – a must-have. Using a sealed container of viscous fluid such as oil or silicone, the head damps camera movement so that *pans* (left and right camera movements) and *tilts* (up and down camera movements) are as smooth as possible. Good camera moves start slowly, gradually accelerate, then smoothly decelerate to the end point of the move. The fluid head makes it much easier to control your moves, and this is especially important when using telephoto lenses. Fluid heads have *drag* adjustments that control the amount of resistance the head has to movement. A large amount of drag will produce smoother movements, but will transfer a greater force (torque) to the tripod, causing it to twist. When this happens, your tripod will create backlash at the end of a move and you'll find it's difficult to bring a move to a smooth stop. For this reason, it's important for a tripod to be as rigid as possible. Many professional tripods use double legs of metal or wood. These form a triangular structure that is inherently rigid, but heaver than single legs. Rigidity is most important when working with telephoto lenses, which is why you'll see the cameras used for covering football games mounted on large, heavy tripods.

In working with lightweight camera equipment, I like to have two tripods available, one that's light and easily carried along with the camera, and one that's heavier for more demanding shots. Both should be built to handle the weight of the camera you're using. A tripod-head combination that's correct for your camera will hold its position wherever you put it without your having to constantly lock and unlock the pan and tilt controls. For example, the springs used to level the camera will make it difficult for the head to keep the camera in position for an "up" or "down" shot if the camera is too light for the particular tripod system.

Better heads have adjustable springs to allow for a range of camera weights and centers of gravity, but this range is limited. If your camera is too heavy for the tripod, it's definitely in danger of toppling over – an accident waiting to happen.

Inexpensive tripods have the head rigidly attached. This means that in order to keep the camera level, you will need to individually adjust the height of the tripod legs. A better solution is a *ball mount* that allows you to level the camera quickly without adjusting the legs. With either tripod type, a small bubble level is usually included to help with camera leveling. Be sure your tripod has one. Also, be sure the tripod has solid, reliable and easy-to-engage locks on the legs.

Beware of tripods that have a center "crank-up" column. (Most inexpensive tripods are built this way.) While a center column can provide an extra foot or so of camera height, it also seriously compromises the rigidity of the tripod, especially if it doesn't have a solid, secure locking mechanism. It's best to choose a tripod that's tall enough without using the column. Center-column tripods do have the advantage of having a built-in *spreader*, a framework that keeps the legs in position. Other tripods may require a separate spreader, particularly for indoor use.

Tripods designed for outdoor use may have sharp spikes at the tips of the legs, intended to push into the ground. These have accessory feet that can be attached for indoor use on slippery surfaces. To improve the stability of your tripod, it's often helpful to weight it down with small sandbags, placing a couple of them on the spreader or frame. It can also help to use a bungee cord to tie the tripod to a sandbag directly underneath it. This simple expedient makes a lightweight tripod much harder to jostle during a camera move. A small collection of sandbags can help keep light and microphone stands under control, too.

Consider, too, having an assortment of *apple boxes* available during your shoot. These sturdy wooden boxes can be either the commercial units manufactured for the purpose, or they can be readily improvised by anyone skilled in elementary woodworking. They're useful for everything from providing a place for the cameraman to stand for a high-angle shot, a place to put your monitor, or for changing the height of furniture, props or actors.

For moving fast and still having some degree of camera support, a *unipod* can be worthwhile addition to your kit. Simply a telescoping pole with a camera head on top, unipods are inexpensive and easy to carry.

Camera heads with ball mounts can also use a *high hat,* (sometimes spelled *hi-hat*). It's really a miniature tripod, just tall enough to allow mounting of the head. Often clamped to a ladder for high angle shots, it's also a very useful accessory for any spot where the tripod just won't fit. If your tripod system doesn't adapt to a high hat, you might want to consider one of the many very small tripods as an accessory in your grip kit.

Camera Moves

While a steady camera is desirable, that doesn't mean that the camera can't move. If you watch a Hollywood movie, you'll notice that the camera is very often in motion throughout a shot, whether it's a simple pan, tilt, or zoom or a more elaborate *tracking* shot where the camera moves through the scene. Achieving smooth camera moves can be daunting, and has been the subject of a tremendous amount of creativity on the part of engineers and technicians throughout the history of the motion picture.

Hand-Held

Of course, the simplest way of moving the camera is going *hand-held*, simply carrying the camera and moving it where you want it during the shot. Hand-held shooting is definitely an art, and unless you are well-practiced, have the steady hand of a surgeon and the strength of an ox, you probably won't be able to do it well. Still, hand-holding the camera is a viable way to get moves, especially if you can work with a wide-angle lens. With any kind of camera movement, the longer the lens the more any unsmooth movement will show.

Larger professional cameras that can sit on your shoulder are considered better for hand-held shots. They gain the extra support of your body and the sheer weight tends to damp fast movements, the kind that are most distracting. The motion stabilizer systems built into most smaller cameras can help a lot here, but it still takes practice to do a good job and to understand the limits of the optical or digital stabilization.

There are a number of products on the market that are designed to steady the camera. One of the more popular is the *Steadicam,* which comes in several versions. The original Steadicam, developed by Garrett Brown in the 1970s, was designed to support large professional cameras. It uses a body harness and an attached spring-loaded arm designed to transfer the weight of the camera to the harness. Simultaneously, it contains a *gimbal* and counterweight arrangement to allow the camera to balance in mid-air and automatically level itself. The camera mounts to the top of a rod attached to the gimbal; the camera battery and a special high-brightness video monitor serve as a counterweight, mounted to the bottom of the rod.

In effect, the Steadicam attempts to harness the ability to hold things steady while moving – a person can carry a full glass of water up a flight of stairs. When properly adjusted and balanced, the camera seems to float in mid air and the operator can control it with the slightest touch. Of course, the original Steadicam is a complex and very expensive piece of equipment. Being a good Steadicam operator also requires a great deal of practice as well as substantial strength and athletic ability.

Fortunately, the development of lightweight cameras with built-in LCD viewfinders has made it possible to create the Steadicam JR, a version that uses the same principles but without the cumbersome and heavy body harness. Steadicam JR is a relatively simple and inexpensive system incorporating the gimbal and counterweight, allowing surprisingly smooth moves with small cameras, and there are several similar devices on the market. There's even a simpler stabilizer: a rod with a tripod fitting for the camera on one end and a counterweight on the other. Any of these devices can dramatically improve the steadiness of hand-held shots. Keep in mind, however, they are never substitutes for tripods. They can help create great shots while the camera is moving, but for very slow moves or stationary shots, they can give your camera a slight rocking motion, as though you were shooting from a rowboat.

Dollies

The best way to move a camera smoothly is using a *dolly*. Professional dollies carry the camera and the operator and often are built to run on prefabricated aluminum track that comes in straight or curved sections. The track can be assembled to follow any desired path. The dollies themselves have special concave or double wheels that ride smoothly on the track rails, hence scenes using this equipment are called *tracking shots*. Some dollies include hydraulic pedestals that allow vertical movement as well. Obviously, laying track is time- and labor-intensive as well as expensive, and the use of a dolly requires more time and more personnel.

Sometimes it's possible to dolly over a smooth floor without laying track. There are two inexpensive units designed especially for this purpose: the western dolly and the doorway dolly. They are used as a movable platform for a normal tripod, and are essentially the same, except the doorway is smaller. Both are simple plywood decks mounted to a metal frame, with front steering and pneumatic tires. Using these soft tires, it's often possible to simply lay plywood as a surface for these dollies to travel on.

In film equipment catalogs, you'll see so-called "tripod dollies", sets of wheels that go under a tripod. While these have sometimes been used to make camera moves, their real purpose is to make it easy to move the camera between shots. They are rarely stable enough for actual dolly moves.

Filmmakers have always been innovative in coming up with smooth ways to move their cameras. Many have built dolly systems from scratch, making use of wheels from the local hardware store and track made from aluminum conduit or PVC water pipe. I've seen cameras moved with wheelchairs, garden tractors, adult-size tricycles, cars, pickup trucks and golf carts, not to mention boats, airplanes and helicopters. One filmmaker even used his model railroad track to move a lightweight camcorder over a complex, curved path, creating a shot that might have been impossible using any other type of conveyance.

Booms and Jibs

The classic broad, sweeping shots of a camera moving high in the air were a trademark in early Hollywood extravaganzas. In the early days, the camera booms required for these shots were huge and expensive machinery, since they had to carry not only a large, heavy camera but the operator as well. Today, with electronic cameras and computer-controlled servomechanisms, it's possible to get such dramatic shots while the operator remains safely on the ground. High-end camera booms, available from the larger rental houses, can reach heights of fifty feet or more and can provide truly spectacular shots. Smaller versions of these booms, called jibs, are relatively inexpensive and some filmmakers construct their own. Like operating the Steadicam, using this equipment requires skill and practice, and most filmmakers hire a specialist when a boom shot is required. In most larger cities, freelance boom operators who have their own equipment are available.

Prompting

While not exactly in the category of camera support equipment, you may have need for a *teleprompter*. Professional prompters are built as shown in the drawing, with an LCD (or sometimes a CRT) display mounted below the camera and a half-silvered mirror providing a reflected image of the display, which appears directly in front of the lens. Using a prompter, on-camera talent can read their copy (lines) while looking directly at the camera. The display is connected to a laptop computer, which runs the prompting software. (My personal favorite is *Presentation Prompter* from NextForces Software, and it's one of the least expensive packages out there.) The prompter operator can vary the speed of the display, keeping up with the talent's pace.

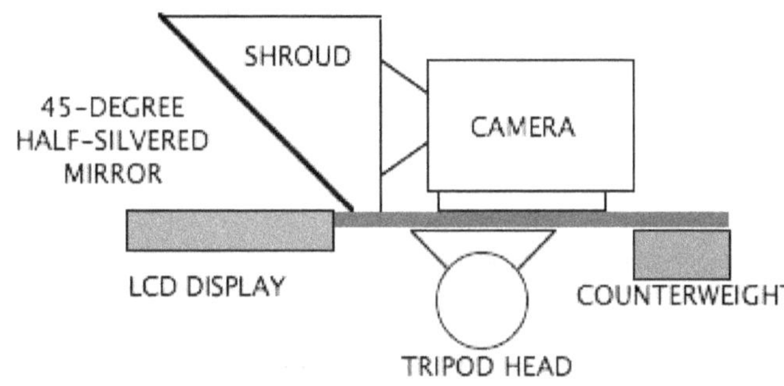

While professional prompters work well in a studio setting, they are expensive and add a lot of bulk to the camera, requiring a heavier tripod and extra wiring. For many shots, I've improvised a prompter by connecting a regular TV set to the video output of the laptop computer and placing it as close as possible to the lens, just below it. This inexpensive cheat works best if you use a 12-20-inch TV set (preferably a flat-panel LCD type) and work the camera as far away from the talent as possible. In this way, the difference in position between the prompter and the lens is minimized and the effect can be quite acceptable; it will appear that the talent is looking at the camera. It's helpful if the talent is cautioned not to shift her gaze from the prompter to the lens, but to always look directly at the prompter.

Of course, cue cards are always a good low-tech solution to the prompting problem. There are two tricks that make cue cards really work:

1. Work the camera as far away from the talent as possible, using a long lens. This helps make it appear the talent is actually looking at the camera, since at a greater distance, the angular difference between the lens and the cue cards is smaller.

2. Be sure the talent fixes his or her gaze on the cue cards, never actually looking into the lens.

It's best if cue cards are printed on heavy paper or card stock. Cards can be hand- or computer-printed, and should be prepared so each ends with the end of a sentence; no sentences should carry over from one card to the next. The assistant holding the cue cards should keep them as close to the lens as possible.

Prompting can also be applied to dramatic films, taking a cue from the way it's done on the soap operas. Instead of (or in addition to) putting the script on a camera-mounted display, the video feed from the prompter computer is routed through a video distribution amplifier and on to two or more TV monitors located on the set but out of camera view. Using these monitors, actors can see their lines while looking in a direction appropriate to the action in the scene. Off-camera cue cards can also be used.

Prompting in outdoor locations can be problematic with any of the video-based systems, not only because of the difficulty of seeing a video display in sunlight, but also because of the bulk of the equipment. A creative solution that's been applied to this problem is the *ear prompter*. The presenter records his lines, then plays them back through an earphone (perhaps the "invisible" IFB earphones TV newscasters use) and simply repeats the lines on-camera. It takes a bit of practice to do this well, but a good actor can learn the skill quickly. Devices like the iPod or similar MP3 players are great in this application.

"If it's green, it's biology. If it stinks, it's chemistry. If it has numbers, it's math. If it doesn't work, it's technology."

Unknown

PART 3 - PRODUCTION

"Every production of an artist should be the expression of an adventure of his soul."

W. Somerset Maugham (1874 – 1965)

If you've done a good job on your pre-production homework (or possibly even if you haven't), the production phase can be the easiest and most "fun" part of creating your film. Easy, of course, is a relative term. Compared to other efforts, there's nothing easy about it, and it can sometimes become intense. One director I know described production as "a total immersion process, during which your mind is totally occupied every waking and most sleeping moments." Furthermore, he feels that it's imperative to maintain this level of complete concentration throughout the process. During one production, he posted a sign on his office door that read:

DO NOT DISTURB EXCEPT IN THE EVENT OF EMERGENCY

Example 1: My mother just died. This is not an emergency.

Example 2: My mother needs a kidney transplant and I'm the only eligible donor. This is an emergency.

This may be extreme, but it gets to the point. The film will take on a life of its own, and you'll be carried along. And this is where all the careful pre-production work will really begin to pay off. In the previous section we talked about the technologies. Now we'll turn to techniques.

3.1 JUST SHOOT IT!

"Shoot for the moon. Even if you miss, you'll land among the stars."

Les Brown

The first day of shooting has arrived. Whether it's your first shoot or your thousandth, there's a feeling of anticipation and excitement. Is everything ready? How will it go?

By now you will have selected and rehearsed your talent, assembled and briefed your crew, lined up your locations or built your sets, gathered all your props and wardrobe, and put together a great complement of equipment. If your shoot is at all complicated, you will have a full production schedule along with daily checklists for every item and person. You've thoroughly checked out your equipment to ensure you don't have any unexpected failures. Your crew has been thoroughly familiarized with the equipment, and where it all is kept and how it's organized. Hopefully you'll have good weather, and a good contingency plan in case you don't.

This is the point where the director's heavy lifting begins. Still, the producer and his staff (if any!) will still need to be sure all the pieces are in place for each day's shoot.

The Director

In Hollywood, the director is the ultimate authority for everything that happens on the set. (It's still "the set" even if you're shooting on location.) There are as many different styles as there are directors, and a director's job will be different on every film.

Ultimately, the director's job is to guide the cast and crew through the production phase with a minimum of crisis management, and ideally, most of the important decision-making has been done before the camera rolls.

At the beginning of a day's shoot, the director finalizes the *blocking* of the first scene, determining where the action will take place, how the actors will enter and exit (if they do), where the camera will be placed for each shot, and how to best capture the sound. Knowing how the scene is to be blocked, technicians can place the lights and other equipment appropriately to avoid later conflicts. When lighting is done (or often while it is being done), the director will take the talent and crew through a final rehearsal, sometimes called a *camera rehearsal*. This will be the first opportunity for the camera operator to see the action and coordinate any required camera moves. The sound person will finalize microphone positions and set sound levels for the dialog.

Sometimes, the camera rehearsal is the first time anyone learns about the *business* the actors will be doing in the scene. Business is what actors do that isn't in the script – things like pouring a cup of coffee, adjusting a tie, hanging up a coat. Directors add business to a scene to keep it moving and more natural, so it's important for the crew to see it and do their jobs to provide adequate coverage of the scene, including the business.

If you're shooting a scripted dramatic film, you'll probably be starting with Scene 34 – or some other scene in the middle of the film, since they're rarely shot in sequence. Though directors differ widely in their approaches, they traditionally start with a *master* scene, usually a wide shot that includes all the action that is to happen. In a way, the master comes closest to the way the scene would be played on stage, in front of an audience. The master serves several purposes. First, it sets the pace for the action. In post, the editor can look at the master scene and understand everything that is to happen, and how the actors' timings play out on the screen. Secondly, it will point up the need for other shots – for example, when actors may be blocking each other from the camera, or when subtle action can't be seen well enough in a wide shot. Third, it provides a "safety net". If you know you have a good, clean master shot in the can, you have a version of the scene you can always use when needed.

The master serves as a reference for the action for the actors and crew, and for *continuity*. Actors in dramatic films need to concentrate on making their performances as identical as possible from shot to shot within a scene. If, for example, an actor takes a swig of beer in the middle of a sentence, he needs to do it in the middle of the same sentence every time, in every angle. It's the job of the Script Supervisor (continuity person, once called the "script girl") to make note of all the little details that are so vital to making every shot's action match every other shot – including such minutia as being sure the same amount of beer is in the glass, or the same amount of a character's cigarette has been smoked. Most directors like to work long enough on the master shot to be happy with all the action elements that are taking place, essentially finalizing them for the actors and crew. Thus, he'll usually do a number of takes of the scene, until it is as good as it can get.

Angles

After the director is happy with the master shot, he'll move on to other *camera angles* (or simply, *angles*). These might include one or more alternate master shots, and a variety of closeups (CU). How many closeups and how close they are is the director's choice. In a scene with two people carrying on a conversation, for example, he may choose to shoot the entire scene in closeup on each of the characters, and he also might want *2-shots* including both characters, which might be similar to the master, but not as wide. There may be more than one set of closeups, too – medium closeups (*MCU*) and extreme closeups (*ECU*). Some directors will shoot the entire scene in each of the closeups; others prefer to shoot some or all of the closeups "line by line", sometimes shooting only the lines where he knows he is going to be using a closeup in the final cut. Camera angles other than the master are usually designated by letters following the scene numbers: Scene 34A, 34B, 34C, etc. These extra numbers are rarely shown on the script, because the director will decide how many are needed during the shoot.

Many scenes will also require *insert shots,* usually closeups of objects, hands, or other important subjects that may be part of the story. To draw attention to a dramatic moment as midnight is approaching, for example, the director might want to use a closeup of a clock. These also include *reaction shots*, showing how a character reacts to an action or to what another actor is saying. These shots are also called *cutaways*, though by definition, inserts are in the same setting as the main action while cutaways are somewhere else. For example, a shot of a sunset put into a scene to indicate the passage of time is a cutaway, while a closeup of a newspaper a character is reading would technically be an insert.

In deciding which angles to shoot and how to shoot them, I find it very helpful to think about how a person watching the scene unfold might look at it. When seeing a stage play (or watching any interaction between people), each member of the audience creates his own angles. When the scene opens, he takes in the entire setting, seeing the characters, the props, the entire environment. As the action proceeds, he will begin to concentrate on the individual players in turn, looking where his attention takes him. The director should shoot the scene in such a way that he anticipates what the audience wants to see at any given moment, and what the viewer needs to see to carry the story along. A well-shot scene will have the exact shot an editor needs to best convey the scene to the audience. And this is perhaps the director's most important task: directing the audience.

It's worth noting that in a live TV show, all the angles are shot at the same time, with multiple cameras. The director switches between the cameras in "real time", taking the shot that best carries the show along. On a few occasions, multiple cameras are also used in filmmaking, for similar reasons – like shooting events that only happen once.

The Line of Action

In shooting any scene, it's important that all the shots (angles) are coordinated. This provides the maximum flexibility for the editor, and helps make the scene flow smoothly across the cuts. One of the most important considerations in accomplishing this is being mindful of the *line of action*. It's an imaginary line

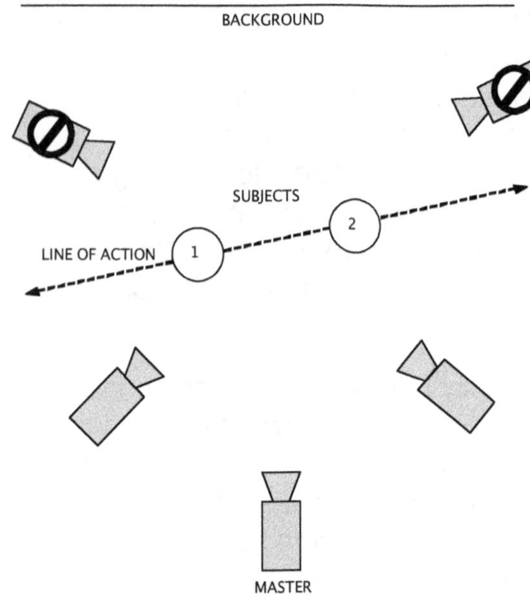

through the scene, extending through the primary subjects. In the drawing, the scene is a conversation between two people. The master scene has been shot from the camera position indicated, with closeups from the other positions, so subject #1 is *camera left* and subject #2 is *camera right*. Notice that this is also true for all the camera positions below the line of action. The other two positions, however, reverse this relationship. If the editor uses one of these shots, he'll immediately see that the shots "don't cut", because the characters will appear to instantly "flip" to the wrong side of the screen or appear to be looking in the wrong direction. For the best flow, avoid crossing the line of action. Imagine, for example, how confusing it would be if you shot a football game with two cameras on opposite sides of the field. If you intercut the footage from these two camera positions, it would be very difficult for the viewer to tell which way the players were running!

Be aware, too, that the line of action can change within a scene. If (in the master shot) we see subject #1 move behind subject #2 (closer to the background), a new line of action has been established, which may make some of the camera positions violate the new line. The line of action changes only if the audience sees it change, or if a new line of action is introduced by a new scene or a different perspective. An example of this might occur when a new character enters the scene. Because the audience immediately sees a new line of action, it may be that two master shots are needed for this scene – one before the third character enters and another for after her entry.

The line of action may or may not be important in insert shots. Suppose, for example that our two characters are playing cards and we want to shoot an insert showing that subject #1 is holding the ace of spades. If we shoot over #1's right shoulder (the one closer to the master camera), seeing her hand, the audience will know immediately that they're looking at #1, because of the established line of action. If we do the same shot, but look over #1's left shoulder, the audience could easily think they are looking over #2's left shoulder.

Other inserts (a shot of a clock somewhere in the room, for example) would have no line of action, as long as neither of the characters is in the shot. Of course, any cutaway or insert gives you the opportunity to establish a new line of action.

The line of action also has to do with screen direction. For example, if your scene involves traveling in a car or airplane, it's best to keep the vehicle moving in the same direction (left to right or right to left) from shot to shot. This keeps the scene smooth and avoids confusing the audience: "Which way are they going now? (Psychologically, too, screen direction connotes subtle meanings: left to right action seems to indicate going away or going East, right to left action is returning or going West.)

The line of action can also be re-established by using a point-of-view (*POV*) shot, also called a *subjective shot.* It's exactly what it sounds like: the camera angle is from the point of view of a character, showing what he or she sees. If a POV shot includes the character's head or shoulder, it's called an *over-the-shoulder* shot. A variation is the *reverse angle.* Literally, a reverse shot is one in which the subject and camera change places. A good example is a scene where someone is using a computer. The POV shot would be of the computer screen, the reverse angle would be of the person from the computer's point of view.

Continuity and Coverage

We've briefly touched on the importance of continuity between shots within a dramatic scene, but the subject applies to any film. What you shoot is what the editor will have to work with in assembling the finished film, so it's important not only to maintain continuity, but to provide enough *coverage* that the editor has sufficient material to exercise the best creative options.

One of the most important aspects of coverage and making all your shots usable from the editor's point of view is avoiding the *jump cut* – the appearance that a character or object jumps from one place or position to another. Suppose, for example, that you've shot an interview and you want to remove a sentence from the middle of a paragraph. If you simply cut the sentence from the middle of a single take, at the point of the cut, there will be a jump – everyone's seen it. On some occasions, it's used for effect, but it's usually jarring.

Of course, in shooting interviews, your subject will rarely say the same thing twice, so it's helpful to vary the shot enough to allow you to cut from one section of the interview to another, thus allowing you avoid jump cuts.

A jump cut also can occur if you shoot a scene from two angles, but they are too similar. In that case, the cut looks like the image just gets larger or smaller, not that you're cutting to a really different angle. One helpful guideline is the "60-degree" rule: If the shots are similar, the camera position should move about 60 degrees relative to the subject.

Another useful consideration in shooting is what I call the "two joint rule": When shooting two angles of a person, include or exclude two body joints to make the angles different enough. For example, if your closeup includes the shoulders but not the elbows, your next wider angle should include the elbows and wrists – not just the elbows. If your closest shot includes the waist, your next wider angle should include the knees. This is an extension of what some cinematographers call the *rule of joints*: shots look best if the bottom of the frame falls between two body joints, not on one.

When shooting, get all the relevant *cutaways* you can. They can be your best friend in avoiding the dreaded jump cut. Every scene has something that can be an interesting cutaway, whether it's a characters hands, a point-of-view shot, or as one director put it, "When in doubt, cut to a bird."

A special case occurs when your subject is directly addressing the camera, something that rarely happens in dramatic films but is common in promotional films and commercials. This breed of scene, often called the *talking head*, presents a unique problem. If you move the camera to a different position, a cut between the angles will always be a jump cut, unless you have the presenter turn to the new camera position after the cut – and even this can look very unnatural. Such turns also present an editorial problem, because you must plan exactly where the cut points are when you shoot. The one solution to this problem that always works is to think of a fixed line of action that's established between the subject and the camera, and don't get away from that line. You can move (or zoom) closer to or farther from the subject along that line. When shooting talking heads (which are usually scripted and often prompted) I almost always shoot two or three angles changing only the lens focal length, zooming to wide, medium and closeup shots. If you shoot talking heads this way, you'll avoid a lot of problems and your editor with thank you.

Slates and Claps

The ways takes are marked and shot carries a lot of history and lingo that you may or may not choose to adopt in your filmmaking. Traditionally, takes are *slated* at the beginning. The slate is practically the symbol of the movie industry. In the early days it was simply a chalkboard with spaces laid out for the title, scene number, take number, camera roll number, director, cameraman, etc. Mounted at the top is a *clapstick*, a small, hinged board that can be slammed down on top of the slate creating a distinctly audible clap. The clapper is traditionally painted with black and white diagonal stripes so that it can easily be seen on film while in motion. It was used for synchronizing the film with the sound, since the film camera records only the picture, while the sound is captured using other equipment. Usually, sound was recorded on some kind of tape recorder that has the capability to run at a very accurate speed. In the old days, these original recordings would have been transferred to magnetic film of the same gauge as the picture, greatly simplifying editing, since the separate sound and picture films could be kept in perfect "sync" using simple mechanical sprockets.

In this traditional scenario, to start a take the director calls, "Roll sound." To this, the sound recordist responds, "Speed," indicating that his sound recorder has reached operating speed. Then, it's "Roll camera" (or just "camera"), and the camera operator also responds, "Speed". The clapper (a person operating the clapstick) then reads the slate: "Scene 32, take 1," and claps the clapstick. Sometimes, particularly in noisy environments, he'll also shout, "Marker" indicating to the editor that the next sound will be the clapsticks. Then, when the clapper is out of the shot, the director calls "Action" (often expanded to: "aaaannndd action" or "ready aaaannnndd.... action!). There may also be a few other commands before "action", such as a call for a dolly move to begin, or for background extras to start their action.

On rare occasions, scenes are *tail-slated,* meaning that the reading of the slate and the clap occur at the end of the scene instead of the beginning. In this case, it's customary for the clapper to call "tail slate" and for the slate itself to be held upside down.

Some modern slates are equipped to display timecode, which is used to synchronize camera and sound. This effectively eliminates the need for the clapper, though it's sometimes used as a backup in case of timecode failure. Either way, an assistant will be logging scene number, take numbers, and timecodes for each take. If "real" film is being shot, camera footage numbers will be logged.

Scenes that are shot without sound are indicated on the slate as *MOS.* According to film legend, the origin of this term comes from an early German director who put this designation on the slate. When asked what MOS means, he replied, "Of course, it means *mit-out* sound." This started a tradition, and MOS became a standard industry designation.

The end of the take is called by "Cut!", meaning the camera and sound recorders should stop, and everyone can relax – at least until the director calls for everything to be reset for the next take, angle or scene. Of course, in digital filmmaking, many of these steps are unnecessary; many directors don't feel a need to use slates at all (since scenes can always be identified by timecode or file names), and the camera is usually the sound recorder as well. Still, "roll camera", "action" and "cut" retain their usefulness and slates can add a certain glamour.

In shooting "real film", it is customary to "print selected takes". If, for example, the director does ten takes, he will say "print that one" at the end of each take in which he feels the action and blocking are acceptable. He can also say "circle that one", since a circle around the take number on the camera log was a standard way of indicating acceptable takes. Putting a star by a take traditionally means that it is probably the best take. What "print that" actually means is that after the film is processed, workprints are made only of the selected takes. The original negative from "bad" takes is simply stored away, saving the cost of making prints of scenes that would likely never be used. The workprints are generally referred to as *dailies*, because during production they are delivered daily from the processing lab. After shooting, the editor (or an assistant) "syncs up" the dailies (workprints) so there is reliable "lip sync".

(Interestingly, on some low-budget films, directors would "process selected takes", a way to save still more money. At the end of each take, the camera assistant would open the camera and punch a hole in the film for a bad take. If it was a good take, he'd punch two holes. Later, a lab technician would go through the film in the darkroom, before it was processed, and physically cut out the raw film representing the bad takes.)

Because videotape stock is so much less expensive than film, these measures aren't necessary, but "print that" or "circle that" are still used, mostly to save time for the editor. Only circled takes need be transferred into the editing system, saving work and conserving storage space. Of course, non-circled takes are always available from the original footage. Again, for the convenience of the editor, timecodes are logged with the take numbers.

On-Set Etiquette and Communication

Although films with small crews and low budgets require that everyone wear multiple hats, it's vital that someone is in charge. Like a ship's captain, the director is that person. He (or she) is the one whose vision is being incarnated during the shoot, and it is a major transgression to do anything that might undermine or usurp his authority. As artists, some directors are offended or even insulted if someone injects unsolicited ideas or suggestions. The director needs an absolute minimum of distractions that might do more harm than good. Restraining yourself from making suggestions is most important when it might affect the relationships between director and talent. The director has a delicate task in coordinating his vision with each actor's unique abilities and individual interpretation of a part.

An actor or crew member who feels the need to make a suggestion should only do so if it's obvious that the director is in a position to accept it. If someone notices, for example, that an actor is wearing a wristwatch while shooting a drama about ancient Egypt, this fact should be communicated discreetly to the director, not shouted out so everyone can hear. On a large shoot, the message should go to the assistant director.

The exception to this rule: speak up when there is a problem or suggestion that is directly related to the job you're doing on the set. If you're the camera operator, for example, and you notice one actor is blocking another in the shot, say something about it. If you're the sound man and you hear that one actor's voice is much softer than another's, point it out. Even under this exception, however, don't take it upon yourself to tell the actors what to do, address the director with a suggestion: "Could we try to even out the volume of the voices? I'm having trouble with their levels."

During the shoot, say as little as possible. It's fine for the camera operator to say, "The mic's in the shot." It's not OK for the gaffer to say, "Wow, that's a crappy piece of dialog."

"Most directors make films with their eyes. I make films with my testicles."

Alexandro Jodorowsky

3.2 Lighting 101

"There is no more worthy, no more glorious or more potent work, than to work with light."

Omraam Mikhaël Aïvanhov

There are as many ways to light a scene as there are cinematographers and videographers. Each will have his own style and technique, heavily influenced (hopefully) by the desired "look" of the film. Back in Chapter 2.6, we talked about lighting instruments and what you might need for your shoot. Here, we'll do an overview the basics of lighting simple scenes. These fundamentals can be expanded to cover the lighting of any scene because the principles remain the same.

The approaches I'll describe are based on relatively simple instruments and setups that can yield professional-looking results. As you gain experience, you'll develop an eye for the subtleties and create your own techniques.

Lighting has very little to do with the *quantity* of light; it's all about the *quality* of light. Digital cameras can shoot almost anything you can see, but they can't create the subtleties of light and shadow that bring life to your images. Some extra effort in lighting can make your work look far more professional regardless of the format or quality of your camera. Good lighting is even more important if you're using consumer-level equipment than with top-line professional cameras because inexpensive cameras are less able to deal with contrast and detail, especially in the highlights and shadows.

Before starting to light a scene, the director and cinematographer will have agreed on camera angles and how and where on the set the action is to be blocked in the scene. (It could be awkward if an actor has to enter a scene and there's a light stand in the way!) Since scenes are often shot from several angles, it's important to plan your lighting so that all these angles can be accommodated without a lot of re-lighting. Undoubtedly, the setup will need to be "tweaked" from shot to shot, but good planning can minimize delays for re-sets. Of course you'll also need to take into account existing or practical sources of light – windows, lamps, or ceiling fixtures that may be included in the scene. For feature films, cinematographers and directors like to do lighting plans, similar to the sketches later in this chapter.

People are prominent subjects in most films, and lighting them to look good is always a challenge, and perhaps your most important lighting task. Indoors, practical lights are designed to give adequate illumination for work, leisure activities, reading, and perhaps to display art or architectural features of the building. Rarely is the direction or quality of light flattering to people. Outdoors, sunlight is likely to be too harsh on a sunny day and too "flat" on a cloudy day. Whether interior or exterior, however, people should be lit to look natural and be flattered by the light. Equally important, the lighting should not be obvious; it must look like the natural light that would normally exist in the environment. The light should appear to have the same character and come from the same direction as "normal" light sources that might exist in the scene.

Interiors

In the town where I grew up, a lady photographer specialized in portraits, and over her long career, she had photographed almost everyone in town. Every other year during my childhood, Mom would take my sister and me to the photo studio for a sitting. I recall that every time we went through the portrait ritual, the studio was arranged exactly the same, with the same three lights – one on each side of the camera and one behind the subject on a high stand, peeking out over the top of the changeable painted canvas backdrop. She had found a lighting formula that worked for her, and it showed in the way her portraits brought out the character, features and personalities of her subjects. She always used classic three-point portrait lighting: *key*, *fill* and *backlight*. Of the three instruments, the key light is the brightest. She used a fresnel type, but any relatively hard source will do, though a focusable type is easier to control. The fill light is a weaker and softer source; it's called the fill light because it fills in the shadows the harsher key light produces. The backlight is a hard source positioned behind and above the subject. It's usually a small fresnel or open-face instrument. Also called a *hair light* or *rim light,* its function is to provide definition to the edges of the subject and to provide a rim of light that separates the foreground (subject) from the background. Ideally, the hair light should be a hard source, without diffusion. Control its intensity with a dimmer or scrim.

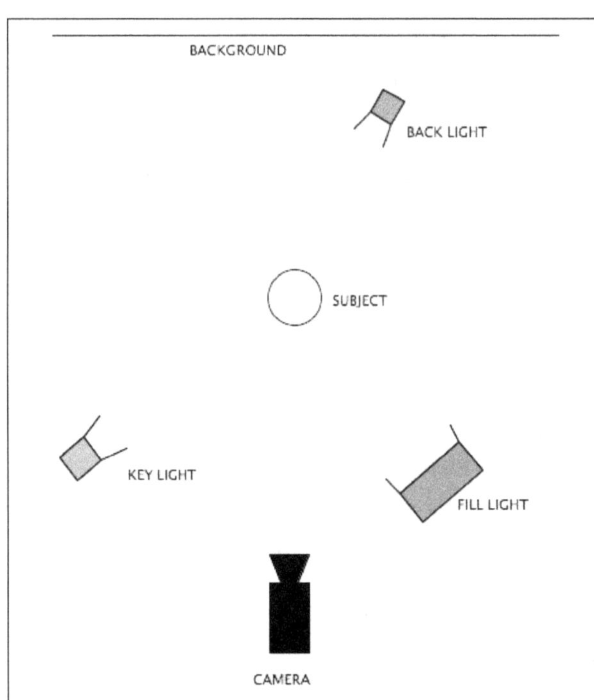

The relative positions of the front lights influences the depth of the shadows created by the key light. If the key light is moved farther from the camera, shadows become larger, providing more *modeling* or texture. Raising or lowering the key light will affect the position of shadows. For example, a higher light source lowers the chin shadow, darkening the neck and emphasizing the nose. Placing the key closer to the camera yields more subtle modeling. Often, the key light is diffused a bit, by adding some translucent material in front of it. Our family photographer used lightweight white fabric (I think it was silk), stretched on a frame like a painting canvas. Some diffusion on the key also has the advantage of enhancing the "catch lights" in the subject's eyes.

The depth of the shadows is controlled by the brightness and relative softness of the fill light. The fill light can be a point source with diffusion material in front of it, or it can be a commercial soft light. Small lights bounced into white or metalized umbrellas are also often used. A larger source (softer) creates less definition of fine textural details, allowing the light to wrap around the subject; a brighter source reduces the contrast between highlights and shadows.

The *lighting ratio* defines the relationship between the brightness of the key and fill sources. For example, if the amount of light from the key is twice the amount from the fill (as measured using an incident light meter), the lighting ratio will be 2:1. A ratio in this range is often used for shooting women because it is more flattering to skin textures than a higher ratio. To bring out the character of a rugged male face, lighting ratios of 4:1 or 6:1 are often used. For more dramatic effects (such as a dark, nighttime look), still higher ratios can be used.

While not usually expressed in terms of ratio, the backlight's intensity will be similar to the keylight, at least in areas of dark colors. A person with dark hair and clothing against a dark background, for example, would require a fairly bright backlight. At the other extreme, a person with white hair and light clothing against a dark background would require much less backlight. My personal rule: The backlight should be bright enough to separate but not so bright as to be obvious.

You may recall that in Section 2, I suggested that a light meter could be a good addition to your tool kit. It can be your best friend for setting lighting ratios, and for keeping flesh tones constant from scene to scene, and especially from shot to shot within a scene. I like to use a spot meter for this purpose, using an area on the key side of an actor's face to determine relative exposure. When shooting a scene, I take a reference reading and correlate this with the *f*-stop setting being used on the camera. On subsequent shots, I use this reading to set the camera f-stop to assure that the skin gets the same relative exposure as in the reference scene.

There are several ways to do this. My favorite is to use *exposure value (EV)* numbers; most light meters provide a scale for this purpose. Each increase or decrease of 1 EV unit corresponds to one *f*-stop. For example, suppose my reference measurement is EV 8 on a particular scene, and I use a lens setting of *f*5.6 for a pleasing exposure. On the next setup, I read an EV of 7. To keep the exposure for this part of the scene consistent with the first setup, I simply set the lens to *f*4. Alternatively, I can adjust the lighting to bring the level on the subject's face up to an EV 8 and leave the lens alone, at *f*5.6.

Keeping exposures consistent from shot-to-shot can vastly improve the quality of your film and, importantly, it can make your life much easier when you get into editing. Some cinematographers get adamant and pragmatic about this point, insisting that every scene be lit so that the *f*-stop is never changed. They want every shot to be done at *f*4, for example. While this is a perfectionist attitude (and one that can add a lot of extra work for the lighting crew), there is some justification for the approach. Not only is exposure consistent, so are the depth of field and relative overall sharpness. You should realize, however, both depth of field and relative sharpness will change if you change the focal length of the lens. (We'll talk about this more in the section on camera technique.)

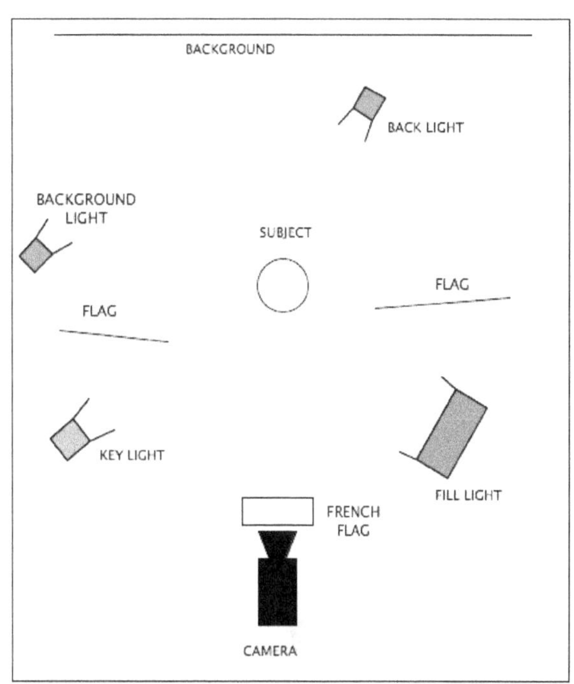

My family photographer took care of lighting the background simply by moving it closer or farther from the main lights until it looked right. She avoided shadows on the background by keeping the subject well in front of it. By this, she also could keep the background slightly out of focus and dark, which helped make the foreground subject "snap out" in sharp relief. In studio portraiture, the background is often lit separately with one or two small instruments, sometimes with colored gels and/or a "cookie" to create texture.

In more realistic environments (on set or location),the actor's key, fill and backlights must be controlled to keep them (and undesired shadows) away from the background. This means using barn doors on the instruments, and may require using flags or cutters to control the stray light.

Notice also that a *French flag* has been placed above the camera lens. Many cinematographers leave a small flag attached to the camera for the express purpose of keeping the backlight out of the lens. (There are commercial versions that clamp on the cameras, or even fit the accessory shoe.) Since the backlight is often aimed directly at the camera, it can produce *flare* in the lens, even though the light is out of the shot. (Flare creates extraneous and undesirable reflections inside the lens, which can show up in the image, as can often be seen in pictures with a bright light in the shot.) The lens shades that comes with most zoom lenses is effective in preventing flare if the lens is set at its widest focal length, but is totally ineffective for longer settings. A *matte box* (an adjustable bellows-like attachment on the front of the lens) can also be used to avoid flare, but it's expensive and sometimes inconvenient to use with zoom lenses. Matte boxes are not usually available for the small prosumer or consumer cameras, but a French flag can always be used to do the job when needed. In any case, it's always a good idea to check the lens before shooting to be sure none of your lighting instruments is hitting it directly. Sometimes flare can be happening inside the lens, but not be readily seen in the viewfinder; it may be undesirably reducing the contrast of your image by adding light into the shadows.

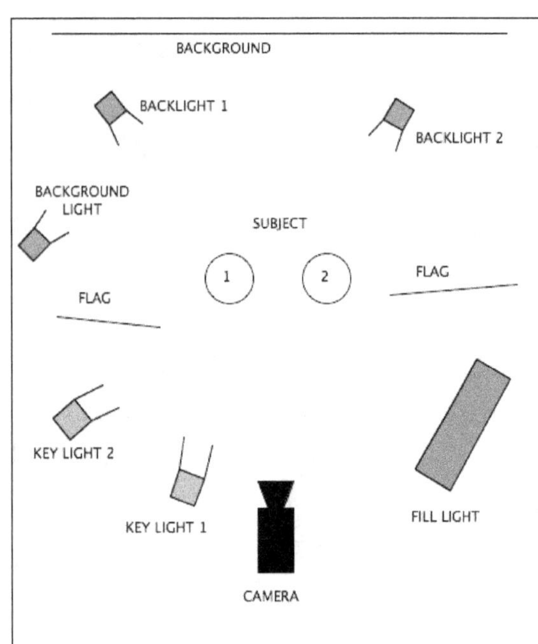

Next, let's add a second actor to the scene. Scenes with two characters are very common, perhaps more common than the classic "talking head". If you have plenty of working room, two people can be lit with basically the same setup as one, except you may want to use larger instruments placed farther away from your subjects. Increasing the distance simply provides a way to get the light falling on both actors to be about the same level and coming from approximately the same effective angle.

Where you want a bit more control, separate key and backlights can be used, taking care that each instrument hits only its intended subject. Notice that barn doors are used to confine the light from each instrument and flags are still used to keep undesired light off the background. Notice also that key light #1 is placed closer to the camera, creating a bit more "wrap" around the subject's face. There is a problem with this position, however. In the position shown, key light #1 will cast a shadow of subject #1 on the background. The solution to this problem is to raise the light so that the shadow falls lower on the background and out of the shot. Both key lights should be kept on the same side of the camera so the light appears to be coming from a single off-camera source, a much more natural-looking approach.

When dealing with separate key lights, it's important to remember that multiple lights create multiple shadows, something that is immediately obvious because it rarely occurs in nature. Beginners often have the idea that you can wipe out multiple shadows by filling them with another light. Wrong. The additional light will just create more shadows. Keep in mind too, that hard lights create hard, more obvious shadows, so one way to reduce the visibility of the shadows is to use soft sources.

Introducing more lights also creates a need to change the lighting setup more for different angles. For some angles, one actor's backlight will become the other actor's fill, and vice-versa. You should be keenly aware of these effects and be prepared to re-light accordingly, always making the lighting appear to match the master shot.

Remember that backlights are artificial; they rarely occur in natural settings. In filmmaking, they are a compensation for the fact that the image is two-dimensional, while we see real objects in three dimensions. They should be just bright enough to create the illusion of depth and separation from the background – never so bright that they appear to give the actors their own halos. (Unless your film as about angels.)

Keep your lighting contextual – the direction of light should match any natural light sources in the scene. If there's a window on the left, it's natural for the key light to be on that side. If there's also a lamp on the right, you may want to consider making the key a daylight source (more blue) and the fill light tungsten (more orange), to match the perceived context.

In the two-person setup, the fill light has been moved farther back and made a bit larger (softer) to keep it even between the two subjects. The same could be done for the key light, although the sketch shows separate key lights.

A single light on the background is often adequate for portraiture or a two-person interview. Perhaps surprisingly, it's also often ideal for a more complex scene, too. Lighting from a single point creates deep and defined shadows. While this isn't desirable for people or most foreground objects, it can add texture and depth to a background. Consider, for example, a scene with two people having a conversation in a typical den. They may be seated on a couch; behind them might be cabinets filled with books and memorabilia. There are pictures on the wall, furniture and woodwork. All these things (as long as they are in the background) get more detail and apparent sharpness from single-point lighting, simply because hard light (especially when it comes from an acute angle) emphasizes texture. This is especially true for scenes staged so that the principal characters are some distance from the background. One cinematographer calls this "blasting the background", and it is certainly a trick that will make your life easier. I've seen him light the interior of a very large church using one instrument, with beautiful results. By using relatively soft light on his foreground actors, he created a warm intimate look with striking background texture.

When you use single-point lighting for a background, it helps to keep the level of light a bit darker than your foreground subjects' key light. Remember the artist's rule: dark colors recede, lighter colors come forward. This adds depth through contrast. For backgrounds with little texture (blank walls, for example), use even less light or consider using a "cookie" to create shadows. Sometimes just casting the shadow of a leafy tree branch or some Venetian blinds on the wall can create the illusion of realism.

You can control how much you make the background "snap" by how close to the camera you place the background light. If it's near the camera and "spotted" in on the background, the texturing is subtle. At a 45-degree angle to the camera, shadows will be deeper and the background will spring out in sharp relief.

Sometimes it isn't desirable to bring out background detail; it may be your objective to make it softer. In this case, you may want to try bounce lighting. Using one or more of your larger instruments, bounce light off the ceiling or a wall outside the shot. You will need to play with the size of the spot on the ceiling or wall (by focusing the light) to get the intensity and softness you want.

Another use of reflected light is to create what I call "virtual light sources". Especially in cramped quarters, you can use a space blanket, foil-covered card, or a mirror to bounce light into problem areas. Small metal flags with polished surfaces on one side are available for this purpose.

Exteriors

Lighting exteriors (at least in the daytime) is largely a matter of using what light is already there, controlling it as best you can, and supplementing it where necessary. You'll really only have control of the foreground; Mother Nature will already be blasting the background for you. Again, the quantity of light is not the issue – it's the quality. Outdoor light seems to always have the wrong contrast. It's either too much or too little; rarely is it "just right". Take a simple example: a scene where two people are having a conversation on a golf course. If it's a bright, sunny midday with the sun high in the deep blue sky, the key light is coming from the sun and the fill light is from the sky and whatever is reflected from the ground (green grass?) and other surrounding objects. The net result is that the key light is too hot and coming from the wrong direction. The fill light is almost non-existent. The lighting ratio can easily be 50:1 – definitely not flattering to people. With the sun overhead, your subjects' eyes fall into dark shadow and seem to recede into their heads. Their noses cast long shadows down to their chins and their ears seem to glow. This is a worst-case scenario for too much contrast.

What can you do about it? The first help is some kind of reflector. For a closeup shot, a large piece of white poster board or foam core held just out of the shot and below the actor's face can make a tremendous difference. For wider shots, several 4 x 8 pieces of foamcore, white-painted 1/4-inch plywood, or even white bed sheets on the ground just out of the shot can work fairly well. To get even better results, you can use a big *silk*. These come in sizes like 8 by 8, 12 by 12,

16 by 16 feet, or even larger. They are laced to a lightweight aluminum frame and suspended above the actors, usually on tall and heavily sandbagged light stands. (Do you know how much lift a 16 by 16-foot airfoil can generate in a moderate breeze?) Some cinematographers have used a military-surplus parachute (a white one, of course!) for this purpose. Plastic film made for agricultural purposes can also be used, though it doesn't provide as much diffusion as fabric.

The silk simulates a more-or-less cloudy day. They come in light, medium and heavy varieties with varying amounts of diffusion. If you use a heavy or medium silk, you may need to use reflectors to bounce sunlight back under the silk. In this way, the direct light from the sun becomes the fill light and the light from the reflectors becomes the key. The objective, of course, is to get the lighting ratio on your actors down to a more reasonable 2:1 to 6:1.

Commercial reflectors are usually about 4 by 4 feet and they have a swivel mount that can be attached to a (sandbagged) light stand. They come with either a hard, mirror-like surface or a textured surface that yields a softer (but weaker) light. Pieces of plywood covered with aluminum foil work as well, but it's more difficult to get the reflected light aimed the way you want it. There are also some commercially available "pop out" reflectors made of reflective fabric. These are built on round, spring steel collapsible frames, so they fold up to about 1 ft in diameter and fit in a small carrying case. When expanded, they are 3 to 5 feet in diameter and usually have a textured metal surface on one side and a white surface on the other. They're aimed by having an assistant hold and direct them during shooting.

Given a larger budget, you can take the Hollywood approach: brute force. The classic instrument for outdoor lighting on big feature movies was the "Brute Arc", a huge 3-foot diameter beast that used a carbon-arc lamp and over 20,000 watts of power. And that baby could put out some light! More recently, similar brutes using HMI lamps are available for those situations where nothing else will do. Needless to say, such behemoths are out of reach for most filmmakers, but use 'em if you've got 'em. Smaller HMI lights can be used outdoors, of course, but are useful only for lighting relatively small areas except on very cloudy days. Tungsten lights with correction filters (even large ones) are practically useless outdoors on bright days because they have insufficient output when used with the necessary filters to bring them to the necessary color temperature to match daylight. To put all this in perspective, full sunlight delivers approximately 1000 watts per square meter of illumination. You don't have to do much math to figure out that most lighting instruments simply don't have the horsepower to compete on anything but the smallest scale.

The cloudy day presents a different set of problems. A heavy overcast can reduce the intensity of sunlight by 90% or more. This is both good and bad for the filmmaker. It's good because it means you can get some benefit from reasonably-sized lighting instruments. It's bad because reflectors become ineffective, and the character of the light is flat and dull. Sometimes, of course, the cloudy-day look is exactly what you're going for. In that case, rejoice for the clouds, and go ahead and shoot in nature's bounty of natural light. If, however, you want a more sunny look, you'll need to add some light. For medium and close-up shots, I have had great luck on cloudy days lighting the scenes almost as if they were interiors and just letting the background go.

If you can use HMI lights (which match daylight color temperature) so much the better, but tungsten lights can add some warmth. If the warmth is too much for you, just fit each light with some *booster blue* gel. Booster blue is not the same as the gel that actually brings tungsten lights to daylight color temperature – it's about half that much filtering. As a result, it lets a lot more light through. If you have thick cloud cover, you can get a wonderful look this way.

Fortunately, for either outdoor scenario, you can probably get away with shooting your wide (and even medium) shots without supplementary lighting. It's a strange phenomenon, but audiences seem to involuntarily accept that actors always look the same in the wide shots as they do in their close-ups, so you can get away with murder with wide-shot lighting. If your close-ups look good, you're probably home free.

The cinematographer's worst curse is the partly cloudy day. You know the kind. It's the summer day with forecast showers and thunderstorms, when the sun keeps peeping in and out from behind the clouds and your exposure keeps changing from an *f*22 to an *f*8. The best advice I can give you here relates to the foregoing paragraph – get the close-ups rights and your wide shots will be fine, too. In this situation you'll need to make a judgment about which is going to give you the most working time – the full sun, or the cloud cover – then light, expose and shoot accordingly.

Mixed Lighting

In the real world, light comes from a variety of sources. As you are reading this book, you may be getting your main source of light from a reading lamp, but across the room there may be another lamp, or a ceiling fixture. There may also be windows letting in more or less natural daylight. Real environments, especially interiors, have multiple sources of light, of different intensity and of different color temperatures. As discussed in Section 2, lighting instruments are made to match the color temperatures of most conventional light sources. Some cinematographers eschew mixing of different color temperatures, while others embrace mixed light as a part of their "look". Sometimes the style of the film more than the cinematographer's choice dictates whether mixed lighting is appropriate.

On a set, on a soundstage, you'd have complete control, mixing or matching to your heart's content. On location, however, it's a bit more difficult. Suppose, for example, you're of the non-mixing school. You're shooting on location in a spacious room in a large house with a view of the mountains out of the living room window. The scene calls for an actor to refer to the view: "Isn't that magnificent?" he says, while seated in his easy chair. As a cinematographer you'd have two choices: either match the light level and color temperature inside the living room to the outside, or bring down the scene outside to match the lighting you've done inside. For a simple close-up, it might be reasonable to pursue the former approach, using a couple of HMIs, but for a wider shot, it might be best to follow the latter. Several companies manufacture gels that can be used over the windows; some of them are made to be self-sticking to glass. (See www.rosco.com) Some can also can correct the color temperature from daylight to tungsten (85) and can simultaneously reduce the light intensity with a *neutral density* (ND) component (85N3 for one *f*-stop, 85N6 for 2 stops, 85N9 for 3 stops, etc.). Using your trusty light meter, you can determine which gel is right for the situation. (Note: each ND or N number represents 1/3 of an *f*-stop, thus 3 ND units equals one *f*-stop or one EV unit.)

"Gelling" windows is common Hollywood practice, but independent filmmakers often look for other, less costly and less labor-intensive solutions. The simplest, of course, is to do a minor re-write to let the action take place outdoors. Another is to only allow the camera to see out the window when the actor is in relative close-up, allowing you to match the light intensity and color for only a small area.

A less extreme and far more typical situation is a scene that's to be shot on location in a typical room with windows and a variety of practical light sources. When including windows in a shot, it can make your life easier if you can choose north-facing windows; it's even better if what's outside the window can be relatively dark, like trees or woods. Remember that the color temperature of light from a north-facing window will be considerably higher than normal daylight, since it will be coming from the sky or clouds, not directly from the sun. The light from the window can be either the key or fill, depending on the effect you're after. The practical lamp (if in the shot) should be put on a simple hardware-store dimmer so it can be set to a level that's convincing without "burning out". The key (or fill) light should be positioned so that it simulates the practical lamp in direction and texture. Also, since the practical lamp is a relatively soft source, the key can be fitted with some diffusion material to soften

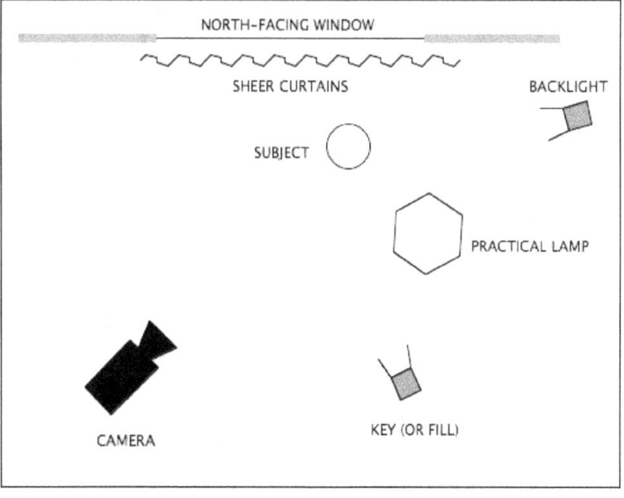

it. It should be barn-doored or flagged so that it doesn't hit the practical lamp, and any shadows it casts on the curtains shouldn't be in the shot. The window is a very broad, soft source, and depending on the intensity of the outside light, it may obviate the need for a backlight, if it provides adequate separation from the background. Still, the backlight can be useful if you let it just "kiss" the curtain, providing a bit more texture to the fabric. The sheer curtains serve several purposes: they add texture, soften the outside light and reduce its intensity, they prevent any real detail from outside showing in the shot, and they reflect back some light from the key, effectively lowering the color temperature of the outside light. (They can also add motion and interest if they're moving in a slight breeze. One grip I know keeps a small, quiet computer fan in his kit just for this purpose.)

So, shall we mix color temperatures on this scene, or not? If the key light is an HMI, we'll be close to a match with the window light, and a bit of booster blue gel on the backlight will bring it into line. The practical lamp, however, may present a problem. Since it will be on a dimmer and thus have a much lower than normal color temperature, it will appear red-orange. It will probably take a couple of layers of blue gel around the bulb to raise its color temperature sufficiently to match.

Suppose, on the other hand, we want a rainy-day look, or just a more natural feel. The cool, bluish light from the window mixed with warmer light from the lamp can lend coziness to the scene, implying that it's cold outside. For this kind of mood, a small tungsten instrument can be the fill. The practical lamp, too, can contribute some of the fill light, providing additional softness. In fact, it might be possible to light this scene beautifully with only a single instrument plus the practical lamp and its dimmer.

When working on location and using mixed light, it's become popular and quite acceptable to let windows "burn". This means that you expose for the interior and let whatever is outside the windows simply go completely overexposed, obscuring any detail outside. Burned-out windows work, of course, only if outside detail isn't important to your story. Some cinematographers take this idea even farther, putting tracing paper or plastic film over the windows (on the outside) to completely obscure details outside.

Remember, earlier I mentioned that video cameras don't respond well to over-exposure? That they clip the whites and obliterate detail? Burned-out windows can look great on film because a little of the detail outside is preserved, making the scene look more natural. To achieve the same effect with a digital camera, it helps to underexpose a little, just to preserve some of the detail outside. Then, in post-production, you can bring up the mid-tones a bit without affecting the highlights. (Some cameras have adjustable *gamma* to accomplish this in-camera, but you can still do it in post with whatever camera you have.) It may take a bit of testing to discover exactly how much you underexpose to get the desired effect with your particular camera; try about one to 1 1/2 *f*-stops for a starting point.

Supplementary Lighting

As I have said before (several times!), digital cameras work amazingly well in low light, so you probably have enough light to shoot just about anywhere. Given that fact, what can you do to supplement existing light – not so much to make it brighter, but to improve its quality? The previous example took a step in that direction. Since you'll probably be working on location more often than in a studio, most of your lighting will consist of supplementing what's already there, not lighting things up from total darkness.

Let's look at a typical office as an example. You know the setup. Rows of desks in a big room with banks of fluorescent fixtures on the ceiling, firing straight down. The light is very flat and even throughout the room, with virtually no shadows. A person seated at a desk under these lights will have deep shadows in her eye sockets, and if she's looking down, her face will be darker than the surroundings. Also, because of the even illumination, if her clothing is a similar color to objects behind her, she'll blend into the background.

To make such a scene look better, we first need to re-direct the existing light, but taking care to keep it soft, matching the rest of the light in the room. A good way to do that is with white cards. A card on one side of the camera can bounce light onto the subject at a more flattering angle, and can serve as the fill source. For the key, you have several choices. Many offices today are lit with "warm" fluorescent lamps, as opposed to the older "cool white" or "daylight" tubes. The newer lamps have a color temperature of around 4000° K, somewhere between tungsten and daylight. Adding a tungsten soft light as a key will give your subject and foreground objects a little more warmth. Alternatively, you can use a fluorescent soft light, or simply use another white card to provide the key source, positioned a bit closer to the subject than the fill card. The backlight may or may not be necessary, depending on the position of the overhead fluorescents and the background.

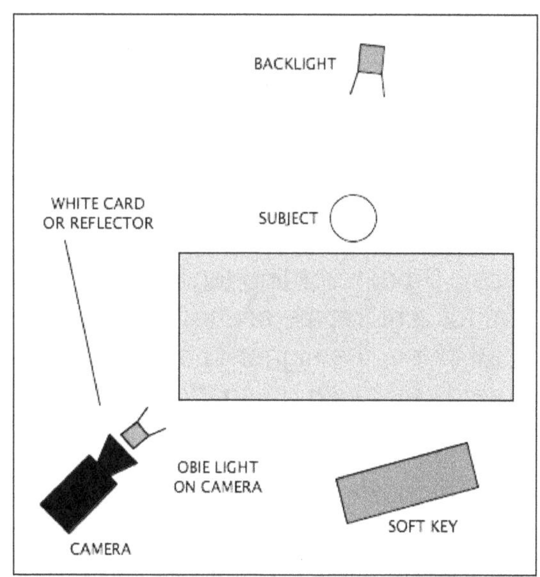

In any situation where the light is very soft, I have found it helpful to use an *obie* light, mounted on the camera, just above the lens. In this case, its purpose is not to increase the light level, but to provide specular highlights – most importantly "catch lights" in the eyes, which are especially important in close-ups. An obie light can work the same for exteriors on cloudy days and can do wonders in adding texture and depth to faces. It's intensity should be adjusted until it can just barely be seen brightening the face and eyes; the catch lights will pop out at you.

Again, the office is a case where one or more hard sources can be used to "blast" the background. The purpose here is to introduce some shadows where there previously weren't any, bringing out texture in background objects. Like the obie light, the intensity should be just enough to see the effect, but no more.

Similar setups work very well in any kind of evenly-lit environment – grocery stores, factories, warehouses. None of the lights need to be big ones. I like to use nothing larger than 650-watt tungsten or 250-watt HMIs. My favorites are even smaller – 250 or 300-watt open-face tungsten units. Larger instruments will overpower the ambient light, and will just have to be reduced in intensity. In most cases, you don't want to bring the light level up more than about one or possibly two *f*-stops. This allows you to get a lighting ratio of about 2:1 in an otherwise flat-light environment. You'll be amazed how much better 2:1 (with light coming from the right directions) will look than the ugly near-1:1 that naturally exists in these locations.

There is another big advantage to using a minimal amount of supplementary lighting: Your close-ups will look great, but you can get away with shooting your wide shots with little or no supplementary light – just what's there. If you do it right, the shots can match perfectly. Remember, too, that keeping your subject slightly brighter than the background draws the eye to the foreground and improves the sense of depth.

Night Lighting – Interior

Classic 3-point lighting tends to look warm and sunny – just the look you don't want for a nighttime scene. The lighting needs to constantly give the audience visual clues, the higher-contrast, harsher look of nighttime. A good night look depends as much on shadows as it does on light, and there's nothing wrong with having large areas of total black in your scenes.

Most obviously, light levels are much lower at night, and for the best look you should work with low-intensity instruments and/or keep light sources far away from the subject. From the camera's perspective, look for exposures that require your lens to be nearly wide open – perhaps *f*2 or *f*2.8. This keeps the depth of field rather shallow, causing the background to go more or less "soft", particularly in close-ups. You can enhance this effect by shooting close-ups with the camera farther away, using a longer focal length (more telephoto) lens setting. For interiors, it helps to include a dark window in the shot, with the lighting emphasizing the lack of daylight.

Some of the best nighttime lighting is very simple, with a single key light and a high ratio – perhaps 8:1 or greater. Any fill you need to help the camera to capture detail in the shadows can usually be obtained simply by using a white or aluminum-foil covered card just out of the shot. Often, your scene will look even more dramatic with no fill light at all. Don't be afraid of the dark!

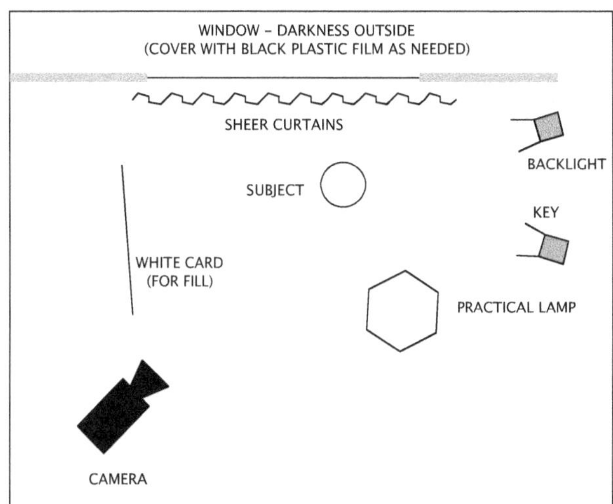

Notice that the key light has been moved (compared to our daytime setup) to a position that is a bit more than 90 degrees away from the camera axis. From this location, the light still simulates the effect of the practical lamp, but produces more shadow on the subject's face. It can also be placed lower, since the shadows it casts will be outside the shot. The practical lamp should be placed on a dimmer (or use a small bulb – 15-40 watts) so that it really becomes another fill source. The key should be flagged or barn-doored off the curtains in the background, to keep them dark. Walls and ceilings (especially white ones) should get as little light as possible to keep the nighttime feel, and since they will reflect additional fill into the scene. The white card merely reflects a little of the key light back onto the subject to fill shadows.

In this setup, the backlight is optional (as always). If used, it should be kept at the lowest intensity possible to maintain separation of the subject from the background. Remember that in most scenes, an equivalent of the backlight usually doesn't exist in the real world. One trick that can enhance the nighttime look is using booster-blue (or even full blue) gel on the backlight. Using blue light (I call it "instant moonlight") is an age-old way to enhance night scenes, particularly when it's mixed with tungsten. Don't overlook other colors, either. Reds and ambers can be effective in warming up a scene or enhancing the environment.

Another interesting way to get a nighttime look for an interior scene involves using a light box. This works best for scenes, for example, of a group gathered around a kitchen table. It's based on the classic pool table lighting fixture – a big rectangular source suspended directly over the table. The easiest way to assemble a light box is from foamcore, taped together, or it can be a simple pasteboard box with the interior spray-painted white. The depth of the box determines how much light spills out onto the walls, so deeper is usually better; I usually go with a depth of about 1/2 the box's longest dimension. It should be a bit smaller than the table and should contain a 250 to 650-watt broad light, mounted so that only the bounce light strikes the subject(s). I've also built boxes with fluorescent tubes, preferably the warm type with about 3200°K color temperature. (Choose a color temperature that fits the mood of your scene.)

Another way is to suspend a soft light over the table, taping fabric, cardboard or foamcore skirts to all the outside edges. Use black fabric if you're after a stark, contrasty look, or white for a softer light. If the shot permits, you can even use a box that doesn't contain a light source at all, by bouncing a tightly spotted and barn-doored instrument into it. (Some lighting fixtures have an available *snoot,* which can further confine the beam.)

I've also used commercial fluorescent fixtures. The best one is the inexpensive 2' by 4' variety, made to be dropped into a ceiling grid. It is lightweight, about the right size for many situations, and usually contain four tubes. You can reduce the intensity by removing two of the tubes (they operate in pairs), but you normally can't use dimmers with them. If it's still too bright, you can put strips of gaffer or duct tape on the tubes, since they run very cool. Of course, you'll need to attach the fabric or cardboard skirts, as described above.

Using the box as the only source of light can be quite dramatic and moody, but this effect can be softened by using some fill light from elsewhere in the scene. I rarely use backlights with a box, because the light direction (mostly from above) tends to automatically separate the subjects nicely from the darker background.

A very stark nighttime look can be had with just a single light bulb hanging from the ceiling. Choose the wattage for the intensity you need – anything from a 15-watt bulb to a high-output *photoflood* lamp. For a moodier look, put the bulb in a commercial shaded fixture or even fabricate a simple cardboard cone. The objective here is to light the subject, but keep the light off the walls.

Lighting a large interior at night can be a much bigger challenge. In many spaces (such as warehouses or churches), existing lighting is often too much. Keeping your story in mind, you'll need to light for the mood of the scene. In most cases, pools of light with areas of darkness are more effective and dramatic than trying to create even illumination. Where there are windows, it's good to see apparent sources of light outside, such as a street light. Being able to see the windows defines the shape of the space more effectively than more light inside. Again, keep the light on the walls at a low intensity, remembering that shadows are your friend; it's easy to over-light. You can still "blast the background", but do it selectively and from the sides, not from near the camera – this creates more and deeper shadows.

A fog machine can be a useful addition to your tool kit for nighttime work, and they can be purchased for as little as $50. Judiciously placed fog can make light beams become visible and add atmosphere. It doesn't take much, so choose a small fog machine for this application. A small household electric fan may be needed, too, to disperse the fog over a large area. (The exhaust of a vacuum cleaner can work for this, too, if you can stand the noise.) The objective is to give the scene a slightly smoky or dusty appearance, not the feeling that a steam pipe has broken! Fog works best when it's back- or side-lit with bluish light, so many DPs will use an HMI light just outside the top of the frame to bring out the fog and create edge highlights on objects in the scene.

Night Lighting – Exterior

The sensitivity of digital cameras comes to the rescue in making shooting outdoors at night a lot easier. In his trailblazing 1976 film *Taxi Driver*, director Martin Scorsese used a special chemical process to dramatically increase the light sensitivity of his filmstock. Through this technique, he was able to use existing light on New York streets for many of the nighttime scenes, a technique that hadn't been used before, but which digital video has made easy today. While he didn't attempt to use only available light, he was able to capture background detail that would have been impossible otherwise. For example, the illumination of the street from the headlights of passing cars was clearly visible, and very natural looking.

In a bright city environment, the challenge is to light for the areas where you must see detail and balance the light you add with what's already there. This is most important in closeups, where the softness and direction of light can complement the background. It's become popular in Hollywood to use tungsten sources in the foreground and supplement the background with HMI light, because of its bluer color. To avoid seeing a black sky, large HMIs are often fired upward (often with fog added) to create a blue simulation of moonlight. Backlights are also often daylight balanced (5600° K) for the same reason, to give them a blue tint.

Darker areas (like residential neighborhoods) require more effort, since streetlights are rarely intense enough and the direction of residential outdoor lighting is usually wrong. In situations like this, you're probably back to "blasting the background", but you'll need to get creative about it. It's amazing what a single, properly-positioned HMI fired down a residential street can do.

In lighting a wide night shot of the exterior of a house, I've used a single 1000-watt instrument on a tall stand to simulate a streetlight, then used a few portable 500- or 300-watt work lights (the kind sold at home-improvement stores, that come with a stand) to get light on the house and shrubbery. I've also replaced the bulbs in porch lights with larger sizes, or even with a high-brightness photoflood bulb. Sometimes just parking a car outside the shot and aiming the headlights in the right direction can fill in a troublesome dark spot. It can also improve the depth of a shot to kick extra light up into the trees, to make the green in the leaves visible. Be sure to get some light behind the house, too, to make it separate from the background. Sometimes lighting the trees behind the house can give a nicer effect than putting light on the roof, which can look unnatural.

As with shooting interiors in large spaces, a fog machine can help. For outdoor use, you'll need a larger fog machine, and probably an operator for it. On a windy night, it can be hard to get the fog to hang around long enough to get the shot, so keep that in mind. Be sure to get side or backlight on the fog. Remember, too, that a large fog machine is noisy, so don't plan on running it while you're recording dialog.

One of the best things you can do to improve a night exterior is to get it wet. Water on pavement or other surfaces increases their reflectivity, so the effectiveness of the existing light and what you add can be dramatically increased. Just thoroughly wetting down a driveway with a garden hose can make a tremendous difference. For larger areas, you may need to get a water truck from a local contractor, or try to get help from a cooperative fire department. And you could get lucky: it could rain!

Even more than night interiors, high contrast (high ratio, low key) lighting on exteriors will increase the drama of your shots. Placing the key light at an extreme angle, almost behind the subject, for example, can accentuate edge texture. Also, you'll want to use mostly hard sources because they create the harder shadows you would normally see at night.

Another tip: a long lens can be your best friend for night exteriors. Because it foreshortens distance from the camera, small areas of light in the background become larger, so even your wide shots can look better if shot telephoto. Move the camera way back and see what a difference it makes!

Day for Night

The ability to shoot during the day and make it look like night is an art that's been attempted (with varying degrees of success) since the first motion pictures. In those early days, the sensitivity of the film stock was so low that full sunlight was about the only available light source bright enough to get sufficient exposure. To make the scene look like nighttime, all they did was underexpose a couple of f-stops. To maintain the illusion, though, it was necessary to avoid shots that included the sky – a bright sky is a dead giveaway that it's not really night.

With the coming of color, cinematographers found that shooting through a blue filter (and underexposing the film) could create an even more convincing illusion of night. This combination turned sunlight into moonlight. And it still works, if you're careful how you do it.

For the most convincing day for night, try to position your subjects so they are back lit and not in the shade; shooting in the shade just makes the picture look underexposed. The key to making it convincing is the same as shooting night for night: high contrast and lots of deep shadows. That's exactly what sunlight does, and it's quite the opposite of what we want the sunlight to do when shooting day for day. Perhaps surprisingly, a bright, clear day is best for day for night.

In shooting day for night, you can use reflectors, too. This can be a very helpful way to get strong light behind or to the side of your subject when the sun is high in the sky. Put the actor in the shade and kick in some sunlight with a hard reflector, or even an HMI instrument.

Day for night works great if you're shooting something like commandos sneaking through the woods, but it's not a viable choice for shots like cars going down a freeway. With night for night, light sources are your friend; they're your enemy if you're trying day for night. Car headlights, flashlights, street lamps, or lights inside buildings are totally overwhelmed by direct sunlight, so the illusion is broken.

In shooting day for night, it's important to actually underexpose at least two stops, or even more. The reason for this is that detail in the highlights is lost in the camera at normal exposures. The idea is to keep detail in the highlights, but allow the shadows to fall completely into darkness. You can't get the same result by darkening the image during editing, because the detail in the highlights has already been lost. The picture will just get dark and muddy.

Adding a blue filter to the camera lens during shooting was the way to do it back in the film days, but with digital cinematography it's usually not needed. Blue can easily be added during post-production, and you have more control at this point. The advantage of using the blue filter during shooting is that you can see a good approximation of what you're getting on your field monitor or color viewfinder.

Post techniques can come to the rescue, too, if you happen to have some sky in your shot. Color correction software can selectively darken specific colors, saving the day on some shots.

Power Sources

In Chapter 2.6, we touched on getting power from generators and tie-in boxes. Getting enough power on location can sometimes be a problem, particularly if you need to use lighting instruments over about 1000 watts. As a rule of thumb, you can count on approximately 1 ampere of ordinary household power (115 volts AC) for every 100 watts of lighting. Most household circuits are rated at 15 amperes (amps), so if you put more than 1500 watts on such a circuit, you'll flip a *circuit breaker* or blow a fuse. Commercial wiring is sometimes a bit heavier, allowing 20 amperes (about 2000 watts) per circuit.

(Note: In this section, we're referring to typical wiring in the US. In other parts of the world, voltages and currents may be different. Typically, other countries use

220 volts instead of 115 volts, with individually circuits being 10 amps. In 220-volt countries, estimate 1/2 amp per 100 watts of lighting power.)

A typical home will have ten or twenty lighting (115-volt) circuits (each with its own circuit breaker) in the incoming power distribution panel, with those circuits being divided between two "legs" of the incoming 230-volt service (see drawing). If you're playing with power, it's important to understand that both 115 volts and 230 volts are present in the distribution panel – AND EITHER CAN BE LETHAL.

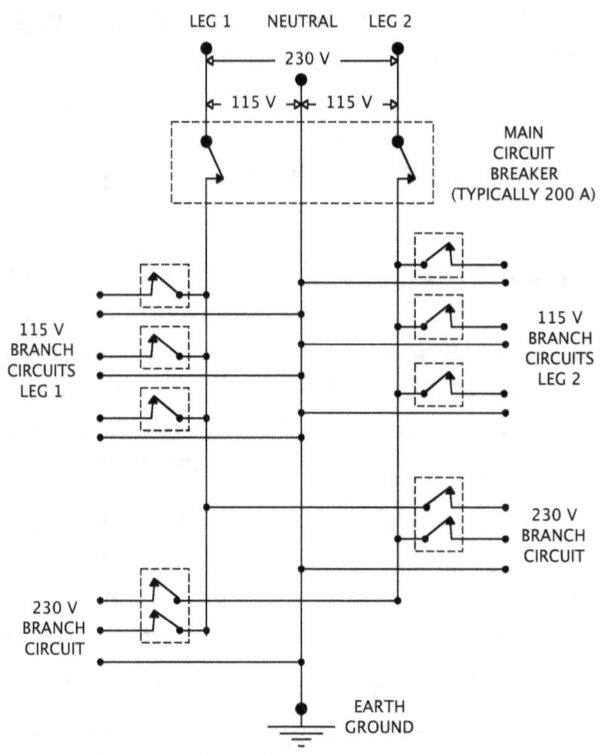

Appliances with heavy power consumption (such as ranges, dryers, air conditioners, etc.) use 230-volt circuits, while lighting and convenience outlets use 115-volt circuits. (You'll frequently hear these voltages referred to as 110/220, though the actual voltages are most often 115-120 and 230-240. Your handy voltmeter can tell you the truth.) The drawing shows a typical wiring arrangement as it might appear in a home or on the output of a small generator. The 115-volt branch circuits usually have 15-amp breakers; the 230-volt branches can have up to 60-amp breakers, depending on what appliances they are feeding. (In some cases, 230-volt circuits will feed other (smaller) distribution boxes elsewhere in the building.)

Notice the three incoming lines: Leg 1, Leg 2 and Neutral. If you connect your voltmeter between Leg 1 and Leg 2, you'll read about 230 volts. If you measure between Leg 1 and Neutral or Leg 2 and Neutral, you'll read about 115 volts. (Legs 1 and 2 are sometimes called the two phases.) If you connect a load (a lighting fixture) to one of the branch circuits of Leg 1, the current will flow through that branch and back to Neutral.

Note that Legs 1 and 2 are the same voltage, but are 180° out of phase with each other; thus, when the current in Leg 1 is equal to the current in Leg 2, the current in the Neutral line will be zero. Keeping the currents in the two legs approximately equal is called "balancing the load", and it's desirable, because it minimizes the current in the Neutral leg. Notice, too, that the Neutral leg is always tied to a solid earth ground.

In offices and commercial buildings, you will often find *3-phase* installations, in which there are three incoming power legs, plus Neutral. In these systems, the legs are 120° out of phase with each other (instead of 180°), but the principle is the same. The voltage between any leg and Neutral is still 115 volts, but the voltage between two legs is about 208 volts, so such systems are called 115/208 3-phase. In larger commercial buildings, you will often find higher voltages as well, so proceed with caution.

A *tie-in box* is essentially the same as the power distribution panel, connected to a long piece of heavy cable and with special connectors for safely clamping onto the incoming power legs. Most tie-ins are based on 115/230 connections, but can be used with 3-phase installations by using two of the legs plus Neutral. They usually have only 115-volt branch circuits, since few lighting instruments require 230 volts. Often, they'll have 115-volt circuits with larger circuit breakers (20, 30 or 50 amp) that allow use of lighting instruments of 2000 watts and more. That's when a tie-in is essential, since ordinary utility outlets can't accommodate these lights. Often, too, tie-in boxes will have special connectors for these high-wattage instruments. Of course, in no case should the total amperage used with the tie-in box exceed the capacity of the incoming service (usually 200 amps or more).

There are definite dangers associated with using a tie-in box, especially in the process of connecting it in the first place. Besides the ever-present risk of electric shock, it's quite easy to damage equipment with excessive voltage if the box isn't connected correctly. For these reasons, if you need to use a tie-in box, it's strongly recommended that you have a qualified electrician on your crew. Similarly, if you are using a generator, hiring an experienced operator/electrician to deal with connection and grounding issues is a very good idea.

Minimalist Lighting

Now that we've discussed the hard way, let's look at some other lighting options. For most low-budget films, there's a shortage of manpower, lighting instruments and time. Face it. Decide what's really important, and go for a "look" that fits both the budget and the story, and always remember *the story is everything.* Be realistic.

I once had the good fortune to meet a Japanese crew working on a documentary in the US. They had made the conscious decision to work in existing light, bringing only the director, cameraman and sound person as their crew. Their subject needed a number of interviews and the philosophy was, "Find a place where the light is nice and shoot there." They cheated a little, using folding reflectors and occasionally re-positioning a lamp or other *practical* light source, but they didn't bring any lighting instruments.

I adopted their methodology for a series of medical history documentaries shot largely in Eastern Europe. With our crew of two, the Prime Directive was: don't take more than you can carry – including your personal luggage. So, we carried a DV camera, lightweight tripod, two microphones and extension cables, wide angle lens, batteries, charger, tape, a "space blanket" to use as a reflector, and that's it. We called it our "ultralight-flight" package. We've since added our "not-quite-so-light-light" package, including an assortment of small lighting instruments, stands, cords, and accessories. It's really not a package to light scenes, it's all about supplementing what's there. After experiencing this way of working, I've found it hard to go back to the more conventional way of doing things. (Isn't interesting that while the new cameras have ten times the light sensitivity of the ones made just a few years ago, people still use the same size lights?)

If you choose the minimalist approach, it's best to be moderate about it. While some filmmakers feel that an "available light only" approach creates the most realistic images, a little supplementary light can improve any scene. Supplementary is the key word, and it means using small lights. Small means compact and lightweight in addition to low-wattage.

The objective is to make the people look good and let the surroundings look natural. Adding too much light will overpower the surroundings, so any light brighter than what's already there will simply be too much. You just want to make the light direction and softness more flattering to your subject's face(s) and perhaps to add some back light for separation and detail. Where appropriate, you can also do some judicious background blasting to bring out texture. Be prepared to mix color temperatures because you'll likely have tungsten, daylight and possibly fluorescent sources. If the primary light is daylight or fluorescent, you'll want to use some booster-blue gel on your tungsten lights, so they don't look too warm. And always remember, too little supplementary light is better than too much. If the light level in your location is just too low to shoot, try bouncing some light off the ceiling, a white wall or a small reflector to get just enough light to bring the scene up to a minimum exposure for your camera – and no more – then go from there with your accents.

Remember that you can get the shallowest depth-of-field if you run your lens wide open. That means you can have your subject in sharp focus with a softer background, an image that is pleasing to the eye and can cover a multitude of sins. Keeping your primary subject just slightly brighter than the background also helps with separation.

Of course you may have to make sacrifices. If you're shooting daytime interior and there are windows in the shot, chances are they are going to "burn out" unless it is a very dark and dreary day. If you're shooting minimalist, live with it or shoot around it.

To sum it up: Add just enough low-angle soft light to your subjects' faces to fill any harsh shadows and just enough back light (if needed) for highlights and separation from the background. And be sure you can see catch-lights in their eyes.

I've searched the web and the catalogs for an appropriate pre-packaged kit in this category, but haven't found what I think is a good solution. So here's a short list of what I'd put in my custom-made minimalist light kit:

- Three or four small focusable lights, 300 watts or less. Add a stand for each light and a couple of extras. Personally, I like the inexpensive Lowel Pro-Light instruments with the available barn doors. Have smaller bulbs available, too (100 or 150 watts). You might also want a stand extension (Lowel makes these, too) for extra height, and a few clamps for attaching reflectors and flags.
- One small and one large reflective umbrella that can conveniently be attached to create a broad, soft light source. The Pro-Lights are designed to accept an umbrella diffuser.
- Indoor-rated extension cords, 20 or 25 feet. These are made for household lamps and are available at any hardware store and are very lightweight. You don't need the heavy ones made for power tools. A couple 3-way splitters can also be helpful. (Note that these cords are light partly because they don't include a ground wire, so never use them outdoors or where they might create a shock hazard. Also remember they are usually rated at 10 amperes, so should never be used for more than 1000 watts total connected to the cord.)
- A couple of table-lamp dimmers, also available at your friendly hardware store. These are usually rated at 300 watts, so be careful to use one dimmer for each light, whenever you need them. In using lightweight cords and dimmers, you will need to use ground-lifters, or simply cut the longer ground pin off the cords on your instruments. Be aware that lifting the grounds from lights can, under some circumstances, create a shock hazard.
- A couple of collapsible reflectors (Flexfill or others). 36-inch round or 32-inch square are good sizes, though smaller works in many situations. The most versatile types are white on one side, silver on the other. Add a few pieces of white and black card stock for bouncing and flagging light, and some gaffer's tape.
- An assortment of color-correcting gels and control media. Rosco offers an inexpensive sample pack with about everything you need for your minimalist package. Get some wooden clothes pins (plastic ones will melt!) to hold the

gels to your barn doors, or purchase gel frames with your lights. You will also want some diffusion material, such as Rosco Tough Spun or Tough Frost.

- If you have room, consider adding a small 15-watt under-counter fluorescent light, the kind that go in kitchens. For under $20 at any home-improvement store, these can give you a compact source of fill light for any room with overhead fluorescents.
- I've also found it handy to add a couple of small (50 watts) screw-in PAR 20 flood lamps that can be put in practical lamps at the location. These can provide enough bounce off the ceiling to reduce shadows and be closer to the same color as your other lights than ordinary household bulbs.
- If your budget permits, get a camera-mountable LED Obie light. The one I use is the Micro from Litepanels. It is dimmable to give you just the amount of fill you need, and can give you up to 4 hours of running time from four AA Lithium batteries. While expensive, these little lights are lifesavers.

If you're serious about traveling light (pun intended), this kit will cover 90% of your low-budget shooting needs. Best of all it will fit in the trunk of the family car along with your camera and sound gear.

"Ouch!"

Benjamin Franklin

3.3 Shooting Techniques

"The sheer ease with which we can produce a superficial image often leads to creative disaster."
Ansel Adams

I'd like to start this chapter with a list of things you should always keep in mind when shooting any scene. I'd say they're rules, but everyone knows rules are made to be broken. Just call them guidelines:

- Think of your camera and tripod as a unit. While you may want some hand-held shots, most shots look best with a solid tripod or other suitable camera support.
- Keep the camera level. The audience usually likes to feel the action is taking place in a place where the ground (or floor) is level and the horizon is horizontal.
- Keep the camera steady. Think of it as a car. If it's supposed to be stopped, it doesn't move. When it does move, the most pleasant ride for the passengers will be when it starts, turns and stops smoothly. Imagine there is a full glass of water on top of the camera. Anything that will spill the water is bad. Any camera move that doesn't support the story is also bad.
- Remember the camera is a camera. It is not a trombone. Zooms should be rare, and be used only for a good reason. Let the editor change the shot, not the cameraman.
- The camera is not a rifle. You don't aim the camera at the subject, you compose an image that includes the subject.
- Remember the best point of view is not necessarily your point of view; just because the viewfinder is at the right height for your eye doesn't mean you are getting the best shot.

With these key points dutifully committed to memory, you'll have a foundation that will help in any shooting situation, even though every shot is different.

Familiarity Breeds Proficiency

When recruits go into the army, part of their basic training requires them to learn to disassemble and reassemble their rifles quickly and skillfully. They do it standing up, lying down, and even in total darkness. The objective, of course, is that they become intimately familiar with their equipment so they can fix problems quickly and know what to do when the pressure is on. The same idea works with the equipment you'll be using to shoot your film. You (or your camera operator) should know instinctively, without thinking about it, where every control and button is located, what it does, how it responds, and when you need to use it. Just as the military recruit needs this kind of familiarity with his rifle, you must build a similar relationship with your camera, tripod, and related equipment.

Practice setting up your camera, mounting it on a tripod, charging and changing the battery, attaching the wide angle lens, plugging in the microphone, headphones and power supply. Learn to go through all the menus to be able to quickly change things like white balance, shutter speed, exposure settings and audio levels. Build a mental checklist of what each setting should be for any shooting situation. Learn to quickly zoom in to a subject, focus, and reset the shot. Practice doing follow-focus as your subject moves in the frame. Get a solid feel of your zoom controls, including the on-camera zoom rocker and a separate zoom controller if you're using one. In short: practice, practice, practice!

Keeping it Steady, Level and Safe

In the section on technology, I talked about having a spirit (bubble) level on your tripod and using it. I'm amazed how often I see shots that are almost – but not quite – level. Usually it's subtle, but it tends to throw the viewer slightly off-balance. Leveling is most important in wide shots because there's more of the horizon (or the floor, or the ground) in the shot. The bigger the screen, the more important it becomes, too. The physics of nature keep the horizon level, and the human sensory system uses it (along with the inner ear) to build a frame of reference. When a shot isn't level, it sends a subtle cue to the audience that something isn't quite right. Leveling your tripod does something else, too. While a shot might look level in the viewfinder, when you pan the camera, an unlevel tripod will show up because the horizon will tip as you pan. A ball mount tripod head makes leveling easier, but for indoor use, simply making all the legs the same length will get you pretty close.

Since many modern cameras are so light (and so are most tripods), I like to add some extra weight to my tripod. I do this with a sand bag tied to the tripod with a bungee cord. This adds some rigidity to the setup and protects the camera from accidentally tipping over. It's all too easy for the camera tilt lock to be off and the camera slowly tips all the way over, causing a light tripod to tumble. The extra weight prevents this. If you're traveling very light, rig your camera bag so it can hang from the tripod for extra weight.

Adjusting the tension on a fluid head takes practice, too. Every head is a bit different. Some have self-leveling springs and some don't; some have separate tension adjustments and locks, some don't. Ideally, the fluid head should provide quite a bit of resistance to either panning or tilting the camera, and the resistance for each should be about the same. If they aren't relatively balanced, it will be more difficult to do a diagonal camera move.

If the tension is set too high, the tripod will tend to flex and create backlash. This will cause your moves to be rough at the beginning and end of motion, as the tripod flexes and "unflexes". So, set the tension as high as possible so that the camera moves but the tripod remains rigid. With center-column tripods, be sure to lock the column solidly, and raise the column as little as possible, since the more it is cranked up the more backlash you're likely to have. Unfortunately, very lightweight tripods require low tension to work properly, and are often not balanced well, so if you set the tension low enough to prevent backlash, the camera may tip over forward when you let go of the pan handle. The problem gets worse if you have any accessories mounted to the camera, such as an obie light or French flag. Some tripods provide the ability to move the camera forward or backward on the head for balancing. If yours doesn't have such a feature, you can sometimes balance your rig by adding weight to the panhandle.

On many shoots, there will be the hazard of cables. Here are some of the cables you may have attached to the camera:

- Headphones or a headphone extension
- Microphones or external audio input
- Video and/or audio to external monitor
- Zoom control (LANC)
- Firewire cable to external recorder or computer
- Timecode cables(s)
- Power cable for camera
- Cable for on-camera light
- Teleprompter cables

In addition to the needed cables, you'll want to have a handful of removable cable ties in your camera kit. (I prefer the ones that use Velcro strips, but the plastic types work fine.) Camera connectors are fragile and it's all too easy to break them, so it's prudent to secure the cables. More than once, I've seen someone trip on a cable and either break it (or break a connector) or send the camera crashing to the floor. This is another reason to use extra weight to secure the tripod. When you tie down the cables, be sure to leave enough slack for your anticipated camera moves.

Obviously, if there are a lot of cables tied to the camera they become hard to manage, and handheld operation becomes increasingly difficult. Since many shoots require a lot of cables, some directors like to use a second camera for handheld shots, using the primary camera (on a tripod) to record the sound, and possibly a second angle. Synchronized timecode can be used to "sync up" the sound in post-production.

Composition 101

It's far beyond the scope of this book to fully describe the fine points of composition, but maybe I can stimulate you to pursue the subject. If you're serious about shooting, you should make yourself intimately familiar with it. While most books on composition (of which there are many) confine themselves to paintings and still photography, filmmaking adds the extra dimensions of motion and time, presenting even greater opportunities to create rich, compelling images.

One of the most important principles of composition makes use of the *golden section*, also called the *divine proportions*. It's based on the idea of dividing a line into two parts so that the ratio between the larger section and the total length of the line is the same as the ratio between the smaller section and the larger section.

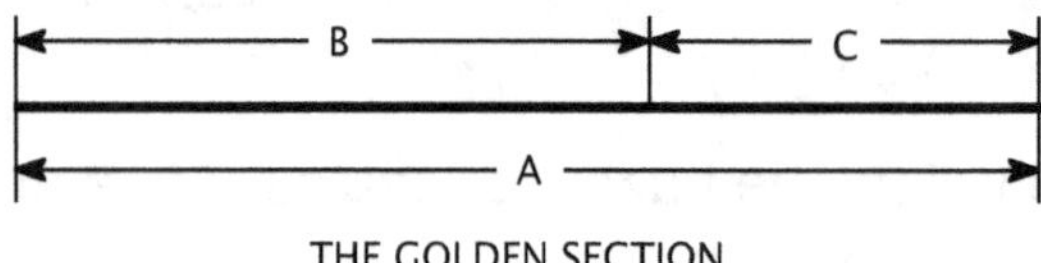

THE GOLDEN SECTION

Expressed as an equation, A/B = B/C. For this to be true, the value of the ratio is about 1.618 to 1. Many works of art and features of living things (including the human face and body) incorporate this ratio. In fact, it seems to built into our genes. Any object or image that incorporates the golden section seems to gain a sense of harmony and unity. Interestingly, the 16 by 9 ratio (1.777:1) comes fairly close to the golden section, too. If you divide a 16:9 frame according to the golden section, it looks like this. Of course, the 4:3 frame can also be divided using this ratio.

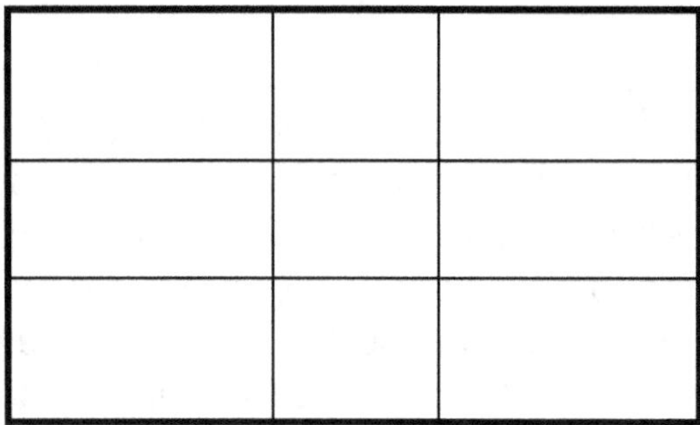

THE GOLDEN SECTION IN A 16:9 FRAME

The golden ratio is fairly close to the ratio of 3 to 2, or 1.50 to 1, so a variation of the golden section for purposes of artwork or photography is called the *rule of thirds*. It's a simpler version in which the frame boundaries are divided into thirds, the image into nine equal parts. Notice that the points of intersection fall close to the same points in the frame.

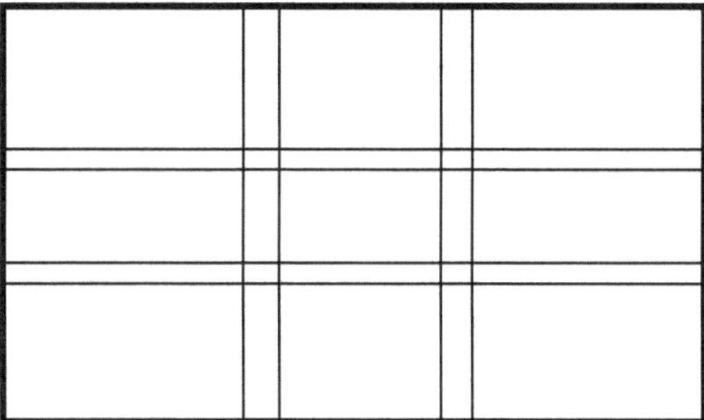
THE GOLDEN SECTION AND THE RULE OF THIRDS

These are the spots to which the eye naturally gravitates when looking at a picture, so the best compositions put a key object of interest at one of the intersections. In a wide shot, it might be a person's face; in a closeup, it could be his eye. Whatever he's looking at could be positioned on another intersection.

For scenic shots, an image looks more balanced and harmonious when the horizon falls near one of the grid lines.

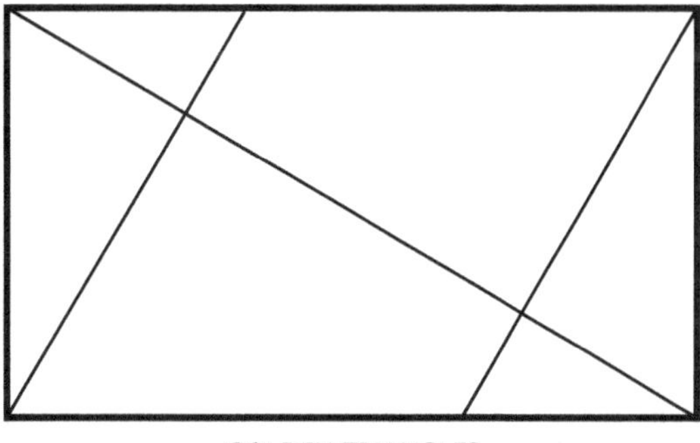
GOLDEN TRIANGLES

A variation on the golden ratio is *golden triangles*. These are formed by lines from the corners that are at right angles to either diagonal. When your composition contains a strong diagonal element, it becomes more harmonious when it lines up with one of the sides of the triangle and leads the eye to a point of intersection. Of course, golden triangles work equally well when "flipped" to opposite corners of the frame.

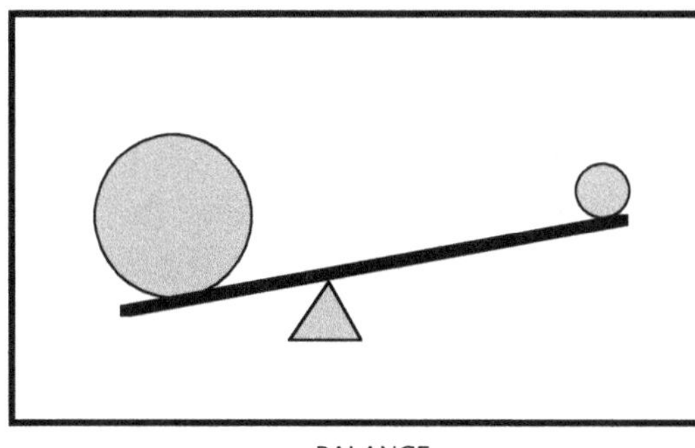
BALANCE

Another important aspect of composition is balance. In any image, objects have relative weights. Big objects are heavy, small objects are lightweight. Foreground and dark objects are heavier than background and light-colored objects. Light objects need space around them; heavy objects can be brought closer together.

Good compositions also create a sense of depth, and many techniques help add a sense of three dimensions to the two-dimensional film image. Objects closer to the camera than the primary subject, such as doorways or arches, can create a frame-within-a-frame. Using shallow depth of field can keep objects in front of or behind the subject slightly out of focus. In the real world, distant objects in the background tend to have less saturated colors and lighter tones than nearby ones. Complimentary colors, too, can cause a foreground object to "snap" away from the background.

When shooting people, I find it helpful to imagine that I'm not just getting a shot of a them, I am also including their personal space, their "auras". One's personal space is a sphere of attention and influence, but there tends to be more of it around the eyes. Some photographers call this *eye room* or *lead space*. In composition, it means allowing more space in the direction your subject is looking or moving, so if she's looking screen left, give her more room on the left – don't center her in the frame. The rule of thirds helps here; put her eye near an intersection. Keeping eye room is especially important when shooting dialog because it not only creates a better conversation, it gives each participant his own space on the screen and maintains a more consistent line of action. An exception to this (where the person is normally centered in the frame) is the talking head, someone directly addressing the camera. (Review Chapter 3.1 for more on shooting dialog scenes and talking heads.)

Another aspect of composition when you're shooting people is *headroom*. Unlike the concept of headroom in the chapter on audio, this headroom is literally how much room there is above an actor's head. It's disconcerting to see actor's heads bumping against the top of the frame, and it's just as bad to see him too low in the frame, making him appear as if he is sinking into quicksand. Just as we talked about allowing eye room and not centering a person horizontally, you'll rarely want to center a person vertically, either. Once again, the rule of thirds can help. Put it this way: if the point of interest falls on an intersection of the grid, you probably won't have too much headroom; if the top of a person's head is either always in the frame or always out, you probably don't have a problem, either. An exception: someone directly addressing the camera will usually look best if he is centered horizontally and his eyes are on or near the top line in the rule of thirds grid.

Composition in Motion

I mentioned earlier that film introduces the elements of time and motion. Composing for action and passage of time is a vital part of creating compelling images. This aspect of shooting is sometimes called *dynamic composition.* Any motion in the frame causes the composition to change from the beginning of the shot to the end. Directors and dolly grips call the beginning of the action #1 and the end #2, so plan to have well-composed shots at both points (or more than just two if the action calls for it) with smooth transitions between.

Imagine a shot of a runner on a beach and several ways it might be shot. You might position the camera so that it is static, with the horizon lined up with the "rule of thirds" grid. As the runner moves through the shot, she will pass through the two intersections on the grid, and the editor might choose to use either or both of these. You could also do a high angle shot with her path and the line of the surf following a diagonal and passing through the golden triangle intersections.

If you choose to follow her with a panning shot, the background will change but the composition of the shot relative to the runner can remain constant throughout. In this case, you could give the shot two subtly different meanings: If you allow space in front of her, you can give her room to run – so-called *lead space.* On the other hand, if you position her on the other side of the screen with more space behind her, you can introduce a sense of menace, as though she's running away from someone and looking over her shoulder to see if he's approaching.

Points of View

In Chapter 3.1 I mentioned a POV (point of view) shot, but now I want to concentrate on <u>points</u> of view, where the camera is located with respect to the action. To reprise the list at the beginning of this chapter: "...the best point of view is not necessarily <u>your</u> point of view; just because the viewfinder is at the right height for your eye doesn't mean you are getting the best shot."

One of the best shooters I've ever worked with is...(how shall I say it?) let's call him a big guy. It's to his credit that on many of his shots he finds himself incredibly contorted around the camera to get his eye to the viewfinder. But that's as it should be; the camera should be put where it can get the best shot. He likes to work with at least two tripods (standard one and a short *baby legs*) and a high hat. When he has a dolly available, he'll use it for static shots (with or without track) just to make it easy to change the height and position of the camera – something he's probably going to do for every shot anyway. He'll use the high hat on the ground or on a few sandbags for low angle shots; he'll scamper up a ladder and c-clamp it to the top for a high one. All this because he realizes the importance of the camera's point of view.

It's obvious that when you want to see all the cars in a parking lot you can only see them if the camera is way up there. What's not so obvious is how the camera's position can subtly influence the dramatic character of a shot. When shooting people, for example, a slight upward angle creates a feeling of authority or power, and makes the person look tall or even menacing. A head-on angle is more friendly, a meeting of peers. Shooting downward makes a character smaller, more humble, more vulnerable. A view through a window can seem voyeuristic, a shot from floor level presents the scene as viewed by the family dog. Extreme closeups can become more extreme to emphasize key dramatic points. Unique shots, such as from inside a refrigerator as the door is opened, can create experiences for an audience that rarely happen in the real world. Good shooters are always on the lookout for the perfect angle that will carry the story forward with the most effectiveness.

Lens Techniques

In all likelihood, you'll be using a zoom lens for all of your shooting, but for purposes of this section, I'll talk about long (telephoto), normal and wide angle lenses – meaning zoom settings. To apply the lens settings to a consumer or prosumer camera without interchangeable lenses, think of telephoto as being about the longer 2/3 of your zoom range, normal as about 1/4-way into your zoom range, and wide angle as a wide setting of your main lens plus a supplementary wide angle adapter lens. As you get more serious about your filmmaking, you may find it useful to consider these designations of some lenses used on 35mm film cameras:

- 16mm or less - Extreme wide angle (very short)
- 20 to 28mm - Wide angle (short)
- 35 to 50mm - Normal
- 75 to 150mm - medium telephoto (medium long)
- 150 to 300mm - Telephoto (long)
- Over 300mm - Extreme telephoto (very long)

For 2/3-inch video cameras (or 16mm film cameras), divide these numbers by two. On cameras using smaller than 2/3-inch imaging chips, there is no easy way to actually read the lens focal length, so you'll have to approximate. Many digital still cameras offer an *equivalent 35mm* focal length specification that indicates which focal length would produce the same image on a 35mm film camera. Alternatively, they offer a *focal length multiplier.* If you multiply the actual focal length of the lens by this number, you get the equivalent for a 35mm film camera. Unfortunately, few video camera manufacturers have offered this information.

Wide angle lenses (or zoom settings) obviously let you see more of the scene than a longer lens. They also tend to be relatively fast (*f*/2.0 or better) and have enormous depth of field. Depending on how wide the lens is, if set to infinity, any subjects farther than a foot or two from the lens will be in focus. Correspondingly, wide lenses can focus very close. Extremely wide lenses tend to introduce distortion, too. Foreground objects look larger than they are; backgrounds look smaller. A closeup of a person will show exaggerated features – the nose will look huge, the ears very small. A shot of the flat side of a building will make it appear to curve away from you at the sides, while shooting up at a building will seem to make it taper skyward and seem to lean unnaturally. Straight lines near the edge of the frame may seem to bulge outward, an effect called *barrel distortion.* Because of these optical phenomena, it's better to use a normal lens and back up the camera when the shooting situation allows it, although distortions are sometimes used to create a visual effect. (Interestingly, you won't see extreme wide angle shots in old movies. It's only been with the advent of computer-based designs that the optical quality of very short lenses has been up to professional standards. When *Gone with the Wind* was shot, the widest lens available for the Technicolor camera was 35mm – a lens we'd say today is in the "normal" range.)

Normal lenses are just what they sound like. They take in a field of view that approximates the area of maximum acuity of your eye, so a shot taken with a normal lens and viewed from a comfortable distance portrays the scene in a scale that seems more realistic than one shot with a shorter or longer lens. Unlike wide lenses, focusing accurately becomes important with normal lenses. With an iris setting of *f/*2.0 for example, a normal lens might be in sharp focus from 9 to 11 feet if set for 10 feet. Like all other lenses, stopping down (increasing the *f*-number) will increase the depth of field. At higher *f*-numbers (*f/*16, *f/*22) depth of field becomes extreme with normal lenses, too, which is why most shots done outdoors have everything in sharp focus.

Telephoto lenses have even more shallow depth of field (the longer the shallower), so it's a good thing they're most often used outdoors when there's plenty of light. Medium telephoto lenses are sometimes called *portrait* lenses because they tend to flatter people, making their features very natural-looking.

A phenomenon known as *diffraction* comes into play with small lens openings (high *f*-numbers). Without going into the arcane details, it turns out that lenses produce the sharpest images (when they're in focus) about midway in their *f*-stop range. For example, a typical lens will be somewhat sharper at *f/*5.6 or *f/*8 than at *f/*16 or *f/*22. If you're working in SD, you probably will not be able to notice or even detect that your lens is softer when stopped down, but in HD it can make a visible difference. For this reason, it's handy to have a couple of *neutral density* (ND) filters in your camera kit. They are identified as ND3, ND6, ND9, etc. (Actually ND 0.3, ND 0.6, ND 0.9, but usually abbreviated as shown), with each ND number being 1/3 of an *f*-stop. Thus, and ND3 filter is equal to 1 *f*-stop, and ND6 is 2 f-stops, and so on. If your exposure was normally *f/*16, adding an ND9 filter would require that you set the lens to *f/*5.6, opening up three stops from *f/*16.

Working with low *f*-stops (with or without ND filters) has another advantage. It allows you to take advantage of shallow depth of field, a technique Hollywood cinematographers long ago discovered can increase the drama and depth of a shot. By keeping backgrounds more or less out of focus, the foreground seems to snap forward and separate. Because of the high sensitivity of modern cameras, you may find that you sometimes may want to stack ND filters (ND6+ND9=ND15, equivalent to 5 *f*-stops) to get the effect you want.

Some cameras have built-in ND filters, and some allow you to reduce the video gain, accomplishing the same result. (Reminder: video gain reduction of 6 db is equivalent to an ND3 filter.) Correspondingly, increasing your camera's shutter speed also reduces the effective amount of light entering the camera; doubling the shutter (from normal 1/60 second to 1/120 second) reduces the light to 1/2, equivalent to one *f*-stop.

Keep in mind that using the shutter will change the way your camera sees motion; short shutter speeds reduce motion blur, the way fast motion causes a smear in moving objects. This is the same effect you get when you take still images of moving objects. Shooting fast-moving action (or fast camera moves) with a short shutter speed will cause objects to appear very sharp and clear, but an effect called *strobing* will also appear, creating jerky apparent motion.

Progressive Scan and Shutter Speeds

In Chapter 2.3, we talked about variable shutters and the characteristics of various frame rates. From an artistic point of view, it's important to understand the effects of various frame rates and shutter speeds. As a starting point, let's go back to the 35mm motion picture camera, usually running at 24 fps. These cameras use a mechanical shutter, usually a rotating metal half-disk. The film is transported by an *intermittent movement*, which moves each frame into position then holds it there for its exposure to light. The shutter is mechanically synchronized with the movement so that it is open when the film is stationary and closed when the film is being moved to the next frame.

Since the shutter is open approximately half the time, it is called a 180° shutter, half of the 360° rotation of the shutter shaft. Since a full rotation happens in 1/24 second, the exposure time for the film is 1/48 second. In fact, only half the action is actually recorded on film; the shutter is closed half the time. (Some film cameras have variable shutters that can be set to less than 180°, but only a few can achieve angles greater than 180°.)

Motion picture cameras do a pretty good job of recording moving scenes, but when action is too fast, and especially when camera moves such as pans are too fast, strobing occurs and the action begins to look jerky on the screen. Just how jerky depends on a number of factors, including the size and brightness of the projected image. Over the years, the motion picture industry experimented with a number of techniques to reduce strobing, including shooting at frame rates of up to 60 fps and developing camera movements that allowed up to 270° shutter angles. Because of the expense of these approaches, they were never widely accepted. Instead, cinematographers are careful to avoid fast camera movements. *The American Cinematographer Film Manual,* published by the American Society of Cinematographers, includes a section of panning tables showing maximum panning speeds for various combinations of lenses and camera speeds (see www.theasc.com).

In digital video, we have the opportunity to control exposure times and use faster frame (or field) rates, thus we have the tools to potentially reduce (or nearly eliminate) strobing by increasing the camera's *temporal resolution.* This simply means that the camera can capture more of the motion and capture it more accurately.

The best temporal resolution is achieved with one of the 60p formats – 60 full frames per second. This is why the 720p format is very popular for broadcasting sporting events in HD. A 720p camera is capable of capturing nearly all the image data for a 1/60- second exposure time. In fact, a 720P camera is the motion equivalent of a 35mm camera running at 60 frames per second with a near-360° shutter. Interlaced cameras (1080i, 480i, 580i) can also have equivalent temporal resolution, although at the expense of interlace artifacts that may show up in some scenes.

Because high temporal resolution is associated with video, many filmmakers prefer reduced frame rates and increased shutter speeds to create a more "filmic look". Shooting 24p with an exposure time of 1/48-second creates a near-perfect emulation of the motion characteristics of film. 60-field interlaced cameras sometimes have a "progressive" or "cine" mode, and while exactly how these work varies with the individual camera and from manufacturer to manufacturer, usually they provide a 1/60- second exposure time which occurs ever 1/30-second, resulting in an emulation of a film camera with a 180° shutter running at 30 fps.

When working with progressive or cine modes (and this varies with the camera, too), you'll usually find that the shutter speed relates to the exposure of each <u>frame</u> of video (30, 25 or 24 fps), not to each field. When you're not in cine or progressive mode, the exposure (for speeds of 1/50-sec. or less) is the exposure time for each <u>field</u>.

In working with various shutter speeds and modes, there is no substitute for experimenting with the way your camera handles each combination of settings. The way you get a particular "look" with a specific camera may be different with another camera.

Special Uses of the Shutter

One important use of shutter speeds other than the normal is when shooting where the power line frequency is different from the field rate of your camera. In most of North America, the power line frequency is 60 Hz; elsewhere in the world, it is usually 50 Hz. If you shoot 30 fps video under 50 Hz lighting (or 25 fps video under 60 Hz. lighting), you may get an undesirable pulsing in the picture, so many cameras offer a solution. 30 fps cameras offer a 1/100-second exposure time for 50 Hz lighting; 25 fps cameras offer a 1/60-second exposure time for 60 Hz lighting.

Sometimes motion in a scene is so rapid that blur during the exposure completely obscures details you want to be able to see. In these cases, the higher shutter speeds come into play – speeds of 1/250-second and up. I once shot a commercial where the object was to see individual corn flakes pouring out of the box. By using a shutter speed of 1/1000-second and running the footage at half speed, the individual flakes snapped into sharp focus as they poured. Often scenes that are intended to be used in slow motion benefit from using the faster shutter speeds. Remember, of course, that doubling the shutter speed reduces the camera sensitivity by one *f*-stop.

How to Shoot Wide Shots

Master shots, establishing shots, long shots, cover shots, scenics, vistas – they're all wide shots (WS). This doesn't mean they will all be shot with a wide angle lens, but it does mean that they take in a lot of visual scope. They are the kind of shots that give the viewer the opportunity to look around the scene and pick out details. For these reasons, wide shots should be sharp, clear and steady. They tend to look most natural when the camera is kept level both vertically and horizontally; this is especially important when using wide angle lenses. Shots that keep the plane of the camera image parallel with vertical planes in the image (such as walls) avoid convergence or divergence that are exaggerated by a wide lens. With a wide lens, objects close to the camera appear larger than normal, those at a distance appear smaller than normal, thus enhancing the sense of depth. That's what we're after in a good wide shot – enhancing depth, but not necessarily exaggerating it. Looking up at a building with a wide lens will make it appear to taper away in the distance, looking down exaggerates the apparent height of the camera. Using a wide angle lens for a shot down a corridor can make it appear to go on forever.

Sometimes a wide shot can be greatly improved by using a normal or even a telephoto lens. Seems counterintuitive, doesn't it? Lenses longer than normal make distant objects appear closer than they would normally look, so they can change the size relationship between foreground and background. Suppose you're shooting a wide shot of a house on a plain, with a distant snow-covered mountain range in the background. If you shoot this scene close to the house with a wide angle lens, the mountains will appear as small hills behind the house. Moving the camera farther away, using a telephoto lens and making the house the same size in the frame, the mountains will suddenly appear much larger and more majestic. In the city, a street scene shot with a long lens will appear to have much more traffic, more people on the sidewalk. In a neighborhood, a telephoto look can make the houses appear closer together, a wide angle makes them appear farther apart. In the forest, a long lens can make distant trees look much larger, creating an image of primordial woods. In a cemetery, a long focal length can create the impression of a forest of tombstones. Remember: a long lens can always be used for a wide shot if you can get the camera far enough away.

Getting Good Medium Shots

The normal lens was made for medium shots (MS). In a classic dialog sequence, it's the lens you'd normally use for 2-shots of actors carrying on a conversation, perhaps from the waist up (on a 35mm film camera, it's the 50mm or 35mm lens). Normally, medium shots keep the camera approximately at eye level, seeing the scene as if you were an observer – seated if the subject is seated, standing if the subject is standing.

There are occasions, of course, when you'll want to use a longer or shorter lens for medium shots. A wide angle lens can improve a shot of two scientists working on a bubbling experiment in foreground beakers – it will make the apparatus bigger and the scientists smaller. It can also make background details look smaller in the frame and make the room look larger. In the same situation, a telephoto lens can put emphasis on the characters' faces, allowing the foreground and background to go into soft focus.

A medium closeup (MCU) falls into this category, too. Shorter lenses can take in more of the environment around a character, longer lenses can direct attention to a character and emphasize objects close to him. Remember that long lenses have less depth-of-field than wide angles, so they're a good choice for visually separating foreground from background.

The Art of the Closeup

You'll see closeups (CU) of people described as just plain closeups, *extreme closeups* (ECU) and *choker closeups* (CCU). They're different in degree only. A closeup is usually considered head-and-shoulders, an extreme closeup is face only, a choker closeup is a part of the face – maybe just the eyes or mouth. It's in the closeup that you can see what a huge difference your choice of lens can make.

A striking example of what changes in focal length can do for a shot appears in the classic 1975 film, *Jaws.* Actor Roy Scheider is on the beach when the first shark is sighted. In one of the most dramatic medium closeups in cinema, the camera simultaneously dollies in and zooms back, making the background seem to fall away from him as his facial expression's changes are emphasized.

The usual focal length choice for closeups is in the short telephoto or "portrait" range (75-100mm on a 35mm camera). These lenses have shallow depth of field and tend to give a natural-looking perspective on facial features. When used at near wide-open *f*-stops, they require critical focusing. Interestingly, if the eyes are in focus the impression will be that everything is in focus. (Remember the importance of catch lights in the eyes!) Shallow depth of field can make closeups more dramatic by concentrating attention on specific features. Since the closeup is very revealing, shallow depth of field can also help mask imperfections without making the shot appear out of focus. (Remember, you'll need to use gain reduction, fast shutter speed or ND filters to get the right exposure with the lens near wide-open.)

Sometimes employed for comic effect, using a wide-angle lens for a closeup will distort the face, making the nose bulbous and causing the ears to look too small and plastered against the head. Also, any motion toward or away from the camera will be exaggerated.

The effect of longer lenses on facial features is more subtle; the nose will be slightly flattened, the ears will appear to protrude. Depth of field will be shallow, and on a choker closeup, it's possible to get one eye in focus while the rest of the face falls into softness.

Closeups may require more careful attention to lighting ratios than longer shots, too. Carefully placed reflectors can help bring out shadow detail and control skin texture; slightly darkening the background can help enhance depth. Shadows under the chin or nose can become too obvious in closeup, so have a white card ready to bounce in a bit of extra light from below. If an obie light is used, its intensity should be adjusted so that its effect is never too obvious. Remember, too, that in working close to a light source, its effect on the subject can change radically with only a small change in distance.

Closeups of objects (as opposed to people) require different treatment. Very small objects will require macro focusing or use of plus-diopter lenses and depth of field of any lens will become shallow, so it's helpful to increase the light level or even boost camera gain for these shots, allowing you to work at *f*16 or *f*22. Remember that it's not the actual amount of light on the subject that counts, it's the exposure; if the exposure is consistent, the shots will match in the cut.

About Exposure

In Chapter 2.6, we talked about light meters and using one to set exposures. We've also talked about how you can use the "zebra stripes" in the viewfinder to set exposure. If you're using a higher-end camera, you may also be able to use a handy little extra feature: a *histogram* displayed in the viewfinder. A histogram is a graph showing the relative number of pixels within each area of brightness. Black is at the left and white is to the right. Here's an example:

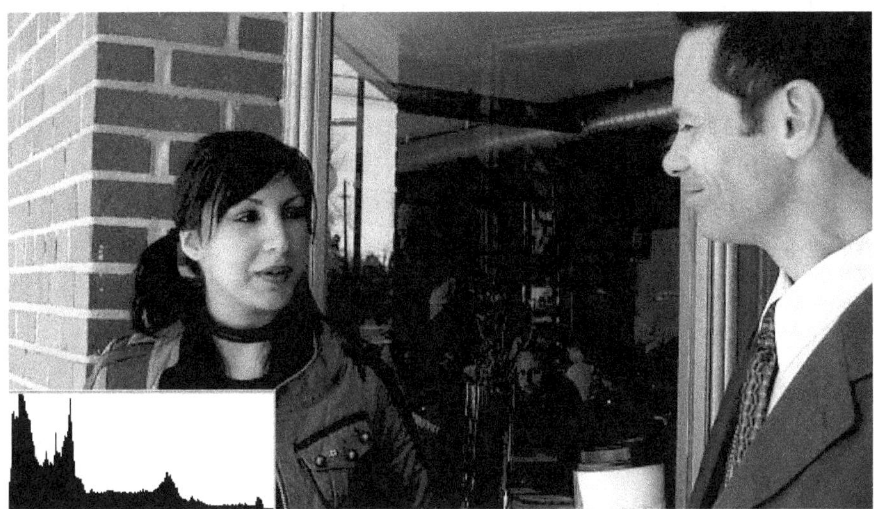

Notice the peak at the left. This shows that the scene contains a relatively large number of pixels in the darker tones. Notice, too, that the peak doesn't go quite all the way to the left. This means that while there are some blacks in the scene, there are more very dark grays. Similarly, there's a small peak at the right, indicating that the lighter tones are near 100% white, but not quite there. This is what you're after for a correct exposure. If you stop down the lens (underexpose) the peaks will shift to left, while overexposure will shift them to the right. Ideally, look for just a little space at the left and right, which indicates that you're not losing any highlight or shadow detail in your image.

With very contrasty scenes, you'll find it isn't possible to "center-up" the histogram. Since most cameras can only handle a 5 or 6 *f*-stop range from highlights to shadows, the histogram can show you where you might need to add light to dark areas of your scene, or when you need to reduce the shadows. Ultimately, you can use the histogram to help you decide whether the highlights or shadows are most important for a particular scene. An interior with windows in the shot, for example, will look best if you favor the shadow areas – because you probably want the windows to "burn out" and keep the indoors properly exposed.

Using the histogram, you can do what the cinematographer does when he tries to get an exposure which maximizes the amount of information the negative can contain. Keep in mind that setting exposure by the histogram may not give you quite the image character you want in the viewfinder or on the monitor, but it will give the colorist the maximum amount of control in post-production. It simply makes the best possible use of the available bits in the image data. With a little practice looking at different kinds of scenes, you'll learn to read the histogram very quickly and it will become your best friend in setting exposure.

Watch the Lens

In addition to the obvious necessity of keeping the lens and filters clean (have lens cleaning tissue in your kit!), be careful of extraneous light from outside the shot that can cause lens flare. You'll see veteran cinematographers waving their hands around the lens while looking through the viewfinder. What they're trying to see is any change in the image. If they're getting flare, the image will change (gain contrast) when the light path from an offending source is broken by the hand. Extreme flare will cause the classic flare circles to appear, but even a small amount of light hitting the lens at certain angles can reduce the contrast of the image. Of course, using a matte box, shade and/or a French flag over the lens can help.

Diffusion and Other Optical Tricks

In designing lenses and camera optical systems, engineers strive to create the sharpest possible image, the maximum amount of resolution possible, and the maximum contrast attainable. Sometimes the cinematographer's objective is to achieve a "softer" look. By this, I don't necessarily mean an out-of-focus appearance, but a reduction of contrast, especially in the fine detail. In the digital age, many effects of this kind can be accomplished during post-production, but they can be (and traditionally have been) done during shooting.

A popular (if heavy-handed) way of doing this has been to stretch nylon fabric from pantyhose over the lens – sometimes called *netting* the lens. White fabric creates a bright, open look; flesh-colored gives a warmer appearance; black is more neutral, opening up the shadows. The density of the fabric and how tightly it is stretched determines the intensity of the effect. The amount of light falling on the fabric from outside the shot also affects the brightness of the shadows, especially with lighter-colored fabrics, so you may need a matte box and/or flags to control stray light.

It's also common to burn a hole in the center of the stretched fabric with a cigarette. This causes the effect to be minimal at the center of the frame, gradually moving to maximum near the edges. The character of the effect varies greatly with the focal length and *f*-stop used, so a lot of experimentation may be required to get the effect you're after. To make the results more predictable, some people have put the net behind the lens, lightly glued around the rear element inside the camera. Of course, this is only possible on cameras with interchangeable lenses.

Another very old effect is accomplished by smearing petroleum jelly around the edges of a clear filter or piece of glass in front of the lens, the results being controlled by how much goo you use and where you put it. Experiment! Of course, never put anything directly on the lens surface.

Commercial diffusion, fog and star filters can produce similar and more controllable effects. When using these filters, keep in mind that with wide angle lens settings and small lens openings, any patterns in the filter can actually be in-focus, creating unexpected results.

Another popular form of filters that have been used since the dawn of cinema is the *grad*. It comes in many varieties, usually in a square format, designed to be used in a matte box. Grad is short for *gradient,* which means that the filter changes smoothly from one color at to top to another color at the bottom. One popular grad is blue at the top and gold near the bottom; it's used to create a bluer sky at the top of the frame while "warming up" flesh tones lower in the frame. Grads also come in ND varieties, usually dark at the top and lighter at the bottom. These are used simply to darken the sky.

Commercial grad filters can be expensive, especially if you buy enough different ones to be relatively sure you'll have the right one when the need arises. One videographer used the gradient feature in Adobe Photoshop to create his own grad filters, printing the images on overhead transparency acetate sheets, sized for his matte box.

In the digital age, the color correction capabilities of editing software can create effects similar to grads if the video is not over-exposed, and that's what most people do instead of stocking up with grads in their camera kit.

Moving the Camera

Perhaps more innovation has been applied by filmmakers to making smooth camera moves than in any other area, because they know that a moving camera adds drama and depth to their shots. Beyond the simple pans, tilts and zooms you can accomplish from the tripod, cameras have been moved by conveyances ranging from model trains to helicopters. The keys to a good moving shot are simple: smooth starts, smooth moves, smooth stops.

Traditionally, the best camera moves are done with a real camera dolly, usually running on track – hence the name: *tracking shot*. Using track has the advantage of allowing smooth moves on virtually any surface; the disadvantages are the expense, extra personnel and time required for assembling, positioning and leveling the track. With some moves, too, it's impossible to keep the track out of the shot.

Inexpensive dollies (such as the *Western* or *Doorway* dollies) are simple platforms that carry a normal tripod. They are built to run either on pneumatic tires or on concave plastic track wheels. More complex dollies have hydraulic lifts or booms to allow the camera height to be changed during a move. There are also miniature dollies used for tabletop shots. Since different types of dollies may be required for various shots, dollies are rarely purchased by filmmakers, but are rented as needed.

I've seen excellent dolly shots done with wheelchairs, tricycles or even a large-size kid's wagon, not to underrate the quality of a smooth move made with a Pontiac convertible pushed by four hefty grips.

Camera stabilization systems such as *Steadicam* can also be used to get smooth moving shots, but they shouldn't be considered a substitute for a dolly. Steadicam moves have a different character from dolly moves, especially at the beginning and end of shots. While they're great for smooth, sweeping moves, when standing still it's difficult to keep the camera from swaying, almost like it's mounted on a boat.

Stabilization systems for heavy cameras (over 10-15 pounds) use a body harnesses to transfer the weight of the camera away from the operator's arms and make it "float" in mid-air. When properly balanced and tensioned, the rig requires only the slightest touch to direct the camera. Mastering such a system requires a lot of practice and more than a little athletic ability and coordination.

With lightweight cameras, the harness becomes unnecessary, and various simple systems have been devised to stabilize these cameras. The idea behind all these systems is to shift the camera's center of gravity to a point well below the lens, to make it self-leveling. One of the simplest ways to do this is to attach a simple rod (a broomstick will do) about 18-24 inches long to the camera's tripod mount. On the other end of the rod, add a simple counterweight, about the same weight as the camera; I've used half a brick. If you're more ambitious, you can fabricate a battery holder as the counterweight. Since the battery is now off the camera and serving as a counterweight, the whole arrangement is barely heavier than the camera alone. With a rig like this, you use the camera's LCD viewfinder and support it by holding the pole near the bottom of the camera.

In many cases, the simplest (if not necessary the best) way to move the camera is to go hand held. Many operators believe using one of the larger, heavier cameras held on the shoulder is the best way to do this. There are some shoulder-mount accessories available for smaller cameras, too. The idea here is that your shoulder is simply a more stable spot for the camera than your hands. When working hand held (or with any less-than-optimum mounting for moving shots) it's always best to use as wide a lens as possible; the longer the lens the more exaggerated any camera motion will become. Fortunately, image stabilizers on digital cameras can smooth out some of the bumps a bit, but they can't accommodate jerky starts and stops.

Since lightweight cameras usually have the viewfinder at the rear (while heavier ones locate the viewfinder nearer the center of gravity) they require the whole weight be supported with the arms. By using the fold-out LCD viewfinder screen, smaller cameras can be cradled in your hands close to your chest, a more stable position than holding the viewfinder to your eye. Of course, this places the camera lower.

Shooting from vehicles creates another set of challenges. A pickup truck (preferably one with an automatic transmission) makes an excellent camera platform. A van works great, too, if you can shoot out the open rear doors. Use a heavily sandbagged tripod, and keep it as low as possible with the legs widely spread. A tripod with an accessory spreader is handy because it makes it easy to keep it rigid.

Need some bags of concrete or fertilizer? Buy them, put them in the truck to make it heavier, shoot, and use them later! Load crew members in the truck, too. If you're working at slow speeds, consider letting some air out of the tires for a softer ride, but be sure you have a way to get the tires back to recommended pressure. For very slow moves, get the grips to push the truck without the engine running. (And don't forget to always have a driver at the wheel!)

I've seen some very good dolly shots done on roller skates, assuming, of course, there's a smooth floor to roll on. The operator shouldn't actually skate, but should be pushed along by another person (the skate grip?). One cameraman puts two or three athletic ankles weights on each leg to lower his center of gravity when shooting from skates.

A wheelchair can make a good dolly on smooth surfaces, too. Choose one with thick pneumatic tires instead of the thin, solid rubber used on lightweight chairs. You can shoot hand held, or better still, clamp a board to the armrests, then mount the camera on a high-hat attached to the board. Alert the person pushing the chair to be sure the guide wheels are straight at the start of each move, or you'll get a jerk.

Industrial equipment such as fork lifts or cherry pickers are usually not capable of smooth moves, but they can be excellent for getting high angle shots, especially outdoors. Be sure to have a tripod with ball leveling for these, because they don't stay level when you change their position. Again, sandbagging the tripod helps.

For those big, sweeping moves, nothing beats a camera boom or *jib*. These come in many shapes and sizes, and are basically a long, rigid pole with a tripod mount and a remote-controlled pan-tilt head on the end. They're expensive, but can be rented in most cities. I strongly suggest that you only rent one along with an operator experienced in using the particular boom. It takes a lot of skill and practice to make smooth moves with these beasts, especially the longer ones.

If you need to shoot from an aircraft (helicopter or airplane), again, you'll probably want to rent. TV stations sometimes will rent their traffic helicopters and cameras during off-news hours. The best of these cameras have very sophisticated gyro stabilizers that can yield rock-steady pictures even in choppy weather and with long zoom lenses. Again, you'll want a skilled operator and a pilot experienced in doing aerial photography. Shooting from the air is one place where it's difficult to cut corners.

If you don't have the budget for a helicopter, you might try a hot air balloon. I've seen some wonderful scenic aerials shot this way. A sandbagged tripod in the basket works very well, but you need to keep in mind some of the limitations of the balloon. First, it can only fly in very calm weather, which in most parts of the world means very early in the morning. Second, you can't really steer a balloon – it goes where the wind takes it, so if you can launch upwind of what you want to shoot, you'll only get one shot at it, and then only if you get lucky. In calm weather, you can get a great fixed high-angle shot from a tethered balloon.

For some unique moving point-of-view shots, try one of the really tiny consumer cameras, maybe fitted with a wide-angle adapter. The better ones are of reasonable quality and present opportunities to get shots that would otherwise be impossible. They can be attached to roller skates, bicycles, vehicles, or helmets, or can even be mounted on a microphone boom.

"A wide screen just makes a bad film twice as bad."

Samuel Goldwyn

3.4 Sound Recording Techniques

"Good sound is the absence of bad sound."
Anonymous

If any one thing differentiates professional from amateur filmmaking, it's sound quality. This is perhaps surprising, since even an inexpensive digital camcorder is capable of better audio recording quality than the most expensive professional analog equipment. Likewise, inexpensive microphones today are at least as good as those used in making all the classic movies. So what's the answer? It's all about technique, and how you use the tools at your disposal.

Rule# 1: I've said it before and I'll probably say it again: forget about using your camera's built-in microphone(s). The quality of these mics varies from bad to awful, and they're located in a terrible place – always too far from the subject and too close to the noise-making mechanisms of the camera. If all you're after is background sound (like traffic, surf sounds, crowds cheering, or a waterfall) you may be able to get away with it. In virtually every other case, an external microphone is essential, often more than one. (Review Chapter 2.5.)

If you're shooting without a crew, a possibility is the camera-mounted shotgun mic. A short shot with a shock mount can work quite well in quiet outdoor situations, or when your subject is kept close to the camera. It will certainly do a better job than the camera's internal mic on ambient sound effects, mostly because it is more directional; it will emphasize the sounds that have their sources in your shot, instead of those coming from behind you.

It's always important to keep the mic as close to the subject as possible. This is relatively easy on something like a simple "talking head". Just place the mic and go. For anything more complicated, it's best to have at least one person looking out for sound.

The Boom Mic for Dialog

In the field or on a soundstage, the audio person's most important job is recording dialog (even if it's a monolog). Many filmmakers prefer suspending the microphone from a boom (or *fishpole*). Personally, I think a boom mic yields the most natural-sounding dialog compared to

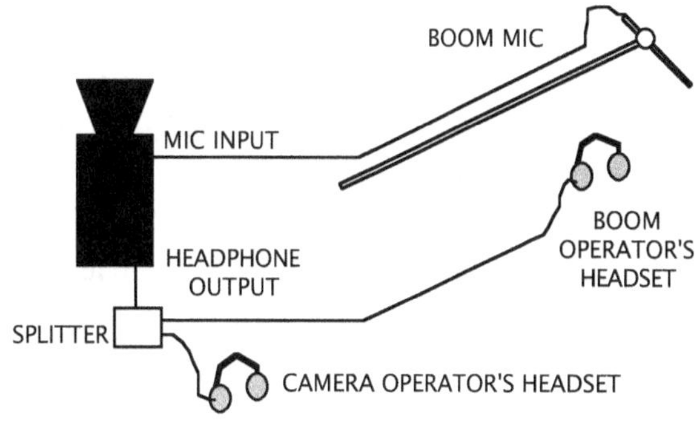

other techniques. The boom operator keeps the mic over the actors' heads, moving and aiming it appropriately to follow the action, listening to what he's getting on headphones. A headphone splitter (and/or amplifier) is used to allow both the camera and boom operators to hear the sound being recorded.

This setup is very straightforward and easy, but has the disadvantage that the boom operator has to deal with two cables. He also has no way of monitoring the recording level and has to depend on the camera operator to be sure the recorded levels are correct.

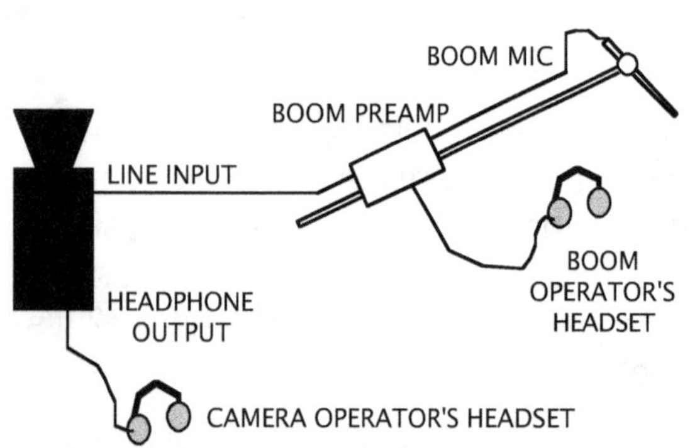

In a more sophisticated arrangement, a battery operated preamplifier (preamp) or simple field mixer is added. This eliminates the headphone cable because the preamp provides the necessary amplification. Choose a mixer with an audio level meter, so if the correct levels are established in advance, the boom operator can be sure that dialog levels are OK. Some mixers can also provide phantom power to the microphone. Notice that the output of the preamp is connected to the camera's line-level input. This is the preferred setup since the line-level signal is much more immune to induced noise than a mic-level signal. Many preamps, however, also provide a mic-level output for camcorders that don't have a line input.

Adding a mixer (the equipment and the person) frees both the boom operator and camera operator from having to worry about monitoring audio levels, and presents the opportunity to use additional microphones. The camera operator should still monitor the audio on headphones, to be certain the link from the mixer to the camcorder is working properly and that sound is actually being recorded.

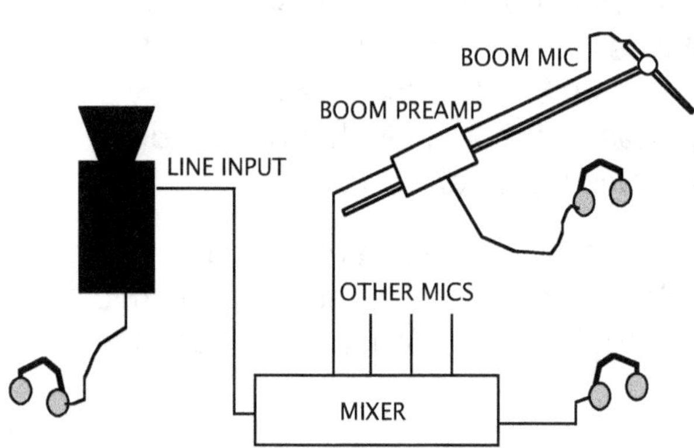

Keep in mind these setups are simplified to show only a single audio channel, though all camcorders allow the use of at least two, the stereo left and right. Often, you'll want to use two mics, and even two booms with operators. I've had excellent results using a stereo mic on a boom in situations where the extra "reach" of a shotgun mic isn't needed. Inexpensive stereo mics will only work when plugged directly into a camcorder using 1/8-inch stereo plugs, because these connectors accommodate both channels plus supply power to the mic.

Professional stereo mics accommodate separate XLR connectors for the two channels.

Which Mic to Put on the Boom

Chapter 2.5 covers the basics of the mics used on booms, the cardioid, short shot, long shot, and stereo. Of these, the cardioid has the "widest" pickup pattern, the long shot the narrowest. At the risk of oversimplifying, you'll get the best sound with the widest pickup pattern you can use given the distance between the mic and the talent. This concept is often misunderstood, and may seem counterintuitive. Why wouldn't you want to always use the mic with the greatest rejection of unwanted sounds?

Shotgun mics are not equally directive at all frequencies; they are much more selective for high than low frequencies. This means that they must be accurately aimed at the talent to sound right. If dialog arrives "off-axis" the high frequencies will be attenuated, making the sound "muddy" or "dull". Also, very low frequencies (sounds such as traffic or air conditioner rumble) are barely rejected at all. High quality cardioid mics, on the other hand, have directional patterns that are quite uniform with frequency, so that a source of low-frequency rumble behind the mic can be effectively rejected, as can sounds bouncing off a hard ceiling.

The directional pattern of a shotgun mic actually only applies to sound originating some distance away; it may behave quite differently for nearby sources. The ability of a shotgun to reject unwanted sound depends to some degree upon the relative intensity hitting various parts of the microphone. In order for an undesired sound to "cancel out" inside the microphone, it must be about the same intensity at the front of the mic as at the back. Therefore, if a source of noise is close to the mic, it will be rejected less than a more distant sound.

Remember, too, that the actual pickup element in a shotgun mic is near the back, the end where you plug in the cable. Some shotguns are 24-inches or longer, which means you could have your actual microphone nearly two feet farther away from the talent than you could get with a cardioid!

In general, use a cardioid mic when you can work fairly close to the talent or when working in confined spaces, use a short shot indoors in relatively spacious rooms, use a short or long shot outdoors or in large indoor spaces, depending on how close you can get with your mic.

Mounting and Using the Mic

First and foremost, use a shock mount! A standard microphone "clip" on the end of a boom will transmit all the handling noise of the boom straight to the microphone. The best shock mounts use rubber bands (usually dressed up with a fabric coating) to suspend the mic, though some use flexible rubber strips.

Secondly, keep everything tight – all the fittings and sections of the mic boom should be tightened securely. Third, secure the cable to the boom using tape or removable cable ties, leaving a good size loop of slack at the mic end of the cable. A few mic booms contain a retractable cable built permanently on the inside of the tubing. While these booms may offer some convenience in cable handling when you change the length of the boom, I don't like them because the cable can rattle around inside the tube during moves.

Usually, you'll want to set the shock mount so the mike is aimed downward at about a 45-degree angle, so it can be easily aimed at the talent's mouth. The more straight-down you aim the mic, the more likely you are to get reflections from the floor, which tend to make the sound "boomy". The boom operator, monitoring on headphones, can quickly get a feel for the right location and angle.

It's best to minimize how much you have to move the mic, too – another reason to use a less-directional mic where possible. In shooting scenes with little action and under controlled conditions, you'll probably want to clamp the boom on a sandbagged light stand. (Quick-release holders for mic booms are available for this purpose.) The advantages are that you can relieve the boom operator of some work and you can accurately position the mic just outside the frame, so you can generally work closer to the talent.

Here's a case where a stereo mic can be useful. Suppose you need to cover three people having a conversation. Mount the stereo mic on the boom, aimed at the middle character. In the final edit, you may be able to use the stereo recording to let the dialog follow the action. Alternatively (if background noise or "off-mic" sound is a problem), the editor can choose to use only the left channel for the left person, the right channel for the right person, and mix the two mics (creating a "virtual short shot") for the middle person.

For closeups and medium shots, you may find that you can get the mic closer by working it from below the frame (or from the side) instead of from above. This may also give you the ability to keep the boom short, giving the operator greater precision in mic positioning. I've found that a "banquet" mic stand to be a helpful addition to the sound toolkit. These stands are designed to be placed on a table to accommodate a standing speaker, so they extend to a height of 2 - 3 feet, just about right for positioning a short shot.

Most sound technicians use windscreens on their mics all the time. While usually not necessary indoors, they do no harm and can help protect the mic (and the actors!) – the end of a boom is a dangerous place. Outdoors, the foam windscreens that come with the mics are adequate in a light breeze, but under windy conditions, you'll want to use one of the "Zeppelin" or "fuzzy bunny" type windscreens that encloses the whole microphone. While expensive, these enclosures provide excellent wind protection and most incorporate their own shock mount. Be sure to choose one that fits your mic; one that's too big may force you to keep the mic farther away than necessary to keep it out of the shot.

Avoiding Off-Mic Sound

If you shoot outdoors on a quiet, still day, you'll find that almost any microphone will pick up clean dialog even from a substantial distance. Taking the same mic indoors (especially into a small room with hard walls) will create a very hollow, unpleasant sound. When you hear sound people talk about *off-mic*, this is the kind of sound they're talking about. It's the result of the mic's receiving both the direct sound from the person speaking and reflections of that sound off the walls and other hard surfaces. In addition to short echoes, the reflections combined with the direct sound create *resonances* that favor some frequencies over others. For some frequencies, the direct sounds arrive at the microphone in-phase with the reflections; for other frequencies they are out of phase. The reflections also create echoes, but in normal-sized rooms, the echoes are so short that they don't sound like echoes, they just make the sound "hollow".

Of course, the easiest way to get rid of off-mic sound is to get the talent *on-mic* – closer. This helps because the closer you get to the mic the stronger the direct sound is in proportion to the reflected sound. A directional mic helps for the same reason; it rejects some of the reflected sound because of the direction it's coming from.

A room with lots of upholstered furniture, drapes, carpet and acoustic ceiling will sound better than a room with bare walls and floors and a hard ceiling. Similarly, a big room will sound better than a small one, simply because the reflecting surfaces are farther away. So, a big room with lots of sound-absorbing surfaces is ideal, which is why professional sound stages are big and have every surface except the floor covered with acoustic treatment to minimize reflections.

When working on location, filmmakers often use specially made *sound blankets* to minimize reflections. Hung on walls or supported by light stands just out of the shot, they can make a huge difference. They also can help on the floor in rooms without carpet. Acoustic foam or carpet works well, too, as do inexpensive packing quilts used by movers.

Surprisingly, the audience can accept "hollow" sound if the situation demands it. For example, it's quite acceptable for a scene shot in a tile bathroom to sound hollow, because such rooms sound that way in real life. Remember, too, that off-mic sound may sound pretty good on headphones, but can sound awful on speakers. The reason for this is that sound reproduced on speakers will necessarily include the acoustic character of the recording plus the properties of the listening room. Psychoacoustics dictates that the ear can accept one or the other, but is uncomfortable with both.

Important: It's always good practice to record a minute or so of *room tone* at every shooting location. Room tone is simply the ambient sound that's present when nobody is speaking, and it's useful in editing to create pauses or to add to scenes when audio edits reveal audible differences in sound texture from shot to shot.

Using Lavalier Mics

For a very up-close and personal sound and maximum rejection of unwanted sound, it's hard to beat a mic actually placed on the talent, and in some cases it's the only practical way to capture usable sound. Because of the mic's position, it will pick up *chest tone*, the sound coming from the actor's chest, in addition to the sound from his mouth. For this reason, it's often difficult to match the sound of a lavalier with the more distant sound of a boomed mic. Also, unlike using a single boom mic, you'll need a lavalier for each actor, which means you'll also need a mixer and operator if you're using more than two mics. On high-budget films, mics are often recorded on separate tracks using a double-system approach or using a video recorder with more than two audio tracks.

Lavalier mics are used either corded or with a wireless transmitter, although some compact recorders are available that allow the sound to be captured on a pocket-size device. Lavaliers come with clips or tie-tack mounts, or can be secured with tape; some are small enough to go through a buttonhole with the cable secured with tape from the back side of the fabric. If you don't mind the mic being visible in the shot, the clips work fine, and you can use a windscreen. These are made of foam, and for some mics, they're available in a variety of colors to blend with the talent's clothing.

Hiding the mic under clothing is more problematic. Many fabrics will cause a lot of noise when they rub against the mic, so very smooth fabrics such as silk or one of the synthetic fibers are a good choices. (So since when does the sound technician ever have a say in the talent's wardrobe selection?) Don't use a windscreen under clothing because its rough surface will make noise when rubbing against almost any fabric. It's often helpful to tape the mic directly to the actor's skin, or to the inside of a garment to minimize this movement. Avoid taping over the actual microphone. Remember, too, that the first few inches of the microphone cable are also sensitive to vibration and handling noise, so it should be taped securely. Some people say that surgical tape is better for this purpose than gaffer tape since it has a softer adhesive.

Surgical tape can also be used to secure the mic directly to the skin. One sound man supplemented this idea by having a machine shop fabricate Teflon "tapeable" skin mounts for his mics. The idea was that Teflon is very smooth and made almost no noise even when rubbing against coarse fabrics, and the shape of the machined disk kept the mic from contacting the clothing. Someone should make these as a commercial product!

Positioning a lavalier mic is always a compromise. Obviously, the closer it is to the actor's mouth, the less background noise you'll get. In the real world, however, putting the mic very close (like on the collar of a shirt) creates highly variable sound depending on the direction the actor turns his head. Turning away from the mic makes the sound muffled and weaker, turning toward the mic makes it much louder and brighter. For better sound texture and naturalness, put the mic a bit farther away so that the change in distance when the actor turns his head is minimized. The best spot seems to be near the bottom of the breastbone. Keeping the mic away from the mouth also allows some of the "ambience" of the room to be captured, making the voice texture more natural.

One creative way of hiding a mic is to make a hole in the fabric behind the pocket of a shirt, snake the cable through the hole and tape the mic on the inside edge at the top of the pocket. As an alternative, you can make a hole almost anywhere in a shirt, put the mic through the hole and secure it to the fabric with a small blob of rubber cement or "Goop" – the kind that's fast-drying and easily removable. Then, cut a tiny bit of fabric from the shirt tail (just slightly larger than the mic) and secure it to the mic's outer case with a bit of cement. Obviously, choose the tiniest mic you can find if you want to hide it. Remember, too, that if you can keep the mic fairly far away from the mouth (maybe 12 inches or so) you will be able to able to avoid having it seen in revealing closeups.

Also, try to help the talent remember that they're wired. I can't tell you how many mics and cables I've seen broken because an actor walks out of a scene to take a break, forgetting he's still hooked up.

About Sound Perspective

Be aware of the picture when recording the sound. Whatever your mic technique, keep in mind that the perspective of the sound should match the picture – sound in a closeup should sound close, in a wide shot it should sound a bit more distant. This is especially important for dramatic films, but remember, perspective must be subtle. Dialog can get far-away sounding a lot quicker than pictures get far-away looking. In a closeup, both the camera and the mic might be 2 feet away from the talent. In a wide shot, the camera may be 20 feet away, but if you place the mic 20 feet away, the sound will be much too distant. You can retain perspective while still getting clean recordings by moving the mic just enough farther away so that you can just hear a slight difference. This tiny change is an audible cue to the audience that the sound matches the picture's perspective. When in doubt, err in the direction of sound that's too close rather than too far away.

If you've decided to use lavalier mics for a scene, perspective is more difficult to control while shooting, so it's usually left to the sound designer to make subtle adjustments in level and equalization to simulate different microphone positions. Sometimes a touch of artificial reverberation is added to dialog tracks for this purpose.

It's common practice for lavaliers to be supplemented by a cardioid or shotgun mic recorded on a separate track. In post production, this mic can be mixed with the lavalier(s) to capture more ambience and create more natural-sounding dialog.

Using Wireless

There's a very strong appeal to using wireless mics. They have become increasingly reliable and, within their limitations, their quality comes very close to the wired equivalent. If you plan to use them, keep their limitations in mind, however.

First, be sure the frequencies (channels) your wireless systems use are clear in the area you want to shoot. This won't be a problem if you're shooting out in the wilderness, but you may very well find that in a city (and especially during a newsworthy event), other people may be using the same slice of spectrum your wireless systems need to work. While inexpensive wireless systems can perform well under good conditions, they are often limited to one or two frequencies. If you have two identical systems, each with two frequencies, you have no choice but to use those two channels. Interference on either of those channels can stop your shoot in its tracks. Even without external interference, you can't add a third similar system and expect to use three mics at the same time. So, in choosing a system for a particular job, be sure you have enough channels for the number of mics you're using, and options of other frequencies should you run into interference issues.

Interference can come from a variety of sources besides other wireless mic systems, including two-way radios, broadcasters, electric motors, fluorescent lights, microwave ovens, wireless computer networks, cordless phones, cell phones, Teleprompters, or even from the camera itself. You can minimize interference and generally improve the performance of any wireless system by putting the receiver as close as possible to the actors (even hiding it in the shot) and hard-wiring it from there to the camera.

About Audio Frequencies

In the technology section, we discussed audio frequencies as part of equipment specifications, but it's also important to have a grasp of what frequencies make up real sounds. What you'll be recording in the field during shooting will be mostly dialog, the human voice. The telephone system, designed specifically for transmission of speech, has always been restricted to a narrow band of frequencies, about 300-3,000 Hz, a range that provides adequate intelligibility, though it has the familiar "tinny" sound.

The bottom end of the energy from the typical male speaking voice is 200-250 Hz, the female or child's voice starts about 400 Hz. This part of the speech spectrum carries the vowels. At the top end are lower energy sounds, mostly the *sibilants,* the consonants. The sibilant energy is maximum around 2,500 Hz., but a lot of the naturalness and presence is carried by the delicate "s","f",and "t" sounds with some energy up to the limit of high-frequency audibility (up to 20,000 Hz). For most of the movie industry's history, theater sound has had very little reproduced sound above about 8,000 Hz, so the extreme highs don't add a lot to dialog, although they can certainly enhance music and sound effects. These subtle sounds seem to be relatively unimportant in everyday life, too, since hearing tests don't ordinarily go past 8,000 Hz; most people over age 50 don't have much hearing above that, even if they have "normal" hearing.

The point is, if you are able to record dialog that covers roughly 100-10,000 Hz, it will be more than adequate and will sound very natural. What you need to learn is how to tell if you have noise in that range that will interfere with the dialog, and if the noise can be effectively removed during post-production.

You'll seldom be bothered by noise over 8,000 Hz, but at the low end you'll encounter a lot. Things like air conditioner rumble, low traffic sounds, or even hum picked up by your mic cables may fall below the critical 200 Hz. low end of speech. Wind noise, too, can be removed if it's low-frequency. One critical factor: if you do have noise, be sure it is recorded cleanly, without distortion. If it is recorded at too high a level or if any part of the recording chain (microphone, mixer, camcorder) is overloaded, *harmonic distortion* will be introduced. By definition, harmonic distortion means that *harmonics* are generated that weren't present in the original sound. These are multiples of the original frequencies. For example, if the original sound is around 100 Hz, harmonics will be generated at 200, 300, 400 Hz, etc., and these harmonics are in the speech range, even when the original sound was not.

Many shotgun mics (and some of the other varieties) include a switchable *low-cut filter*, also called a *high-pass filter.* Most field mixers include similar filters, and they are also available as "in-line" units that can be inserted in an XLR cable. Their function is to "roll off" (reduce) the frequencies below the speech frequencies and will do a lot to keep your original recording as clean as possible. When recording dialog in the field, it's a good idea to use the filter. It will keep the worst of the low-frequency noise from ever getting recorded, or at least will minimize the possibility of harmonics of the noise frequencies being recorded. While some sound technicians feel that the in-mic filters reduce the warmth and richness of speech, others feel they keep the recordings from getting "boomy". In either case, the low frequencies can be adjusted for tonality in audio post-production. Also, one low-cut filter is enough. Don't use two (the one in the mic *and* the one in the mixer), or you'll begin to lose the low frequencies in the dialog.

You should also be able to recognize constant-frequency noise, since it can often be removed during post-production using currently available software tools. Devices that operate at constant speed (such as fans and other electric motors) create such noise, and the software can identify them from samples of the sound and effectively reduce them.

Looping

When it's not possible to record usable dialog in the field, it's necessary to resort to *automatic dialog replacement* (abbreviated *ADR*), done after the completion of editing. Some editing software has the ability to do dialog replacement, also called *looping*. In this process, the actors (working in a recording studio) listen to the originally recorded dialog in headphones while watching the picture and re-voicing the dialog in sync with the picture, usually one line at a time. It can be a laborious process, but not nearly as difficult as it was when film was spliced into physical loops, one for each line of dialog — hence the name "looping".

Even if you're going to be looping all the dialog in a scene, it's still important to get the cleanest sound you can during shooting. Why? The original location sound is the reference for the actor during looping. It conveys the timing, tone, texture and quality of the performance. In cases where actors deviate from the exact written words in the script, it's even more important to know exactly what was said. (More about looping in the Post-Production section.)

Recording Sound Effects

In Hollywood, there are many specialists who make their living recording high-quality sound effects. Just because you're recording dialog in a scene doesn't mean the incidental sounds will always be what you want them to be. You'll also want some additional sound effects. Getting these sounds in the field can make the sound designer's job during post-production much easier. I find it helpful to imagine what I'd want to hear with the scene if there were no dialog, and that's what I record.

If, for example, you've shot a dialog scene on a busy street, you need to remember that when the scene is cut, the traffic sounds will change at each edit, as will microphone's position and sound level. To keep sound consistent throughout the scene, it's a good idea to record some "ambient" sound of the traffic, to be mixed in with the finished scene to "cover" the edits in the dialog track. Getting good ambience is vital for any scene shot in a noisy location. Unlike dialog, ambient sounds benefit from the full audible frequency range, so take out the high-pass or low-cut filters you would use for recording speech. Strong low frequencies (especially) can add richness to the depiction of the scene. During post-production, these tracks can be mixed with the dialog, but have their levels and equalizations adjusted separately, allowing the background sounds to be "wrapped around" the actors' voices without interfering with them.

Some incidental sounds, such as a clock striking, bacon frying, a bat hitting a baseball or a toilet flushing, will sound much better if recorded "up close" to get the right texture. Other effects, such as tires squealing or gunshots sound much better if recorded from a distance.

Recording Narration

While professional narration is recorded in a studio, it's sometimes necessary to do the recording in the field. Because you can work the mic much closer to the talent when you're not worried about it being in the shot, almost any quiet location in a relatively echo-free room works just fine. I've used my living room, a hotel room, or even my walk-in closet.

The classic mistake in recording narration is micing too close. For the most natural-sounding voice recording, a distance of 12 to 18 inches from the mic is best. Another common mistake is having the talent speak directly into the mic. While all mics are directional (at least at high frequencies), the human mouth is less so. Keeping this in mind, the mic should be aimed directly at the lips, but positioned at a 45-degree angle. This simple step will avoid the dreaded pops from the Ps, and can eliminate the need for a windscreen. If you hold your hand in front of your face and say the phrase, "Peter Piper picked a peck of pickled peppers," you can feel these pops – the *plosives.* Hold your hand at a 45-degree angle to your face and try it again. You'll find that you can't feel the pops at all, so the trick works with any mic, with or without a windscreen. (For the purist, it's true the any mic's performance is audibly and measurably degraded, however slightly, by a windscreen.) In studios, mics are often fitted with pop filters – they look like crochet hoops covered with pantyhose fabric. These are very effective in stopping pops, but are unnecessary if the mic is properly positioned and the talent is mindful of the problem.

For recording narration, I use a cardioid mic, preferably a condenser type. Ask the talent to hold their copy (script) on the side opposite the mic. This does two things: it keeps the plosives away from the mic, and the surface of the paper reflects some of the high frequency elements of the voice into the mic, creating a slightly crisper, more "open" timbre. Be sure the script is printed on only one side of the paper, and ask the talent to simply drop pages on the floor after they have been read. Using a slightly heaver-than-normal paper stock can help here, since it lands quietly. (In the golden age of radio drama, a special "silk paper" was developed to avoid paper noises.)

Position the mic near the center of the room, where possible, and ask the talent to stand rather than sit, or use a tall stool. I like to use a lightweight collapsible music stand (available from music stores) to hold the copy.

Try to avoid seating the narrator at a table because the reflections of the voice off the hard surface can introduce coloration into the sound. For the same reason, keep away from any hard surface, such as an untreated wall. If you must use a table, cover it with a heavy tablecloth, a piece of heavy felt, or even a blanket.

Before recording, turn off any noise-making devices: air conditioners, computers, ceiling fans, refrigerators.

It's fine to record narration on a camcorder (even one of the less expensive ones), though many people opt to record directly to the hard disk of their computer. For a laptop, there are high quality USB audio input adapters to make this easy, and a wide variety of simple audio recording (and editing) software is available for this kind of use. Portable solid-state recorders also do a great job. As in any recording, be sure to carefully monitor everything you record with good-quality headphones.

"Everything in the world has a spirit which is released by its sound."

Oscar Fischinger

3.5 Special Effects

> ***"Special effects are characters... effects are essential elements. Just because you can't see them doesn't mean they aren't there."***
>
> ***Laurence Fishburne***

The Willing Suspension of Disbelief

Samuel Taylor Coleridge coined this phrase in writing about drama. The willingness of an audience to suspend their disbelief is a requirement for successful storytelling in any medium. Viewers of Star Trek must (at least temporarily) accept the existence of Klingons and warp drive. The purpose of effects is to reinforce disbelief, or, conversely, to make belief easier for the audience. It follows, then, that once an audience has suspended their disbelief, effects must be invisible and seamless to be successful in moving the story forward. Effects are illusions. The objective is to create a realistic result in a scene that couldn't happen in real life, or would be too dangerous or expensive to actually stage and shoot. Be warned that they are almost never easy, but today's tools make them far less daunting than they once were.

Special effects really consist of:

1) *Practical effects*, those that work like magic tricks that are performed before the camera and require no further processing,
2) *Visual effects* (called *optical effects* in pre-computer days) that require special shooting but are not fully accomplished until post-production is done,
3) *CGI* (computer generated imagery) which is created entirely in a computer, and
4) Hybrid effects that combine two or more of the above.

In reality, most effects are hybrids, requiring special attention during both shooting and post. Like so many topics we've discussed, special effects are really special and an in-depth treatment of them is beyond the scope of this book. This chapter will simply offer a few points to get you started in planning and shooting effects. Like everything else in filmmaking, planning and design are key to successful and believable effects.

Practical Effects

As implied above, practical effects occur in the camera and are accomplished on the set, even though the resulting shots may need to be "doctored" in post. The simplest practical effects are very common and fairly obvious – thinks like spraying water on a window to simulate rain, flashing strobe lights to create lightning, creating platform shoes to make an actor appear taller, "levitating" objects with monofilament thread, use of puppets and miniatures – the list goes on and on.

Practical effects can be extremely complex, too. In the 1951 film *Royal Wedding* (certainly long before computers were applied to filmmaking), Fred Astaire appeared in a famous 4-minute sequence where he was dancing in a hotel room and got carried away, eventually dancing on the walls and the ceiling, suspending the law of gravity. The effect was accomplished by rotating the entire set (including the camera) 360 degrees. Early filmmakers were incredibly imaginative in creating effects, and like magicians, they were often reluctant to reveal how they were done.

A wide variety of practical effects were used countless times in filming classic western barroom brawls. A small industry developed in Hollywood, making props for action scenes, everything from liquor bottles made from sugar to breakaway balsa wood and styrofoam furniture. These props are still available, along with large sheets of "fake" glass that stuntmen can jump through, and explosive "*squibs*" that can simulate bullet hits. They also sell blank ammunition for hand guns, rifles and shot guns.

Hollywood has also spawned a small army of special effects experts, including *pyrotechnicians* and stunt men who can create a burning building, a fire or a "crash and burn" car chase. They also can create "breakaway" props, radio controlled automobiles that can be safely driven off cliffs, and convincing models for impossible-to-build or impossible-to-burn sets. Other shops offer smoke, dust, fog, wind, rain, and snow effects. There are also "monster shops" that create effects and props for science fiction and horror movies, and a host of shops that make realistic models of virtually anything. If you need complex practical effects, I'd strongly advise you to seek out one or more of these experts to assist with your project.

Practical effects are appealing because they are predictable and easier for non-experts to accomplish; you can be sure they're going to work, and you know they have worked when the shot is in the can. Also, if you have an amateur or professional magician in your Address Book, you may be able to get some help in designing your effects. Your creativity will be your best friend!

Basic Visual Effects

Today's movies are filled with visual effects, most of them made possible by computer technology. *CGI* (computer generated imagery) and sophisticated *compositing* have made virtually any effect possible. Like so many other topics, this one is very complex and it's far beyond the scope of this book to explore any but the most basic techniques. My effort here is to concentrate on a few ideas for doing convincing effects that you have a reasonably good chance of getting right on your first or second attempt. I'll also try to confine this discussion to effects you can do with your camera and the resources available inside most editing systems.

The creation of CGI is usually done in post-production and is a subject of yet another book, but during shooting it essential that you know exactly how any live action you are going to shoot will combine with the CGI. Equally important are scenes that are *composites*, a combination of two or more camera shots into a finished scene.

Any composite scene, whether used with CGI or not, requires careful planning if it is to succeed. *Read that last sentence again!* It's vital that all the elements in multiple shots that are to be combined match in lighting, texture, exposure and environment. Where possible, you should simulate the effect you're trying for and do a test, or better still a lot of tests. You want to know the effect is going to work before you commit time and resources to doing it for real.

If you're doing a low-budget film, keep the effects simple. The first rule is: Keep the camera position fixed if possible. Moving the camera will make creating the effect much more difficult, requiring accurate tracking and synchronizing of camera moves for the various elements. For the purposes of this chapter, we'll assume a fixed camera for all the visual effects. (If you want to move the camera, be prepared for a lot more work and be ready to hire an expert!) We'll start with some simple compositing effects that are easy to do, effective, convincing and don't require special skills. These effects will require an editor with the skills to do them, but for now, we'll assume your editor will be up to the task. The point is to be sure the elements are shot in a way that will make the editor very happy. You don't want to find problems with the shots when you get to post-production!

For any special effect, there are three words to remember: Test, test and test. Take the time to be sure it's going to work before you commit.

The Split Screen

Here's an effect that's been done since the beginning of cinema. It was hard on film, but it's very easy in digital. Also, it's the foundation for many different kinds of composite scenes.

Imagine a scene: Martha enters the kitchen to find her twin sister, Wilma, seated at the table reading the newspaper. Of course, the actor playing Martha doesn't have a twin sister, so the purpose of our effect is to create a convincing illusion that she does. The script says that all that's supposed to happen in this particular shot is that they are surprised to see each other. Actually, what we're creating is two different shots, one of Martha and one of Wilma, which will be combined during editing. It's done by creating a "wipe" or simple *matte* between the two shots, but for the effect to work, the matte must be invisible. That's why is vital that everything in the scene except the two characters must be identical. It's also important that neither character ever moves into the space in front of the other – this would obviously spoil the illusion. (Overlaps like this are quite possible and not terribly difficult, but not in this simple version of the effect.)

Think of a matte as a separate image that defines the foreground and background. In a simple split screen, the background is the first scene you shoot, the foreground is placed in front of it – in this case, the second scene. In the matte, that part of the frame where the foreground is to show (be opaque) is white, the rest is black. All composites are based on mattes, as you will see.

Here's how to do a simple split screen: First, put the camera on the tripod, frame the shot to include where the action is to happen, and lock it down so it's impossible for the camera to accidentally be moved. Set the focus for the approximate position of the two characters (hopefully at a point that will keep them both in focus), then lock the focus. Get the exposure and white balance right and lock those, too.

Next, shoot a *clean plate*. This is simply a shot of the background with neither of the characters in place. While it's not likely to be needed in this particular shot, it's a good habit to get into because sometimes an editor or compositing artist may need background elements to make "fixes" during post-production.

Now, shoot the first character (say it's Wilma), getting the action the way you want it. If one character must react to the other based on dialog, have someone else read the second character's lines for timing purposes, getting the pace as close as possible to the way you want the scene to play. (To enhance the effect, you might want to let the first character cross the second character's "space" when she enters – nothing says the matte has to be there at the beginning of the shot. Remember, too that the matte can move during the shot if necessary.) Pick the best take and note where Wilma was, maybe taking a still photograph for reference.

When you shoot the second character (Martha), the main consideration is that she doesn't cross in front of Wilma at a time in the scene where the first character will be there. Make sure their shadows don't overlap, either.

The effect will be easiest if the editor only has to do a simple straight-line "wipe" between the two shots to create the matte for the composite, but in actuality, the matte can be any shape or can even change shapes and/or move during the shot – depending on the skill of your editor.

Bluescreen and Greenscreen

Remember, I said the split screen is basic to all composites? Well, bluescreen and greenscreen are just a variation on a theme. (For convenience, I'll refer to these effects just as "bluescreen", though they have the same effect. Later, we'll discuss the choice of screen colors.)

The classic use of bluescreen is the *chromakey* (or *chroma-key*), and you see it on TV everyday: the weatherman in front of his map. In this case, the weatherman himself is the foreground image, shot in front of a solid blue background (the bluescreen itself), and the weather map is the background. The chromakey system looks at the foreground image and everywhere it finds blue, it substitutes the background image (the weather map). In effect, the system has created a matte in the shape of the weatherman. This matte works in the same way as the wipe described in the previous section on split screen – it defines what part of the final composite comes from the foreground image and where the background shows through.

So you don't get too confused: In the film world, it's called a matte, in the video world it's called a *key* and in the computer graphics world it's called an *alpha channel* – all are functionally the same thing. When you shoot a foreground in front of a bluescreen, you're actually shooting plain old video, but the compositing software can detect the blue and create a matte from it. If the foreground image is created in a computer, it can be made to contain an alpha channel (or matte), which automatically tells the editing system what part of it is supposed to be transparent and what part should be opaque.

Note that more sophisticated compositing software can work not only for solid objects, but can also handle transparent/translucent objects, such as glass or smoke (within limits). It can also handle shadows.

Choosing a Screen Color

There are many factors involved in choosing a background color for bluescreen or greenscreen effects. The first consideration is the color of the foreground objects. If you're shooting a girl in a bright green dress, it's obvious that you don't want to use green as your screen color since the background will show through her clothing and she'll partially disappear. Same with blue – no bluescreen with blue clothing. It's true, however, that modern compositing software can distinguish quite subtle differences in color, so the match of clothing color to screen color has to be fairly close to cause serious problems.

Hollywood uses green almost exclusively because the green layer in color negative film captures somewhat more resolution than the blue layer. The same is true of most video cameras. It's also true that blue clothing is more common than bright green, so the odds are in your favor if you use green. Green also works better for metallic foreground objects, which tend to have a blue component. One disadvantage of green is that with some compositing software use of a green background can cause color shifts in yellow tones in the foreground. Another less technical reason to choose blue is that working all day on a large greenscreen can make you nauseous.

It's important that the screen color be as close to ideal as possible. For good results, buy a background or paint that's designed for the purpose. Rosco's (www.rosco.com) Ultimatte blue and green are some of the best. (Ultimatte is the company that created the first high-quality bluescreen equipment for television.)

Also, keep in mind that the screen doesn't have to be blue or green. It can actually be any saturated color, even red or yellow. Because flesh tones contain minimal amounts of blue and green, that's why those colors are normally used.

Bluescreen Shooting Considerations

Background, lighting and exposure are very important to achieving a convincing result with bluescreen. The color background must be lit as evenly as possible. This is especially important if shadows are to be seen in the final composite since any shadows you can see will show and it may be difficult to remove them later. The light level on the screen background should be the same (in foot-candles) as the foreground subject key light. Shadows on the background should be no brighter than the foreground fill level. Your light meter can be your best friend when shooting for bluescreen. Maintaining correct background light levels will not only provide the best composite of the foreground, but will make shadows cleaner and more convincing. Incidentally, imperfections in the background lighting can produce unwanted shadows, so be careful to avoid them. Good, clean shadows can enhance the effect and can help prevent the illusion that the foreground is "pasted" on the background.

If shadows are important to the effect you're after, remember how they behave in the real world. It can be very disconcerting for a foreground shadow to fall flat on a studio floor, while the subject's placement against the background would seem to demand that the shadow fall on a wall! Use Ultimatte-painted flats or boxes to avoid this problem. Tape the joints between these "pseudo props" and the floor and paint over the tape to be sure you don't have seams that don't line up in the final composite. Imperfections or foreground objects (such as a mike boom) can be probably masked in post, but are very troublesome if their shadows are in the shot.

The texture of the foreground lighting should match the intended background as closely as possible. If the background is a cloudy-day scene, for example, the foreground lighting should be very soft and even. Of course, shadows should fall in the same direction in both foreground and background. General color of light should also be matched. For example, warm lighting colors would be appropriate if the background is a sunset. Don't depend too heavily on color correction in post to match lighting.

It's also important to avoid too much lighting contrast. Lighting ratios should be kept at no more than 6 to 1, especially if shadows are to be preserved in the final composite. It's vital that there's enough light in the shadow areas on the background that the camera can get a clean image of the screen color in the shadows – otherwise electronic noise can make the shadows "grainy".

In general, try to keep the foreground subjects as far from the screen background as possible to minimize color contamination. For the same reason, it is often helpful to shield the foreground from any light reflecting from areas of background that are not in the shot.

It is sometimes helpful to color-compensate subject backlights by using straw gel. Since the background will show through hair, transparent objects, and around soft edges (causing them to fully or partially disappear or get "ragged"), colored backlight tends to cancel this color contamination and leads to a cleaner looking composite. Be careful to shield backlights from the camera. Lens flare can produce unpredictable results, so try to avoid light sources in the foreground shot.

Remember, also, that shiny objects can be troublesome, since they can reflect the background color into the lens, producing "holes" in the foreground. Dulling spray and touch-up in post can help solve these problems.

Matching foreground and background camera angles and focal lengths can be critical to producing a good illusion. This is particularly true if a foreground subject is to be seen head-to-foot, or if a person in the foreground is to move toward or away from the camera. Mismatched angles will result in distorted perspective such as a person who appears to rise off the floor as he walks. When matching perspective between foreground and background it is very helpful to keep detailed notes of camera height, distance to subject and lens focal length. Focus settings and f-stops can also have an impact, particularly when long focal lengths are used.

Bluescreen generally requires a locked-off camera for both foreground and background shots, for obvious reasons. Camera moves can be accomplished with some difficulty if the scene demands them. Convincing dolly moves are not too difficult if the foreground does not include the floor. An actor can simply simulate walking during the move, for example, with convincing results. Similarly, shots such as close-ups of a person on a motorcycle on a highway can be accomplished with relative ease through proper coordination of foreground and background.

Limited pans and zooms can be accomplished in post by digitally enlarging the scene and moving the image, but this demands the very highest quality foreground and background images, since the finished composite must be "blown up", which may reveal any imperfections.

A more sophisticated alternative for moves is motion control of the camera. Computerized *motion control* systems can operate pan, tilt, focus and zoom, even camera cranes and dollies. When a foreground or background is shot using the system, the computer "memorizes" the camera move and repeats it exactly during the shooting of the complimentary scene. While the use of these robotic systems is difficult, costly and time-consuming, the results can be very impressive. If you want to try it, hire a pro!

Another popular use of bluescreen is putting images on TV sets or computer monitors when they're not actually there during shooting. To do this, create a simple blue (or green) graphic field that will fill up the monitor and display it during shooting. Alternatively, just cut a blue or green card the shape of the screen and cover the screen with the card. In post, the appropriate image can be placed on the screen. If camera moves are needed, *motion tracking* can keep the image in the right place.

Bluescreen Exposure

In ordinary field videography, exposure can be determined quite accurately by simply opening the lens until the "zebra" indicators appear in the viewfinder. Bluescreen requires more precision, and a waveform monitor is very helpful. There should be no "clipping" in the camera; white levels should be held at or slightly below 100 IRE. Ideally, the background color (blue or green) should show 50-60 units of luminance, and in no case should it fall below 30 units of chroma. Upper limits of background chroma should not exceed 100 IRE. The camera should be balanced using its automatic white balance or 3200K preset (depending on lighting). Camera "painting" with a camera-control unit should be avoided, since this action can distort the critical background color. Make adjustments in the color of the subject through lighting or color-correction in post.

Is Your Camcorder Good Enough?

The camera and lens used for bluescreen shooting are critical to a high-quality finished result. Good subjective picture quality is not necessarily enough to ensure that satisfactory composites can be made. Here are a few things to watch for:

- The camera should use true RGB processing internally. Some cameras (including low-end single-chip cameras) use a hybrid approach here which produces reduced resolution in the color channels, yielding poor results.
- A high-quality lens is vital for good bluescreen performance.

- Fog, star or soft-focus filters should be avoided if possible. If a soft-focus effect is desired, it is strongly recommended that the softening effect be applied during post-production.

A recording format that uses 4:2:2 (or better still 4:4:4) color sampling will do a better job with bluescreen, simply because there's more color information in the signal. This includes all the major digital formats except DV, DVCam, DVCPro-25, and prosumer-level AVCHD, which use 4:1:1 (or 4:1:0) color sampling. While reasonable results can be achieved in some cases with these formats, you're much safer with one of the other formats. This limitation only applies to foreground scenes shot on blue or green; the background format doesn't matter since the matte is not derived from it.

On high-end projects, 4:4:4 color sampling is used, with the recordings being done direct to hard-disk arrays. (No tape format can handle the necessary quantity of data.) While it's visually difficult to see the difference between 4:4:4 and 4:2:2 on normal scenes, 4:4:4 provides twice the color resolution and thus can yield higher-quality composites.

If possible, shoot progressive for bluescreen, using a camera that supports 480p, 720p or 1080p. Interlaced formats (480i, 1080i) will produce inferior results. (See Chapter 2.3.)

Difference Mattes

A relatively new compositing technique is the *difference matte* or *subtraction matte*. Some compositing software can create a matte by subtracting one scene from another. Let's see how this method could be used. Suppose we have a shot of an airplane (with the camera locked down!) flying through the frame against a clear sky. In the final shot, we want the plane flying in front of a mountain range. We take a still frame of the empty sky and use it as our reference in creating the subtraction matte. When the airplane comes into the moving shot, it creates differences between the frames in which it appears and the shot of the sky. These differences are used to calculate the matte. Now we have a scene of just the airplane against a transparent background, and this new shot can be placed in front of any background, such as the mountain range.

It's important to understand the limitations of this process, however. For example, if you want a shot of a car flying through the air, you can't just shoot the car driving through a parking lot and hope to subtract out the parking lot. Why not? Because the shadow of the car will create differences, too, and thus will show in the finished composite. You could use the technique to create a parking lot full of identical cars, however.

A difference matte could have been used for our original split screen with Martha and Wilma (see above), however. If the clean plate (the shot with neither character in it) were used as the reference, Martha could have moved in front of

Wilma, no problem. Can you figure out how it would be possible to use subtraction mattes to allow either character to pass in front of the other?

While recording format doesn't matter for subtraction mattes, it's important that your camera is creating the cleanest possible video. Any noise in the image will create differences between frames and lead to unsatisfactory or unpredictable results. Always test first!

Overcranking and Undercranking

Film cameras can easily run at speeds other than the normal 24 (or 25) frames per second. Running the camera faster than normal is called *overcranking,* and creates slow motion effects. Similarly, *undercranking* speeds up the action. For example, shooting 48 frames per second and projecting the film at 24 fps will make the action on the screen take twice as long to happen as it did during shooting.

Except for a few special purpose cameras, there's no video equivalent to overcranking. However, since interlaced video cameras actually create sixty (or fifty) images per second, – instead of the 24 images produced by a film camera – convincing slow motion effects can be created during post-production, particularly when *frame-blending* is used. When shooting video for slow motion (often called *slo-mo*), use the normal shutter speed for the smoothest motion; use a fast shutter speed to minimize motion blur. Again, do some tests to be sure you can accomplish the effect you want.

Undercranking is easy. In post production, speeding up the action merely eliminates frames. For example, to get double speed, you would delete every other frame from the shot. Use of frame blending can convincingly simulate the motion blur you'd see in undercranked film. Editing and special effects software can also do *time mapping* (changing the speed within a shot), an effect that's very difficult to accomplish using film.

Other Techniques

Here are some other techniques you may want to use. They all require an advanced level of skill to use, so consult a pro (or read a lot more books!) before you try them in your film.

- *Wire removal* is getting rid of wires that suspend props or actors. Many software packages contain wire removal tools.
- *Motion tracking* involves placing *targets* on props, actors or backgrounds. They're used in post-production to track movement within a scene or camera moves. Current compositing software contains trackers that can keep objects aligned to the sub-pixel level, even during camera and subject moves. The purpose of the targets is to provide high-contrast

points in the image that the software can readily identify from frame to frame throughout the shot. Often they are simply Xs made from pieces of black or white tape, though any high-contrast point in the image can be used. There should be enough targets or tracking points to assure the changing geometry of the object being tracked is accounted for. For example, if a person is carrying a picture frame and you want to put moving video in the frame, it helps to track all four corners, so the frame can be tracked in any position. It's also a lot easier if none of the tracking targets go out of the camera's view during the scene.

- *Double exposures* were used in early films by running the film through the camera more than once. In the digital world, the separate exposures are combined during post-production. An example might be adding smoke or flames to a scene, or Marley's ghost in *A Christmas Carol.*

"One man's magic is another man's engineering."

...Robert Heinlein

PART 4

POST-PRODUCTION

"If I wanted to be frivolous, I might say that everything that precedes editing is merely a way of producing film to edit."

Stanley Kubrick

The digital age has had its most profound effect on filmmaking in the post-production arena. A significant aspect of editing in the digital domain is the ability to visualize your film, to instantly see the results of everything you do. Equally important is the ease of making changes. Unlike traditional film techniques, digital editing is non-destructive. You don't destroy your media when you make a cut.

The ability to edit pictures and sounds and to create complex special effects on an affordable personal computer is genuinely revolutionary. Equally important, software allows the same computer to create the final release in nearly every possible form.

In filmmaking, it's now almost possible to satisfy your champagne tastes on a beer budget!

4.1 Editing 101

"Editing is the creative act of combining two discreet ideas to create a third, disparate concept in the mind of the viewer"

Jay Ankeney

The Puzzle of Editing

One fact stands out: if you give the same production elements to ten different editors, you'll end up with ten distinctly different films. This chapter looks at some aspects of the artistic side of editing, then in the next chapter we'll turn to the technical side and how-tos for actual editing systems.

Award-winning editor, Jay Ankeney, talks about editing's Holy Trinity: Context, Contrast and Rhythm. These demand shooting for coverage, as described in the Production section, and we should consider each of them.

Context relates to the way scenes are assembled to propel the story forward. In a dramatic film, it's driven by the script; in a documentary it defines the relationship of one scene to the next. It's all about what happens and what's said, and it's driven by the director's vision for the film.

Changing the order of scenes can make them tell profoundly different stories. For example, take these three seemingly unrelated shots:

1. A big explosion
2. A group of people running down a city street
3. A man going to a window and looking out.

In the order shown, when we see the explosion, it's implied that the people are running away from a dangerous situation, and that the man is going to the window to see what's happened, having heard the explosion.

If we put shot 3 first, followed by shot 1, we imply that the person knows what is going to happen, but if shot 2 is next, we will think he's heard the people and is wondering what's going on, especially if the sound of the people comes in before the cut. You can see the possibilities.

Contrast refers to the relationships built from shot to shot within a scene, or between scenes. Back in the section on shooting, we talked about coverage and getting shots that were different enough from each other to "cut" nicely. Cuts between scenes that are too much alike look like a mistake or glitch, which is why we avoid the dreaded jump cut except for a deliberate jarring effect. Even when they're not jump cuts, going from one wide shot to another on the same scene doesn't provide the contrast that qualifies a good cut. Skillful juxtaposition of varying points of view is key to cuts that "flow smoothly past the eye". Use of cutaways and insert shots builds contrast.

Rhythm refers to the pace of the cut and how it relates to the action, dialog, music and sound effects. In a dramatic film, the rhythm of the cut should match the mood of the scene – a quiet scene of a mother rocking her baby to sleep will have a slower tempo than a frenetic chase scene. Rhythm also has to do with showing the viewer what he wants to see when he wants to see it. Think about how you might look at a scene as an observer. Where would you look? And when? What would motivate you to change what you're looking at? Beginning editors tend to make scenes too long. As one editor put it, "Shots should be long enough to see what needs to be seen, and not a frame longer."

Matching

A part of the rhythm of your cut has to do with matching. When you look around at a scene in real life, your act of looking doesn't affect the pace of the action going on around you. Cuts should work the same way, so motion flows smoothly past the cut. Matching demands that the action is at the right point in time before and after the cut. There are points at which cuts are most graceful. Suppose you have two shots of a man chopping down a tree. One is a wide shot showing the man, the tree and the surrounding forest. The other is a medium shot of the man and his ax. The shots have the right context and contrast, but to get the rhythm right, the cut between the shots must take place at the right point in time. With repetitive motion like chopping wood, the best cut points are at the stops – the top of the stroke or when the ax hits the tree. If you choose frames where the ax is in the same position, the cut should match properly.

Making a cut during motion is a bit different. If you match the exact position on both outgoing and incoming shots, the motion will appear to pause or jump at the edit. For cuts during movement, it helps to leave out a frame or two, depending on the speed of the motion.

If you've read Chapter 3.1, you know that a lot of the credit for the success of the cut belongs to your director, and to the footage that's been provided for the editor to work with. A review of that chapter can help you make the best use of the shots, avoiding the dreaded jump cut and maintaining the line of action.

Who Takes the Lead?

One of the hardest parts of editing is deciding where to start. Assuming you have all your elements (footage, narration, graphic images, etc.) loaded on your computer, the first step is getting rid of everything that's obviously no good. You may have done this in advance, capturing only the good stuff, or you may capture everything and then sort it all out.

What you do when will depend on the film, of course. A documentary will probably be arranged by location or subject while a dramatic film will be broken down into scenes. In either case, you'll want to organize your footage into some kind of easily-manageable categories. Once that's done, I like to pick a starting scene. It may be at the beginning of the film, but it also may be a scene that I find particularly interesting, challenging, or one that's pivotal for the story.

The first thing to decide about any scene is whether it's driven by picture or soundtrack. An action scene may have very little dialog, so the entire pace is determined by the order of events. For example, a horse race might show the horses getting into the starting gate before the race, the start, the race itself, and the finish. While chronological order is important, length isn't. Here's where one of films greatest strengths, *the manipulation of time*, comes into play. A cut can cover a multitude of sins. Maybe a horse balks going into the starting gate. No problem. Just put in a cutaway of the crowd, or another horse and rider. In any filmed sequence, you can rest assured that the audience will lose track of time. A 2-second cutaway can cover the two minutes it takes a rider to get from the stable to the track.

Sometimes scenes are driven by music. The Music Video is a classic example. In this case, the music determines (or at least supplements) the rhythm of the cut, along with context that might go along with the lyrics. Cuts follow beats and can reinforce key elements in the music. Quick cuts can track with drum flourishes and soft dissolves can embellish soft musical transitions.

Documentaries are often driven by narration. By carefully matching the length of scenes to phrases or sentences in narration, an editor can create interesting transitions between narration and on-camera dialog.

Scenes with dialog are always driven by the soundtrack. In starting to edit a dialog scene, I'll have a pretty good idea of which camera angles I want to use for which sections, so I like to build the first rough cut by simply putting the lines in order, concentrating on making the dialog sound natural with clean edits, and paying little attention to the picture cuts. Once the scene *sounds* right, then I adjust the picture, sliding edits and putting in cutaways and reaction shots that reinforce the story.

The Importance of the Split Edit

Beginning editors will usually make audio and video cuts occur at the same time – when actor A is speaking, we see actor A; when actor B talks, cut audio and video to actor B. Contrast this with the way you'd watch the conversation between A and B. If A interrupts B, for example, you would hear A before you look at him. If A says something to which you think B might react, you look at B while A continues to speak. In a live TV show, the director will freely switch between shots independent of the audio, cutting to the camera angle that seems most appropriate at the time. In either case, audio and video cuts often don't happen at the same time. In fact, they usually don't.

In live TV, *split edits* (edits occurring at different times for sound and picture) happen quite naturally. In cutting together different coverage angles of a scene during editing, however, it's common to start with simultaneous audio and video edits. The objective here is to make the audio sound right, with the proper pace and tone. Then, in polishing the edit, moving the video cuts away from the audio edits can improve the flow. Skillful use of split edits is a major differentiator between amateurish and professional editing, particularly for scenes containing dialog. Let the audience see the shot that drives the story, not necessarily the person talking.

Modern editing software makes split edits very easy; they allow you to "roll" a video edit's position without affecting the audio. When doing split edits, it's often necessary to sync up sound from one take with picture from another. An example might be when cutting from a closeup to a 2-shot. If you're on a closeup of actor A, for example, and you want her dialog to finish a sentence in a 2-shot with actor B, it will often sound best if the closeup audio is what you use. This makes it necessary to sync up the 2-shot video with the closeup audio, slipping it to match. If your actors are consistent in their performances, this can be easy; if they're not, it can be impossible, so you may need to make an audio edit in the middle of a sentence or even in the middle of a word.

Some software packages offer a multicamera option that allows you to simulate what happens in a live-switched TV show. Although designed for switching between multiple cameras that have been used to shoot the same action from different angles, some editors use the multicamera tool for film-style shooting as well. You can approximately "sync up" your master shot and closeup takes and get an instant rough cut. Once done, the cut can be polished just as if you'd done it the old-fashioned way.

Transitions

Harking back to the differences between film and television cultures, it's still true that filmmakers use the simple cut more than all other transitions combined. One reason for this is that for most of the history of film, a cut was the only easy transition – accomplished with a splice in the film. All other effects were created during printing processes; they were expensive, time consuming, and couldn't be previewed by the editor.

Video editing systems offer a bewildering variety of transition effects, from dissolves through page turns and flips, wipes of any shape and size, ripples and defocuses. Before the advent of computer-based editing, these effects were accomplished in video switchers and expensive digital effects hardware. Video editors sometimes were guilty of using extravagant effects simply because they had the tools to accomplish them, not because they added anything to the story. These effects have their place, but use them sparingly and judiciously, especially in dramatic or documentary films. If they propel the story, use them. If not, don't.

After the straight cut, the dissolve (or cross-dissolve) is most common. Traditionally used to indicate a passage of time, dissolves are also frequently for montages. A dissolve from or to black is called a *fade*, either a *fade-in* or a *fade-out*; a fade-out followed by a fade-in is called a *dip-to-black*.

Always consider using an unexpected transition. While tradition calls for opening a scene with an establishing shot, breaking this rule can create some wonderful transitions. Starting a scene with an extreme closeup of a character delivering a key line, or even a cutaway of a key element can quickly set the stage for a new scene. Imagine starting a chase scene, for example, with a tight shot of a hot car's wheel spinning and kicking out a plume of smoke as it speeds off down the street.

Experiment!

Editing is not a quick process, no matter what system you're using. With experience, editors learn to do the cut in their head. They learn to visualize how various scenes and transitions work together and can have a good idea how the cut is going to go before they ever start editing. Even so, it's a good idea to try variations, and editing systems make this much easier than was possible with traditional film or video techniques. Veteran editors often assemble each scene into a sequence, then put the sequences together to create the final film, a technique sometimes called *nesting*. What approach an editor uses is a highly individual choice. Over time, you'll develop a way that suits you and is appropriate for each project.

"When in doubt, leave it out."

Anonymous

4.2 Editing Technology

"Cut!"

Alfred Hitchcock

Of Sprockets and Rewinds

In the golden age of movies, rolls of film were shipped to the laboratory for processing after each day of shooting. Once processed, a positive print was made of the footage, or of selected takes, and the "edge numbers" placed on each foot of film during manufacture were printed along with the images. This "workprint" was sent to the editor. Simultaneously, the original sound recordings (usually on 1/4-inch audio tape) were sent to a sound technician for transfer to 16mm or 35mm magnetic film. The editor's first step was the laborious task of "syncing up" the workprint with the soundtrack(s) for the screening of the "dailies" – the first time pictures could be viewed with sound. Only then could actual editing begin – the process of literally cutting the film into a finished movie. (The word *cutting* is still applied to film editing.) It was done on a *Moviola* or flatbed editing table, mechanical devices that allowed the picture to be viewed, the sound to be reproduced, and kept "in sync". Effects (even simple dissolves or titles) required "*opticals*" – selective combination of multiple negatives using optical printers.

After all this labor of cutting the workprint, the original negative was cut to match the workprint edit, using the edge numbers as a guide, a process called *negative cutting*, *matching*, or *conforming*. A special *interpositive* print was made from the original negative, and one or more *internegatives* were made from this. Final "release" prints were made from the internegative. At the same time, the multiple magnetic film soundtracks were played back together on special synchronized players (called *interlocked dubbers*) and mixed into a final master magnetic track. From this "mix", an *optical soundtrack* was created, to be printed onto each release print. All this was extremely expensive and time-consuming, but it's the way all movies were made until the 1980s when computers began to have their impact.

In the early days of television, everything was either live or on film, so making a TV show that wasn't live was literally making a film, just like it was done for the big screen, though often on 16mm instead of 35mm. Videotape arrived on the scene in the mid 1950s, but it was to be many years before tape could be edited with anything near the flexibility that film offered, so TV recording was really just "live to tape".

Early analog videotape editing was (like film) "cuts only". A system consisted of a "source" VTR and a "record" VTR, and editing was done by selective copying. The machines were synchronized (more or less accurately) by cuing both machines a few seconds before the edit point, rolling them, and starting the recording at the right time, copying the selected scene from the source tape onto the assembled master. The coming of SMPTE Timecode in the 1970s made it possible to make edits that were frame-accurate, consistently occurring in the right place. Simultaneously, the development of the *digital timebase corrector* made it possible to use multiple synchronized source machines, creating the opportunity to do dissolves and other special effects. Soon after, expensive digital effects devices (most notably Ampex's *ADO*) made it possible to change the position, size and shape of video elements in real time. At the peak of this technology, a high-end analog video editing system would have used three or four VTRs, one or two channels of digital effects, a sophisticated edit controller and a complete production switcher. Such a system could easily cost a half million dollars (1980 dollars, remember!) or more, just for the equipment.

This approach, called *A-B-roll* or *A-B-C-roll* editing, was a *linear* process – you started at the beginning of the show and proceeded in order to the end. It's easy to understand that in a linear system, if you decide you want to change the length of a scene, it's necessary to re-assemble the entire show from the point of the change all the way to the end, or make copies with the inevitable loss of quality. While timecode and sophisticated edit controllers made it possible to automate this process within certain limits, it was a serious disadvantage.

Because of the high cost of an A-B-roll linear system, and the difficulty of making changes, complex program editing became a 2-step process: offline and online editing. Offline tape editing required the creation of low-quality copies of all the source footage (usually 3/4-inch U-Matic or VHS cassettes) with timecode that matched the original. Using the less expensive equipment, the show was edited in "electronic workprint" form. Once the edit was complete and approved, the offline editing system produced an *edit decision list (EDL)* which would allow the show to be re-assembled online from the original high-quality source footage, depending on the accuracy of timecode to accomplish this feat. The EDL was simply a text file consisting of a list of the timecodes for the beginning and end of each scene paired with the timecodes of the position of the scenes on the edited master tape.

Early computer-based *nonlinear* editing systems (as pioneered by Avid Technologies and a few others) didn't offer "master-quality" video recording, so they were used entirely as offline systems, still creating an EDL for use in assembling the program in a full-quality linear online suite. They had a huge advantage over tape-based systems, however, because they were truly non-linear; changing the length of a scene within a show no longer required changes to any other part of the program. The non-linear nature of computer-based editing offered the same flexibility as film editing, with far greater speed and convenience. In addition to an EDL for video assembly, non-linear editing systems were soon able to correlate timecode with film edge numbers and output *cut lists* for film negatives (the film equivalent of the EDL).

In the digital age, the picture and sound are ready to see right out of the camera, the sound is already in sync, and editing can begin immediately. In the digital editing system, all of the functions of the analog edit suite are done in software, and even a high-end editing system is dramatically smaller and less expensive. With increasing computer power, offline editing of video is done less and less often. Modern systems can be both online quality and random-access, and many effects can be created in real time. The technology is a lot easier to use and less expensive, but the brainpower required to tell a story with sound and picture hasn't changed.

How an Editing System Works

Every modern nonlinear editing system, from the high-end Avids to Apple's iMovie (provided with every computer they sell) works essentially the same way. The program is presented to the editor in the form of a *timeline.* Source material and the finished program are shown in windows, sometimes called *viewers.* The display the user sees is called the graphical user interface (GUI). Actual edits are made by placing source footage, sounds, and graphic elements onto the timeline in one of a variety of different ways. There are a few differences between how particular actions are handled by different editing systems, but the net result is the same. To put in a scene, the editor must define the scene (its beginning, or *IN point* and its end, or *OUT point*), and he must define where it goes in the program. Optionally, he can define an IN and OUT point within the program and either an IN or OUT for the source scene. Any combination of three IN and OUT points can define the fourth needed point – the system will automatically calculate it. Most systems also allow the editor to define all four points and use a *fit* utility to change the speed of the source footage to make it fit the defined length.

The timeline display in the editor is actually representative of a *playlist* – a set of data stored in the system that tells it what to play and when to play it. When the editor creates a cut from Scene 1 to Scene 2, for example, the system creates data that tells it to play Scene 1 from IN point to OUT point, followed immediately by Scene 2 from its IN point to its OUT point. Every playback from the timeline works like this, regardless of the complexity of the program.

When you want to include a transition between two scenes (for example, a dissolve), the system creates a new piece of video for that period of time when two images (two pieces of source video) are on the screen at the same time. This piece of video may be calculated by the system "on the fly" and stored in memory or the system will create a *render* file containing this piece of video.

From the software's point of view, then, the transition simply becomes another scene included in the playlist.

One way or the other, any scene containing more than one piece of video source footage or which contains footage that has been modified will be rendered into a single scene that can be included in the playlist. Such rendered scenes might include dissolves, wipes and other effects, color corrections, changes in size or position, and (sometimes) changes in playback speed or direction.

You should note that with a few exceptions, processes done on a nonlinear editing system are non-destructive. This means that your original scenes as stored in the system are not changed by any operations the editor does during cutting. The render files describe above are modified duplicates of the original scene(s). The non-destructive nature of the process means you can change your mind without major consequences – a big advantage over all earlier ways of editing.

If your system has fast disk drives and processors (or special hardware accelerators), many of the effects requiring rendering appear to happen in real-time, ready to playback immediately after you define them. As the effects become more complex, however, you'll eventually reach a point where the system needs to stop and take extra time to render the effects to a render file. It's render speed that separates the men from the boys. In fact, there's very little difference between high-end and low-end systems in their actual capabilities, just in the speed of getting the job done.

The "need for speed" really depends on the kind of material you're editing. Simple cuts with a few dissolves can be done on any system, and many projects contain little else. One editor said, "Nobody has ever invented a transition better than a cut, and to prove it, watch any Hollywood movie." It's true that the major studios can afford to use any kind of transition they want, but what do they use 99% of the time? A simple cut.

Choosing Editing Software

If you're working on a simple project with a low budget, it's quite possible to do professional work using the "freebie" editing software that comes with many new computers. These platforms also give you a good taste of how editing works if you're a beginner. If you're serious about editing, however, you'll probably want to move up to a more serious editing system. Some manufacturers offer "Express" systems that leave out some features but offer most of the capabilities of their more expensive cousins. One of these systems might be all you need, and they have the additional advantage of not requiring any external hardware or plug-in cards. This means they can be used effectively on a laptop, too.

Beyond that, selecting your system becomes largely a personal choice. Debatably, the Avid (Avid Technologies) software has been something of an industry standard, and some say that if you want to become a "hireable" editor, you should be intimately familiar with it. Avid has a huge user base, which is both good and bad. It's good if you have an Avid system and want lots of editors to be able to use it. It's bad because Avid has had a problem with making changes and improvements to their software because the user base (isn't it human nature?) has resisted changes that affect the way they use the software. In this sense, Avid is "legacy bound" and has been reluctant to change the way their software behaves, even if the changes would ultimately make things easier or faster. That said, Avid systems are very capable and should be adequate for any project.

In the professional world, Apple's Final Cut Pro (my personal favorite) and Adobe's Premiere Pro represent the main (and fast-growing) competition. Final Cut Pro (which runs only on the Mac) is fast becoming dominant among the new generation of filmmakers. It comes in a package called "Final Cut Studio", which includes a great kit of tools for editing, soundtrack production, color correction, motion graphics and special effects. Final Cut Studio also has the advantage of coming in only one "version", so even if you are using the least expensive computer capable of running the package, you have access to all the features and can learn to use them. Then, when you upgrade your hardware, you won't have to re-learn anything and you'll already have the knowledge to use the full capabilities of the new system. Final Cut also works in all the current formats.

Other manufacturers offer attractive bundles, and you may want to explore these if you're not too "brand sensitive". In terms of capabilities, systems from any of the major manufacturers offer similar features.

It's certainly beyond the scope of this book to teach you how to use any particular software – that's what tutorials and editor training are about. Our focus here should be on the organizational and creative aspects of editing.

Editing Workflow

Whatever format you're using to shoot, you'll undoubtedly be using a nonlinear software-based editing system. With any system, the first step in the editing process is *capture*, or *log and capture,* often called *digitizing* (a holdover when all video tape was analog – capturing the footage was when the video became digital). More recently, with disk- and memory-based recording, getting the media into the editing system is called *transferring*. Here's where you'll have to make some choices about how you will be working.

If you're working with mildly compressed formats (DV, DVCam, DVCPro, HDV, AVCHD) you'll probably want to store your footage in its native format and working with it that way throughout the process. On the other hand, if you're working in an less-compressed format (Digital Betacam, D-9, D-5, HDCam) or if you have a lot of source footage, you may want to consider capturing in a compressed format to save disc space and speed up your editing software.

Every editor has his own style, and it starts with the capture process. Some editors like to capture all the footage, making decisions about what to keep later in the process; others like to log individual scenes and capture only the best takes or footage they know is usable. Which approach you may take is a matter of individual choice. As an editor, I do it both ways, depending on the project.

With the advent of DV, HDV, AVCHD and inexpensive Firewire and USB-2 hard drives, my approach has become very simple. For every project, I purchase a new Firewire drive and dedicate it to one film, building it into the budget from the beginning. For a small project, I buy an 80 GB drive (a bit over 6 hours of DV or HDV footage). Similarly, I expand the drive size to suit the project. While they're slightly more expensive, I strongly recommend using Firewire-800 (800 Mbps) drives which offer twice the speed of the original Firewire (400 Mbps).

Single Firewire drives are available up to over 1 TB (terabyte, 1000 GB), which holds over 80 hours of HDV or DV footage – think of it as a 40:1 shooting ratio for a 2-hour film. I keep all the elements of the project on this dedicated drive in a folder with the project's name. It's helpful to keep all the elements in one folder so they can easily be moved to another drive if you ever want to – which you probably will at some point. It also helps when you want to back up your footage and other elements.

Most editing software has an "autosave" feature, saving the project periodically in case you want to revert to a previous version. FinalCut Pro has an "autosave vault" which can be on any drive. Keeping the main project file on the external drive while putting the autosave vault on the internal drive offers protection from a drive failure. In a worst-case scenario (loss of a disk drive), I can recover the project from either drive, though it might mean I will have to re-capture the footage. (If you want to clean up a drive after completing a project, most editing software has media management features that will let you delete all the unused footage from a project, while still keeping all the active elements intact.)

I often find that I have room for two, three or more projects on a drive, so after some time has passed and I think it's unlikely that I'll be revisiting a project, I usually move it to another drive which has enough room for it. Once I've moved all the projects off a particular drive, I can reformat that drive and treat it like a new one – saving money and space at the same time.

I also like to have a spare drive that's dedicated to backing up my current projects. At the end of each workday, I copy the entire project I'm working on to the spare drive. This process has saved me more than once, because drives can and do fail. For those really important projects (aren't they all?), having two copies all the time can be worth its weight in gold. This is especially important if you're working with a disk or memory-based format, because you won't have access to the original footage once the media has been erased for re-use.

If you're dealing with uncompressed video or any format with a greater bandwidth than DV, HDV or related formats, you may need to use a disc array that is fast enough to accommodate the format you've chosen. Most such arrays are in the form of a *RAID,* an abbreviation for *Redundant Array of Inexpensive Disks.* Inexpensive is a comparative term; these drives are considerably more expensive per gigabyte than either your computer's internal disk or an external Firewire, USB or SATA disk. Without getting into great detail about how RAIDs work, just remember that working in an uncompressed format requires faster drives and a lot more disk space, and the disks are quite a bit more expensive per gigabyte. Remember, too, that if you have a computer capable of holding multiple internal disks, these can often be configured as a software-based RAID, fully capable of handling uncompressed video.

With all this in mind, I have often used a hybrid approach, in effect mixing and matching different formats. If I shoot a project in HDV, for example, but if I need to do extensive effects, I can work uncompressed on those "problem" scenes. In this way, I can keep the vast majority of my footage on a Firewire drive, but use the computer's internal disks while doing the effects. Source footage needed for effects can be exported to uncompressed using the editing software. (More about this in the chapter on special effects.) Remember, too, that a Firewire or USB-2 drive can store uncompressed footage copied from another drive, even if it isn't fast enough to actually work with that footage. Copy it to the Firewire drive for storage; copy it back to a faster drive if you need to work with it again. In fact, I use Firewire or USB drives for archiving all projects, uncompressed or not.

When you begin to capture footage, you'll need to specify to the editing software how and where you want it stored. Also, you can specify whether to capture video only, any of the audio tracks by itself, two audio tracks as a stereo pair or all audio tracks separately. Obviously, if you are only using one of the audio tracks, it saves disk space to only capture that one. If the audio track is really stereo (recorded, for example, with a stereo mic) then it's helpful for that track to behave as stereo once it's being used in the edit. Likewise, if you want to control the levels and equalization of the tracks separately (as when you've used a wireless mic for each of two characters) it makes sense to capture them as separate tracks.

The edit system will give you the opportunity to enter a reel number, scene number, take, comments, and quite a bit of other data. It's a good idea to provide as much of this information as you feel may be needed, particularly if you have a lot of footage. If you're using a prosumer camera, all your timecodes on all your reels may start at zero, so you'll have lots of duplicate timecodes. In this case, it's essential to have a reel number if you need to re-capture.

While many editors will disagree, I think it's a good idea to spend extra time logging footage, capturing individual scenes and takes instead of long sections of source material. In the long run, I think this approach makes things easier to find and is worth the extra effort at the front end. Alternatively, you can capture all your footage while you drink a beer and organize it later by making *subclips*.

In any case, the edit system will keep track of the source footage timecodes, allowing re-capture or locating scenes. Note, however, systems are also capable of capturing video from sources that don't have timecode, like VHS tape or even a live camera. For such scenes, the system will generate its own timecode for internal purposes, but (obviously) the timecodes don't relate to the original source.

If you're working with a disk- or memory-based camcorder, things get easier. Your software will allow you to transfer all or selected takes directly to your hard drive, a process that's much faster than working with tape. Since camera disk drives and memory are always re-used, remember that the copy you make to your hard drive may end up being the only copy! This makes it vital that you back up your hard drives!

Setting up a Project

When you create a new editing project, the system will want to know its format. That is, what format you want the system to use during editing. Usually, the project format will be the same as your source footage; if you are shooting DV, you'll want your output to be DV. Keeping source and editing formats the same has many advantages, the main one being that no rendering is required for scenes that are simply "passed through" in the captured format.

There may be occasions when, for example, you want your final output to be uncompressed even though your source footage is DV. (Uncompressed is better, right?) There are two ways to get this result. You can capture the DV footage in an uncompressed (or a better, higher-bit-rate) format using a hardware add-on with this capability, or you can export your finished project in an uncompressed format. The first method will require five times as much disk space and a lot more processing power, but has the advantage of allowing your effects to be done without re-compression. If you're not doing complex effects, there's no disadvantage to the second method and it's definitely more economical. Of course, there's always the hybrid approach: edit your show in the native DV format, then export it to uncompressed and do your effects last. Either way, it can get complicated but it's something to think about before you start.

Organizing Your Footage

During capture, the system gives you the opportunity to organize footage into *clips* which can be placed into *bins*, and bins can contain other bins. How you organize your clips and bins is a personal choice, but it's something you should think about before you begin. The simplest and most intuitive approach is to create a bin for each scene or segment, named to match the script. Such bins can hold other bins, such as one for all the closeups of each character in a scene, or for cutaways. Remember, too, that bins can also contain still images, titles, sound effects, or music – anything that can be imported into the system. Also, scenes can be copied and placed into more than one bin, sometimes a great convenience for the editor. Note that copying a clip doesn't mean that the footage itself is physically copied; like the timeline, clips are only indicators (references) to where the actual clip is stored on disk.

Some editors will start on a dramatic film by assembling the master scenes in script order, either in sections or for the whole film, the first cut. Especially with films that are dialog-heavy, this approach sets the pace of the film as determined by the director and actors, and lets the editor get a feel for the flow. From there, the closeups, transitions and cutaways are put in, creating the first *rough cut* of the film. This is followed by "fine-tuning" or "polishing" the cut. For a documentary, a similar approach works, assembling all the elements containing audio (interviews, conversations, narration) in the desired order, creating a visual outline of the film's context.

In a fashion similar to creating bins within bins to hold shots within scenes, all the shots related to a particular scene in the editing timeline can be *nested*. Once this is done, each scene becomes a separate *sequence*, which can be treated as a single entity. Sequences can then be strung together in a new sequence representing the final cut.

Importing Other Elements

In addition to capturing footage, edit systems can also import a wide variety of elements you may be using in your film. Software differs with regard to flexibility of importing graphic elements and sound; some can import nearly any sound, graphic or video elements and can render them properly for the format you're working in. With any system, however, it's best to prepare elements for import in a compatible size, frame rate, sample rate, etc. With DV, for example, the native image size is 720 by 480 pixels, audio is uncompressed with 48 kHz 16-bit sampling.

When you import graphics or animation elements, they will often include an alpha channel (matte) to allow them to be easily composited with live-action scenes.

"Films are only tiny slices of time."

Charles Ashby

4.3 Color Correction

***"These rose colored glasses that I'm looking through
Show only the beauty 'cause they hide all the truth."***

John Conlee

Realer Than Real

It's called color correction in the video world. In the film world, it's called *Color Grading* or *Color Timing*. The person doing it is called a *colorist*, a *color grader,* or a *timer*. Whatever you choose to call it, color correction is really a special effect used to enhance perceived image quality. Until recently, video editors rarely had access to anything beyond the most rudimentary color correction capability. Filmmakers (the kind that use real film) have traditionally had the ability to color-correct every shot during printing. This difference is largely responsible for the perception that film has a better "look", even when shown on television.

In designing a digital camera (or a film stock), engineers strive for the most accurate reproduction possible, but accurate doesn't necessarily correspond to "pleasing". On television and in the movies, everything is idealized and bigger than life; skies must be bluer and people should exude a healthy glow. As filmmakers have long known (and videographers often failed to appreciate), color correction is an important tool in making your film "snap" and look professional.

Through most of the history of color photography, Kodak marketed two different types of color slide film: Ektachrome (intended mostly for the professional photographer) and Kodachrome, the consumer's favorite. One difference between the two was that Ektachrome attempted to match the colors in a scene as accurately as possible while consumer Kodachrome was color-balanced to flatter people. "Make it look like Kodachrome" became a credo of color filmmaking. The same tip applies to digital video.

How Color Correction Works

Here's an image showing the user interface for the 3-way primary color corrector in Apple's FinalCut Pro software. It's typical of color correction systems in nonlinear editors.

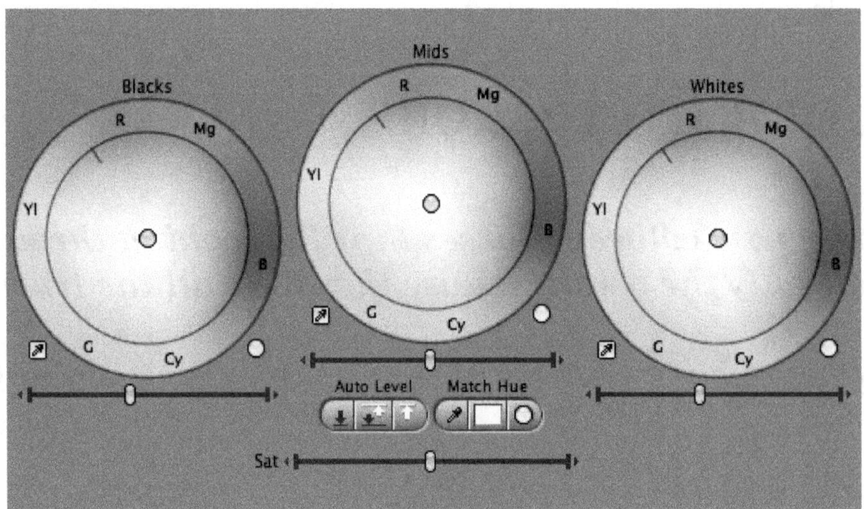

The three circles represent the color balance for the blacks, mid-tones and whites. This is a bit of a simplification, since they all actually cover a range of light levels and interact to some degree. The indicator dot inside each circle is centered (as shown) when no color correction is being applied. Using the mouse to move the indicator circle adds color in the direction it is being moved, and simultaneously reduces the color in the opposite direction. For example, moving the indicator toward green (G) increases the green and reduces the magenta (Mg), its complementary color.

Notice the little marker at about the 11:00 position. This is the *flesh tone vector*, the approximate color of human skin. Interestingly, all human skin is nearly the same basic color; the main difference between races is the luminance (brightness) of the flesh tone. (Note: The flesh tone vector is marked on many vectorscopes, including the emulations in most editing systems, and it's a great aid to matching skin tones from scene.)

Assuming your footage is properly exposed and white-balanced, the first step toward getting that Kodachrome look is to add a bit of color along the flesh tone vector; move the indicator of the mid-tones control in that direction. (Flesh tones are mid-tones; they are neither the brightest nor the darkest part of the image.). Just adding this flesh tone boost will make the skin look better, but will also add an orange cast to the rest of the scene. To compensate, move the highlights control away from the flesh tone vector about the same amount. This will add a bit of blue to the highlights and give the scene a wider range of colors and more "snap", especially on exterior shots where it will make the sky bluer.

Notice that we haven't adjusted the "blacks" control at all. That's because blacks should remain pure black unless you're going for some kind of special effect. This control can, however, be used to correct for defects in the black balance of the camera. Use it with discretion.

Beneath the color circles are three sliders used to control the relative luminance, also corresponding to blacks, mid-tones and whites. These controls have no effect on the actual color signals, but can make colors appear to be more or less saturated because they are darker or lighter. The black and white controls adjust the absolute black and white values in the image. Most scenes look best if there is a pure black and a maximum-brightness white somewhere in the shot. Here's the place where you use these controls to compensate for any exposure errors during shooting. I mentioned earlier that it's a good idea to slightly underexpose your shots to avoid losing highlight detail. Using the luminance controls gives you the ability to decide during post production just where you want absolute white and black to be. You'll definitely want to use your editor's built-in waveform monitor emulation when setting these controls.

Ordinarily, the black control should be set so that the darkest shadow areas hit absolute black, while slightly lighter areas retain some detail. Lowering this control farther can make the shadows go jet black, if that's the effect you're after. Similarly, raising this control causes the blacks to become gray, creating a washed-out appearance. As with the black color balance control, use the black level control carefully. The white level control should be used similarly, to set the brightest part of the image to hit 100 units on the waveform monitor.

Most editing systems have automatic level-setting capabilities as shown here, with buttons for black level, black and white levels together and white levels. These buttons are helpful in getting you to a good starting point for color correction.

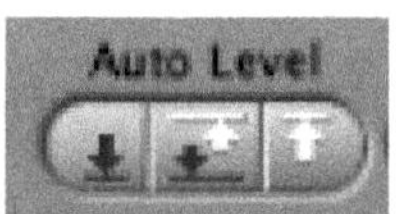

The midtones level control actually adjusts the gamma curve, though it does interact to some degree with the black and white level controls. If you've slightly underexposed your shots as I have recommended, it's this control that will establish the look you want. Raising it is very similar to increasing the exposure on the camera, but with a significant difference: Increasing exposure in the camera will cause loss of highlight detail, while raising the gamma during color correction does not. While the mid-tones control will interact with the black and white levels to some degree, it is easy to reset those levels or use auto levels to get the look you want. As part of the "Kodachrome look", you may find that your scenes look more pleasing if flesh tones are set to be a shade darker than you normally see on TV, similar to the tones you see on movies or other film-originated material.

At the very bottom of the color corrector panel is the *saturation* control. This is the exact equivalent of the "color" control on a monitor or TV set. (Electronically, this control is adjusting the level of the R-Y and B-Y chrominance signals without affecting the luminance.) The third part of the "Kodachrome look" is raising the color saturation a bit – stronger colors are bigger than life.

There as many “looks” as there are films, and the colorist’s job is at least as much artistic as it is technical. There is a great deal more to creating a “dark” look than simply reducing the highlights and midtones. Of course, your cinematographer needs to shoot with the “look” in mind, but it’s up to the colorist to make it work on the screen.

Whatever the “look”, colorists try (within the limits of the context) to get at least some pure white and some pure black in every scene. In a realistic viewing environment with some ambient light, the visible ratio of whites to blacks in a scene is limited to about 1000 to 1 at best. Editing and color correction systems offer some tools in achieving this goal in the form of a variety of “scopes”. Below is a sample scene and what typical scopes show.

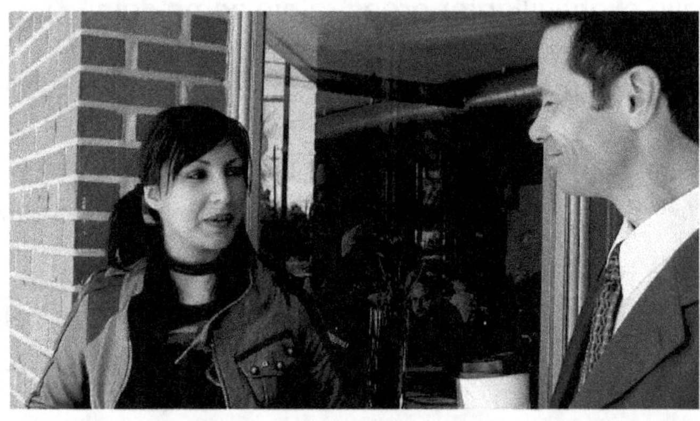

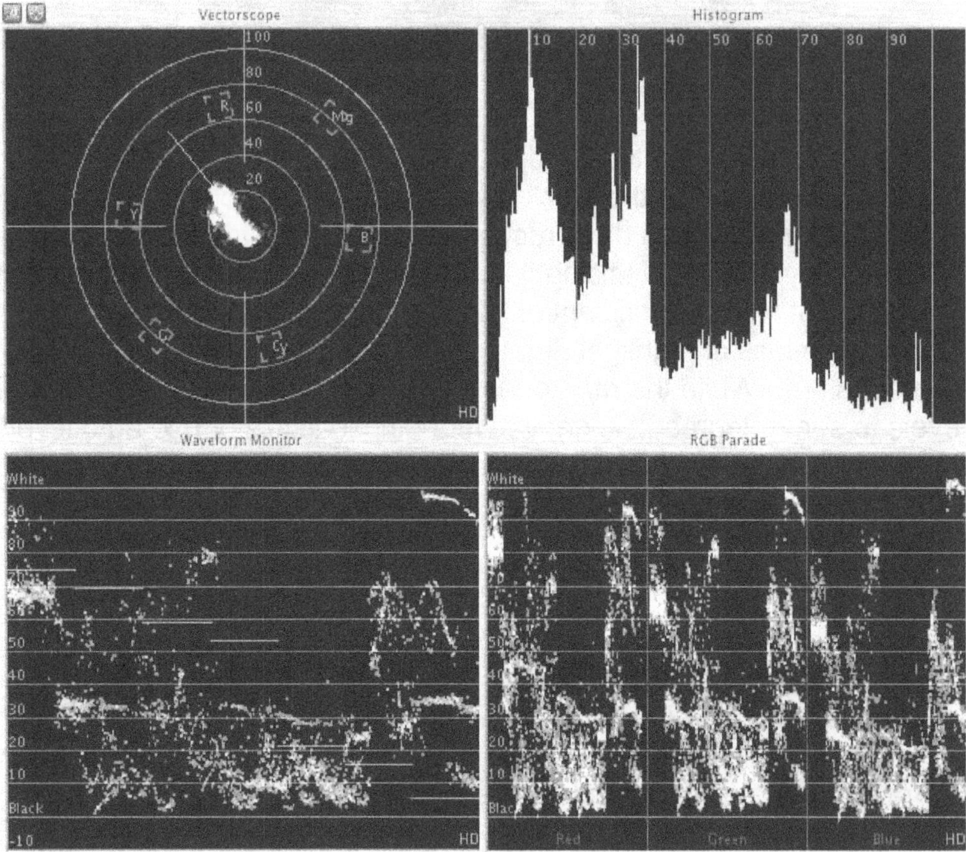

The **Vectorscope** shows only the color components of the scene similarly to the classic *color wheel.* The saturation (how much) of the color is shown as a distance from the center "zero" point. The maximum saturation is at the outside circle. The hue (what color) is shown by the direction. The six boxes labeled R (red), Y (yellow), G (green), Cy (cyan), B (blue) and Mg (magenta) show the vector (direction) of each color and also the maximum saturation of each color as allowed by the NTSC (or PAL) video system. (If the NTSC Color Bar test pattern is shown on the vectorscope, there will be a bright dot in each of the boxes, indicating the correct colors.) This particular scene has somewhat muted colors, so the color vectors are relatively short.

Note the line at about the 11 o'clock position. This is called the *flesh-tone vector* because it's the color of human flesh. If the color balance is correct, flesh tones will fall along this vector, regardless of exposure or if the person is light- or dark-skinned. (Yes, everyone's skin is approximately the same color. The difference is only in brightness.)

We talked about how the **Histogram** can be used during shooting in Chapter 3.3. It also comes into play during color correction. The scale across the top represents the brightness range from zero (black) to 100 (white) plus an extension of white (*superwhite*). The graph indicates the relative number of pixels in each of the brightness ranges. The scene shown has a near-ideal exposure, so there are pixels very near black and very near white, but virtually none at either black or white. Because the large peaks are not "clustered" near the edges, there will is good detail in both highlights and shadows. The superwhite area at the extreme right indicates pixels that might be eliminated (clipped) if your film is broadcast on conventional television. These pixels will be rendered by the broadcast system as pure white with no detail.

The **Waveform Monitor** section shows the luminance of the scene from left to right. Vertically, black (0) is at the bottom and white (100) is at the top. Note there is also a region of superwhite above 100. For an ideal scene, the waveform should "kiss" the 0 and 100 lines – continuing the idea that most scenes need both black and white areas, no matter how small. The black areas at the left represent the actress' black sweater; the white peak at the right indicates the brightness of the actor's white shirt collar. Note that both the waveform and histogram displays in this example represent only the luminance (brightness) of the image and have nothing to do with color.

The **RGB Parade** is similar to the waveform but displays the three (red, green and blue) color channels separately. The parade looks very much like three copies of the waveform display side-by-side, but there are subtle differences. You can see that the blacks look almost identical because there are no saturated colors in he dark areas of the scene. The value of the parade can be seen by examining the whites. Notice that the white peak at the right (representing the actor's white collar) is different in the three parade waveforms. The peak is lower in the red, about the same in green and somewhat higher in the blue channel. This indicates that the scene is balanced such that there is some blue tint in the whites – exactly what you'd expect if we added blue to the highlights.

Beyond the color correction offered in editing software, much more intensive color grading is possible with more advanced tools, such as Apple's *Color*. These make possible more complex primary, secondary and tertiary color grading, and include the ability to track and correct individual colors within a scene. Such features might be needed for a particular "look", or for artistic changes. For example, suppose a scene was shot with two actors, both wearing similar blue shirts. It's possible to change one shirt to yellow while leaving the other blue, throughout a scene. You could also darken or lighten the skin tones of actors individually.

Solving Color Problems

A common problem with footage is incorrect color balance. It's fairly easy to overlook white balance settings while shooting, especially if lighting conditions change. As advised earlier, many professionals prefer to shoot with their camera's pre-set color balance settings, 3200ºK, 5600ºK, or one of the fluorescent light settings. In either case, scenes can be just a little "off" from the most pleasing color balance — sometimes a lot "off". Most editing packages offer semi-automatic white and midtone color balance utilities. To use this feature, you select the tool and click on an object in the scene that you want to be true white. This sets a good starting point for white balance. You can also find a mid-tone color that should be gray and using the same procedure, balance the mid-tones. Then, using the color controls, balance the colors so it's both pleasing and matches other shots in the scene. Ordinarily, you can copy the color corrections from one scene and apply them to others shot at the same time.

With most systems, you can apply more than one color corrector to a scene. You can use this approach to apply secondary and tertiary color correction. As an example, you may have an exterior scene where everything looks good, but the grass is just not green enough. Using selective colors, you can increase the saturation and vary the tones of only the green areas of the image. You can also invert the color selection for effect. This gives you the ability to create a scene which is entirely black-and-white except for a specific color.

By duplicating a scene and stacking it "on top" of the original, you can color-correct specific areas of the frame, using *slop mattes,* user-created shapes that define the areas. The shape of these mattes can be animated to correspond to camera or subject moves.

As with everything else in this book, we can only scratch the surface of the complex field of color grading.

About Monitoring

During color grading, it's vital to have use a monitor you can trust. Most computer systems use LCD displays, and while some of them offer excellent picture quality, most suffer from some change in color rendition depending on the viewing angle. These limitations are more pronounced with laptops, since the displays are designed for maximum efficiency and minimum battery drain. While I won't suggest brands or models, keep these limitations in mind when choosing a monitor, and consider an external monitor for grading if you're using a laptop.

It's also important that your monitor is accurately calibrated. You computer probably has one or more utilities for this purpose. For most purposes, you should calibrate your monitor for a color temperature of 6000-6400°K with a gamma of about 2.0. This will give a good compromise for creating content for CRT, LCD, DLP and plasma displays. It's also a good point to start for projects that will be later transferred to film. To get your monitor as close as possible to the ideal settings, monitor calibrators are available which attach to the screen and accurately measure the monitor's characteristics.

Another tip: Before you start a project, look at some DVDs of your favorite movies on the monitor you'll be using. That way you'll learn what to expect from your monitor and be able to accomplish a particular "look". Being intimately familiar with the way your monitor handles a wide variety of scenes is probably more important than the actual quality of your monitor. Know what to expect from it! Your viewing environment is also important – a brightly lit office is not at all like a darkened home theater.

"Through the magic of motion pictures, someone who's never left Peoria knows the...color of a Nile sunset...and that Big Ben has not yet gone digital."

Vincent Canby

4.4 Sound Design

"Who the hell wants to hear actors talk?"

H. M. Warner, 1927

In Chapter 2.5, we talked about audio technology, how sound recording works. Then, Chapter 3.4 covered techniques to capture good, clean sound. Sound Design is the post-production phase, the combining of sound recorded on-location and in studio with sound effects and music, and processing the sounds for best effect. It covers the gamut from completely creating the soundtrack from scratch all the way to simple "sweetening" of field-recorded sound.

On many low-budget films, the editor is able to complete a good soundtrack entirely within the editing software environment. For more sophisticated sound work, the track finishing goes to a Sound Designer using tools specifically designed for audio. Perhaps the closest thing to industry-standard software for this purpose is Digidesign's *ProTools*, a product of Avid Technologies. ProTools offers a comprehensive package for editing, recording and processing of field-recorded sound, plus everything you might need for music production and surround sound. Other software, including Adobe *Audition*, Apple's Soundtrack Pro and Logic provide similar tools. While modern audio software allows full access to all the controls through the keyboard, mouse and screen (graphical user interface), most high-end mixing environments include a *control surface*, interfaced with the computer. Control surfaces also work with free standing Digital Audio Workstations (DAW). These can be anything from a small mixer emulator to a massive full-function mixing console installed in a cavernous *mixing theater*. They work with the software to follow the motion of the controls and "remember" them, with motorized faders that reposition themselves dynamically as a mix is played back or modified. Working with a fancy control surface provides the ultimate speed and convenience and the ability to precisely fine-tune your mix. While a glorious luxury, many excellent films have been mixed without them.

The Listening Environment

One of the most important considerations in sound design is simply being able to accurately hear what you are doing. Just as color correction and grading require accurately calibrated monitors, it's vital that your monitor speakers and listening room accurately simulate the environment in which viewers will experience your film. In Hollywood, millions are spent creating "mixing theaters". These are literally what the name implies: Actual small theaters with speakers and speaker placements similar to what you'll find in your local quality Cineplex. Low-budget filmmakers will rarely have the luxury of working in this ideal environment, but there's a lot you can do to create high-quality soundtracks without the expense.

Non-feature films will usually be done with simple 2-channel stereo soundtracks, but current feature films almost always include surround sound with six or more channels. Let's start with a simple stereo setup, then we'll expand that into surround.

Digital recording easily captures the entire audible range, roughly 20-20,000 Hz for people with acute hearing. Quality microphones are generally capable of covering this entire range, too, as are analog audio amplifiers and mixers. The weakest link in the chain is universally the loudspeaker, a mechanical system that has to deal not only with electrical signals but also with the physics of moving objects, air, and the acoustic environment.

How Loudspeakers Work

Everyone has seen loudspeakers, and most of them are essentially unchanged from when they were first invented, in the 1920s. They consist of a round metal frame with a paper (or other flexible material) cone suspended inside. At the apex of the cone is a coil of copper wire, suspended in the field of a powerful magnet. An electric current (representing the audio to be reproduced) is passed through the coil, which causes in or out movement of the cone. When the current flows in one direction, the cone moves out, compressing the air in front of the speaker. When it moves in, it rarefies the air in front, reducing its instantaneous pressure. An audio signal from a power amplifier flowing through the coil causes it to move at rates from 20-20,000 times per second. This vibration creates pressure waves in the surrounding air corresponding to the instantaneous amplitude and polarity of the audio signal. The energy in these waves depends on several factors, including the strength of audio signal and its wavelength in air.

Sound travels at about 335 meters per second at normal atmospheric pressure. A little intuitive math shows that the wavelength of a 300 Hz. audio signal is a little over one meter, because 300 individual waves would fill up a distance of about 300 meters. That means that for every meter of distance away from a loudspeaker, each one-meter space contains an equal amount of energy in the form of a pressure wave in the air. For a 600 Hz signal of the same strength, each one-meter would contain two pressure waves, each with half the amount of energy of the 300 Hz wave, but with the same total energy.

Low Frequency Problems

Back to the loudspeaker for a moment: if on the 300 Hz tone the cone moves a total distance of 1 mm, it must only move 0.5 mm on the 600 Hz tone to transfer the same amount of acoustic energy to the air, but it must do it twice as often. Conversely, to create the same energy at 150 Hz, it must move 2 mm, for 75 Hz it must move 4mm, for 40 Hz it must move about 8mm, and for 20 Hz, the distance becomes 16mm.

You can see where this is going. Moving a speaker cone 1 or 2 mm isn't difficult, but if it has to move 16mm, bad things begin to happen. For one, the cone will have more resistance to movement the farther it has to move. For another, it's difficult to generate a uniform magnetic field over the entire 16mm distance. The final result: the speaker begins to distort the wave and it simultaneously becomes less efficient.

Bottom line: if you look at a speaker catalog and review the specifications of various models, you will find that the number of speakers that have useful performance down to 20 Hz approaches zero. Quite a few work fairly well down to 40 Hz, and almost all work fairly well above 80 Hz.

So how do you make a speaker work better at lower frequencies? The most obvious way is to make it larger. Double the diameter of the speaker, and it will have four times the area. Thus, it will only have to move 1/4 as far to create a particular sound level. Another way is to use multiple speakers, four small speakers can equal one big one.

Another problem enters the picture: If a speaker is small relative to the wavelength of the sound, the high pressure from the back of the cone can "spill over" to the low pressure in the front and effectively cancel out the wave, dramatically reducing the efficiency of the speaker. This problem is universally mitigated by putting the speaker in a box – some kind of enclosure.

Enclosures work several ways:

1. They are designed to absorb (or disperse) as much of the sound from the back of the speaker as possible, eliminating the problem of cancellation but reducing the efficiency, or
2. An enclosure can be designed to delay the back radiation in such a way that it can be brought "into phase" with the front radiation at low frequencies, or
3. Enclosures can be "tuned" to increase low-frequency efficiency through resonance.

Of these approaches, the first can produce the best results, but to be effective at very low (extreme bass) frequencies, the enclosure needs to be quite large compared to what is required at mid- to high frequencies.

For stereo monitoring, the best quality can be achieved by using two speaker systems capable of handling the lowest frequencies possible, but there is an alternative (and one that's universal in surround sound): the *subwoofer.*

Perhaps fortunately, the human auditory system becomes less and less capable of determining the direction of a sound's source the lower the frequency. This means that a pair (or more) of small speakers (which are quite efficient at mid- to high frequencies) can be supplemented with a single low-frequency speaker. Such a speaker can be hidden away almost anywhere in the listening room without adversely affecting its performance, while the other (smaller) speakers can be optimally placed, even in a small room.

A system using two smaller speakers plus a subwoofer is often called a 2.1 system, meaning two main speakers plus a supplementary bass channel. Surround systems are often designated similarly, such as a 5.1 system with five main channels plus a subwoofer. Such hybrid systems with very small main channel speakers (such as the popular Bose systems) can sound quite good on music, but they often do not work as well when dialog is involved.

This phenomenon relates to the system's crossover frequency – the frequency at which the subwoofer begins to be the primary source of sound. While it's true that the ear's ability to locate a sound's source direction diminishes as the frequency goes lower, it still is quite effective in the range of the male speaking voice, something films contain a lot of in the form of dialog and narration. Because the male voice contains substantial energy as low as 100 Hz, it's vital that the crossover to the subwoofer be below that threshold for satisfactory dialog reproduction and stereo (or surround) imaging. Keep in mind that if you can't use full-range speakers for all channels, be sure the crossover frequency for the subwoofer is as low as possible. Secondarily, select a subwoofer that has a useful low-frequency limit as close to 20 Hz as you can afford.

Speaker High Frequency Performance

Just as typical loudspeakers' performance degrades at low frequencies, other factors come into play as the frequency goes up. A loudspeaker cone, just as any other physical object, has mass. Power is required to move that mass, and the faster you want to move it the more power is needed. Just as our 300 Hz signal required a 1mm movement of the cone for a specific volume level, a 3000 Hz signal will require only 0.1 mm. Since inertia is a factor at faster speeds, a small speaker actually works more efficiently at high frequencies than a large one. For these reasons, most speaker systems are two-way or three-way, meaning they will have a "woofer" and a "tweeter" (2-way) or a woofer, mid-range ("squawker") and a tweeter (3-way). In most hybrid systems (2.1, 5.1, 6.1, 7.1) the main speakers are 2-way, with the larger driver being between a woofer and a mid-range, with an added tweeter for the extreme highs.

Since there is another crossover point that determines at what frequency the tweeter takes over, it's also important that that frequency is not near the middle of the dialog range. Although there are some exceptions, speakers that sound best on dialog will usually have a tweeter crossover frequency about 3,500 Hz.

Other Considerations

Some popular speaker systems use multiple drivers for the midrange. While this can make them more efficient, it introduces a factor called "comb filtering". Imagine a system with two speakers separated by one meter and reproducing identical signals. If you are seated directly in front of such a system, equidistant from the two drivers, everything works fine. Now suppose you are seated at some angle relative to the line of the speakers such that you are 3 meters from one of the speakers and 3.5 meters from the other, and you are listening to a 300 Hz tone. Since there is a difference of 1/2 wavelength between the path lengths to the two speakers, a compression wave from one speaker will arrive at your ear at the same time a rarefaction (low pressure) wave arrives at the other. These two waves will be out of phase, so the sound will essentially cancel. The same will be true for multiples (harmonics) of the 300 Hz tone. As you move around the room, the frequencies where these cancellations occur will change. If you plot this on a graph, you'll see it has lots of peaks and valleys, resembling the shape of a comb – hence the name. Because comb filtering effects are worse in small spaces, I recommend that your main speakers use a single midrange driver instead of the pair or trio of speakers often used in consumer audio systems.

Setting Up You Monitoring System

Recording studio designers will tell you that a listening room needs to be fairly large for good performance, at least six by six meters (about 20 by 20 feet), with larger being better. Remember that 1/2 wavelength at 20 Hz is about 4 meters (13 ft.), so in small spaces, very low frequencies bounce off the walls and reinforce the direct sound from the speakers, resulting in a phenomenon called "bass buildup". At the same time, mid frequencies bounce off the walls and create comb filtering, for the same reasons as described above. Wall bounce can be minimized by using sound absorbing panels, and low frequencies can (to some degree) be controlled by using "bass traps" or tuned resonators. These solutions always work better in large spaces, but even in a small space you can get creative. Use upholstered furniture, carpet, acoustic ceiling tile, and use things like bookcases and pillows to absorb reflections and avoid parallel surfaces. Commercial sound-absorbing foam can help, too.

Where space is limited (isn't it always?), the recommended alternative is *near-field* monitoring. That simply means: place your listening position near the speakers, maybe only a meter or so away. Near field monitoring can be very good, but has one serious drawback. It gives you only a very small "sweet spot" where sound reproduction is accurate and stereo (or surround) imaging is properly balanced. Your sweet spot should be equidistant from all the speakers, including the subwoofer. Because you are so close to the speakers, a movement of only a few inches off the sweet spot can destroy balance and imaging, just because of the Inverse Square Law. (Remember that from the chapter on lighting? Yes, it applies to sound, too.) Two or more people may have some trouble hearing a proper mix in a near field monitoring environment, but here's the plus side: it takes the worry out of being close. If you're working with surround, you'll obviously need more space, and you will almost certainly need to use near field monitoring.

Notes on Surround

Earlier I mentioned that the subwoofer is universal in all the surround sound formats. The ".1" part of 5.1, 6.1 and 7.1 surround systems represents the "low-frequency effects" (LFE) channel that traces its genesis to the 1974 film *Earthquake.* The road show exhibitions of this film added "Sensurround", a bank of huge subwoofers brought into theaters just for this film. During the earthquake sequences, frequencies down to 20 Hz shook the building, creating a quite convincing earthquake experience. The engineers called this 4.1 or 6.1 sound, the added low-frequency channel for the 4-channel 35mm prints or the 6-channel 70mm prints. Prior to Sensurround, theater systems were rarely able to reproduce anything below about 50 Hz, so experiencing the deep-bass lowest octave became something new for audiences.

Historically, surround sound was first used on a large scale in the *Cinerama* process, which used 6-channel sound on 35mm magnetic film synchronized with the projection. With the coming of *CinemaScope*, the first popular single-film widescreen process, 4 channels of sound were used, with three speakers behind the screen and one surround channel, used mostly for effects. 70mm processes emulated Cinerama, with six channels in several versions. Some used five speakers behind the screen and one surround channel, others used three screen speakers and three surrounds.

The most common surround system in use today is *Dolby Digital*, which was introduced in 1992 and now comes in a variety of flavors, used on DVDs and HDTV broadcasts. It uses five full-range channels for left, center, right, left rear and right rear, plus a LFE or subwoofer channel. Dolby digital is encoded using a process called Dolby AC-3. Through software, AC-3 encodes all the channels into a single audio file. An important feature is that AC-3 not only produces 5.1 (or 6.1 or 7.1) surround, it also contains properly mixed stereo and mono components that can be extracted by DVD players and other surround decoders so the sound works properly in mono, stereo or surround playback. Equally important, AC-3 works with a bit rate no greater than standard stereo CD audio. Another available format is DTS Digital Surround. In all likelihood, however, you will be working either in stereo or in Dolby Digital 5.1.

Getting the Sound Out

Using any of the popular software packages on a modern computer, you'll need a way to get the sound out to your array of two to six monitor speakers. For stereo sound on a budget, the stereo output on better computer sound cards is more than adequate. This output can be used with free-standing 2.1 speaker systems with built-in amplifiers, or with a full-range stereo system.

For optimum quality or for surround, you will need some kind of external decoder. These connect to the computer either with USB or (on suitably equipped computers) with an optical (fiber optic) cable called *Toslink*. Free-standing decoders provide line-level outputs, so you'll need a number of amplifier channels to drive your speakers. Many consumer surround sound "receivers" are also available. These provide the necessary decoding and amplification in a single unit, and the better ones offer very high quality. As mentioned earlier, the speakers and monitoring environment play a much bigger role in the overall quality than the electronics.

Who's the Editor? Who's the Sound Designer?

Once again, in the Digital Age, the line is blurred. In Hollywood, there has been a separation between the editor's and sound designer's jobs. Roughly speaking, the editor puts the dialog and sound effects captured during shooting in place relative to the picture and sends those elements to the sound designer. In the Hollywood model, the editor will usually make level adjustments to ensure good dialog "flow" and to be sure effects are not too loud or too soft. He would leave effects, equalization and noise reduction to the more specialized tools used by the sound designer. The object in this chapter is to describe the tasks needed, not to explain how to do them in any detail, since this will vary depending on the tools used.

With the capabilities of current software, however, it's quite possible for your budget-conscious editor to build a fully-finished stereo soundtrack. Most editing software, however, only deals with mono and stereo, so tracks must be exported to other software in order to position and mix them in the surround sound field.

Dialog First

Since most films are "driven" by dialog, cleaning up field recordings of on-camera voices is the first order of business. As the dialog flows from shot to shot, differences in background noise, microphones and mic placement will be all too obvious. Critical listening will reveal many of the cuts, especially if the shooting was done in an even slightly noisy environment.

The first step is to minimize differences in level across the shots. Next, attempt to match the texture of the sound, the relative balance between high and low frequencies. This is done with equalizers (EQ), which simply vary the relative intensity of high, mid and low frequencies. Listen carefully to the entire scene and try to decide which shot's audio is best, set the level and EQ to optimize it for best sound, then match the others to this "reference" shot.

Sometimes voices are recorded with multiple microphones. For example, a wireless lavalier can be on one track while a shotgun mic on a boom is on another. This is a bit of a luxury, allowing the use of either mic alone or a blend that provides the best texture and ambience.

For most dialog (or any speech), you'll probably want to use a high-pass (or low-cut) filter, which removes the frequencies below the range of the human voice. In almost any shooting location, there will be low-frequency rumble caused by heating and air conditioning systems, traffic, airplanes and the like. The objective is to remove as much of this as possible without noticeably affecting the texture of the voices. You can also use *noise gates*, filters that reduce the volume during pauses. Similarly, software is available that can analyze a sample of the background noise from each shot and minimize it. If the scene takes place in an appropriate setting, you may also want to add a bit of echo or reverberation to the dialog, to imply a sense of location.

Where possible, it's nice to have a stereo or surround recording of the room tone to enhance spaciousness. If your original recording has multiple channels available, it's common to have three or more perspectives of the room tone. If two or more mics in addition to the primary mic are recorded, mixing these in at a low level can provide further enhancement to dialog. It's important that the sound designer communicate with the editor to be sure all these elements are retained throughout the editing process.

Looping

We touched on *looping* (Automatic Dialog Replacement, or ADR) in Chapter 3.4. Sometimes the dialog recorded in the field is just not good enough – it's just too noisy or too off-mic to be used. Looping is simply recording the actors re-speaking the lines in a studio, in sync with the picture. During looping, they watch the picture on a video monitor and hear the original dialog recording plus themselves in headphones. The sound designer (or sometimes a specialized ADR artist) sets the beginning and end of a single line of dialog. The scene is set to play back with a *pre-roll*, a few seconds before recording starts. Audible "beeps" at one-second intervals play through the headphones – beep, beep, beep, go. The actor tries to recreate the same pace and tone for the new recording, doing as many takes as necessary to get it right. Of course, the new studio recordings replace the field recordings.

When recording looped tracks, keep sound perspective in mind. Remember dialog is not the same as narration. Microphone distance should create a texture that matches the picture and the rest of the sound in the film; in a studio it's all too easy to get sound that is inappropriately "up close and personal". This is particularly important when only a few scenes or lines need to be replaced. The new recordings must match the "feel" of the rest of the film.

In a few films, all dialog is looped, with the goal of creating uniformity and controllability throughout the soundtrack. Personally, I'm not an adherent to this school of thought for several reasons. First, I feel actors' performances suffer a bit in looping. Secondly, it is expensive and time-consuming. Third, it usually means sound effects and ambient sound must also be re-created.

Foley

Named after Jack Foley, a sound engineer at Universal Studios in the 1920s and 30s, *Foley* is the art of re-creating sound effects in a studio (Foley Stage) to match or improve on sound acquired during shooting. For recording Foley, the setup is the same as for looping, but instead of actors' voices, sound effects are synchronized with the picture.

Often (and sometimes for the same reasons as dialog), sound effects recorded during shooting are noisy, too distant, too subtle, or otherwise unconvincing. Fist-fights staged by stunt actors, for example, will have none of the sounds that accompany real hand-to-hand combat. Footsteps will be obscured by traffic, breathing sounds may be too quiet to hear. A Foley artist's job is to create and supplement these "natural" sound effects. The Foley studio is equipped with whatever props are needed to simulate real effects. Ripling water gently in a large tub can add texture to a lakeside scene. Smashing a watermelon on the floor can sound like a body hitting the street after a fall from a skyscraper. Crinkling plastic wrap will create a convincing campfire. Dropping a golf ball into a plastic cup sounds better than a real hole-in-one. A skilled human chewing celery can sound better than a real pig eating corn. Hit a wet sponge with your fist for a fight scene. Drop a stack of phone books on the floor to simulate a body falling down a flight of stairs. A canvas bag full of pie plates and scrap glass can hit the floor with the sound of a multi-car pileup.

The possibilities are endless, and a person who's good at Foley deserves the moniker, "artist". In truth, doing Foley is a true talent, and it's also one of the most creative and fun things to do in filmmaking.

Sound Effects

In addition to sound effects recorded in the field during shooting, or specifically for your film, there are thousands of "library" effects available, many in surround versions. Some libraries can be purchased for royalty-free use, others are available on the Internet. Judicial use of so-called "stock" sound effects can add dimension to any film. Bird tracks make the woods seem more like a big forest, traffic sounds can make a small town feel like New York. The hum of power generator can make the mad scientist's laboratory more ominous.

Skilled sound designers rarely use stock effects without modification, embellishment and layering. For example, a closeup of a shot being fired at a person may contain the gunshot itself, an explosion, a thud and a splash. In turn, each element may be equalized, compressed, filtered, pitch shifted and speed adjusted.

Sound Effects Synthesis

Sound designers often take a cue from music recording and integrate samples of sound effects into a musical keyboard, much as musicians use samples of pianos, organs and voices. Totally synthesized sounds, like lasers and light sabers can also be included. By assigning sounds to musical notes, the sound designer can literally 'play' sound effects into scenes.

Mixing

Once all the pieces are in place, the dialog, sound effects and music are blended into the final sound mix. At this phase, the two main parameters are level (volume) and pan (position in the stereo and/or surround sound field). Every sound designer has his own special way of creating the mix, and software and hardware packages vary as to how each component is handled.

From the point of view of the audience, the most important aspects of the mix are consistency, balance and position. Consistency refers primarily to dialog, and it simply means that the volume and texture remain the same throughout the scene with the natural variances of the actors' delivery controlling the peaks and valleys. In reality, there is a tremendous difference between in loudness between a shout and a quiet whisper, but on the screen it's vital that both be easily understood and not distorted yet still maintain believable differences in volume. Similarly, multiple characters within a scene should be heard with similar volume and texture. To keep these factors under control, the mixer "rides gain" throughout a scene, bringing up soft passages and reducing loud ones. Of course, technical assists such as audio compressors and limiters can help, but most sound mixers manually ride gain, sometimes on a word-by-word basis, to get the dialog mix consistent. The consistency of loudness of dialog from scene to scene throughout the whole film is equally important and the same considerations apply. A scene where people are shouting at each other during a battle is naturally louder than a quiet love scene, but for consistency the variations must be smaller than they would be in real life.

Consistency also must be correlated with context. An outdoor scene just sounds different than one shot indoors where room echoes and hollowness may affect perception, so consistency doesn't necessarily mean that all the dialog sounds the same. The environment of the scene has a bearing on what makes a scene consistent, too. For example, in a scene with heavy background sound effects, it may be necessary to compress the dialog heavily to be sure it can be heard over the sound effects of the runaway train. In real life, of course, the actors probably couldn't hear each other, but this is the movies!

Remember that camera perspective relates to sound, too. The texture of sound should be slightly more distant for wide shots than for closeups. If you have dialog recorded with multiple mics, the wide shots can be mixed with a little more of the more distant mic, and the reverse for closeups.

For dramatic films, a good rule of thumb is that "average" dialog should be about 15 decibels below peak level, very loud dialog about 6 to 8 db down and very quiet dialog at 20 to 25 db down. Things like breathing, clothing rustle or very soft room tone, the very quietest sounds, should be no more than 40 to 45 db down. Of course, the loudest sound in the film should not exceed peak level. Music levels are normally kept consistent with dialog – substantially lower than the loudest sound effects.

Balance has to do with the relationships between the various elements of the soundtrack. Sound effects should be at a natural-sounding level but never overriding the dialog or music. It's not just volume that counts, but also the frequency content. For example, an explosion containing mostly deep, low-frequency sounds can be much louder "by the meter" than dialog without overpowering it. Sound designers take this into account in equalizing both sound effects and music where they are mixed with dialog. By carving out space in the intelligible speech spectrum (about 300-3000 Hz.) it's possible to make music and sound effects "wrap around" the dialog. Using an equalizer, you can create a "U-shaped" curve that "fattens" the music or effect so it can bigger under dialog.

When dialog is recorded, it's likely the background noise will change from shot to shot, so that's where "room tone" come in. Whether the room tone comes from the original location or somewhere else, it should be kept at a natural-sounding level, but just loud enough to cover up the variations. Sound effects and music can also be used to exploit this effect, commonly called *masking*, the ability of one sound to prevent the hearing of another. An example might be a scene shot on a busy street. While shooting the master scene, a truck might have gone by while it wasn't there during the closeup. Adding another truck sound that peaks at the audio cut can effectively mask the fact that the first truck disappears from the soundtrack at that moment. Sometimes, too, the sound designer will ride gain on the dialog so that virtually all the ambient sound disappears between actors' lines, making some kind of room tone or ambience a necessity to mask these volume changes. You never want complete silence within a scene!

Panning refers to placement of a sound within a stereo or surround field – where the sound comes from. Editing software generally allows only stereo panning while full-featured audio software allows 360° panning through all the surround channels. During mixing, you will actually be dealing with a number of discreet monaural tracks, even though they can often be treated as stereo pairs or surround clusters. Whether you're working in surround or stereo for your finished track, it's easy to get carried away with panning.

Many older films were mixed so that the dialog "follows" the action – if a character is speaking from the left side of the screen, the sound is panned left, for example. More current practice is to keep the dialog panned center, or very close to center. There are a number of reasons for this. Until fairly recently, it was unlikely that a film would be seen with stereo or surround sound anywhere outside a theater. On a very large screen with speakers actually positioned behind it, directional dialog makes sense, but with smaller screens and unpredictable viewing environments, dialog moving around in the sound field can become distracting, or even downright unpleasant. In TV viewing environments (where your film will likely be seen) the sound field is likely to be considerably larger than the screen, that is, the speakers will be farther apart than the width of the screen. Also, surround systems have a front-center channel (often referred to as the dialog speaker), and this channel is the only one that really creates the illusion that the sound is coming from the screen. My advice: leave the dialog centered and use pans for effects and ambient sound. It's ok for the voice of an off-camera actor to be panned somewhere other than center, but on-screen dialog wants to live near the middle. Music should be allowed to have its full stereo or surround spread, since it's not localized to the screen. The main reason for stereo and surround is to enrich the environment where the action takes place.

One final note that bears repeating: Spend a lot of time listening to known-good soundtracks on your system. Listen to DVDs of your favorite current movies and notice how the dialog, music and effects sound. Is the dialog smooth and natural-sounding? Is it slightly muffled or strident? Is the music bright, clean and full? Are the sound effects rich and realistic? Are these characteristics the same on most of the movies you watch? If you're happy with the way Hollywood movies sound, then you should strive to make your tracks sound the same. If not, you may want to "tweak" your monitoring system so that the Hollywood movies sound their best.

Also, pay attention the relative levels in the mix. Notice how quiet the quietest sounds are, and also the maximum level used. If you have a way of monitoring the actual audio levels on a meter display, so much the better. On most movies, there will be some point where the maximum allowable volume is used. Take note of that, and then compare the quietest passages. You may also want to listen with the volume a bit louder than you might expect to hear them in a theater. This way you can hear those marginal imperfections that might only be noticed by that occasional viewer who likes to play the soundtrack really loud. If you are intimately familiar with what to expect from your monitoring system, you can do a better job than if you have the finest system money can buy but aren't fully aware of what you can really expect from it.

"I'm not confused, I'm just well-mixed."

Robert Frost

4.5 Ready for Release

"Are we there yet?"

...my kids

Once you've finished all the post-production steps, you will be needing ways to get you project out there, and to preserve the best image and sound quality for each of the different ways it will be seen. You will also want to preserve your work so that if the hard disk in your editing system crashes, you haven't lost everything. If you haven't already done it, go buy an external hard drive and backup all the elements of your project!

Next, output a "master" file that will be used to create all the versions you'll need. If you're editing in your camera's native format, such as HDV or DV, you can output a file in that format, or you can choose to use a higher quality format (even uncompressed) to minimize any compression artifacts. You can also output your project to tape. For all my projects, I output using Apple's ProRes 422 format. It's virtually lossless, makes somewhat smaller files than uncompressed, and can be readily translated to any other format you may need. For short films, the files are small enough to be stored on data DVDs.

Making DVDs

Most current computers come with "super drives", capable of reading and writing DVDs (and CDs). Often, too, software for making simple DVDs is provided. Apple's iDVD, for example, allows virtually any type of movie file to be used to create DVDs, and it includes features to create menus for navigation. For all the Hollywood bells and whistles, a wide variety of more advanced DVD authoring software is available, such as Apple's DVD Studio Pro. All these authoring packages can easily make great SD-DVDs from HD original files.

Recordable DVDs come in several varieties: DVD-R, DVD+R and DVD±RW. Some DVD drives will write all of them, others will work with only one or two. DVD-R and DVD+R are "write once" media – once they are recorded, they are not re-usable. DVD-RW is a bit more expensive than the other two, but can be erased and re-used. Of the three, I've found that DVD-R disks will play just fine in most computers and consumer DVD players while DVD+R and DVD±RW can be a bit more "iffy", so I'd suggest using DVD-R where possible. (This discussion is only about SD DVDs; we'll talk about HD a little later.)

A standard recordable DVD holds about 4.3 GB of data, but you can double that by using a dual-layer DVD. Single-layer disks are sometimes called DVD-5, dual layers are DVD-9. (Dual-layer, double-sided disks sometimes used in manufactured movie DVDs are called DVD-18.) While current software does a great job of figuring out how to get your material on the DVD with the best compression rates, it's a good idea to be sure you aren't trying to put too much stuff on the disk. Here are some rough estimates of how much a single-layer DVD will hold. Just double the numbers for double-layer.

- 60 Minutes at maximum quality
- 90 Minutes at medium quality
- 120 Minutes at reduced quality

To accomplish these levels, DVDs use the MPEG-2 compression standard. For a 60-minute DVD, the bit rate can obviously be twice as high as for a 120-minute one. For a 60-minute disk, the average bit rate works out to about 9.3 Mbps, which is considered to be the maximum for DVD. To get longer recording times, the average bit rate is reduced proportionately, but this is not as bad as it sounds. DVD files use MPEG-2 and *variable bit-rate encoding*, which means that the bit rate can change depending on the complexity of the scene. Since scenes with very little motion don't need a high bit rate, the encoder reduces the bit rate during these scenes, leaving more bits for the "harder" parts of the movie. The result is that even with a 120-minute DVD with typical content, you'll rarely see compression artifacts. With most encoders (and most DVD authoring software), any DVD of 60 minutes or longer should totally fill the disk, using all the available bits. In the early days of DVD authoring, artists called "compressionists" manually worked out the "bit budget" for DVDs, manually adjusting the bit rate from scene to scene. While some high-end DVD authoring is still "massaged" in this way, current software does a great job of figuring out the bit budget for you. Note that with a bit rate of only 9.3 Mbps maximum, DVDs have a substantially lower data rate than any of the acquisition formats (compare with the 25 Mbps data rate of DV). In spite of this lower data rate, however, the quality of a properly compressed DVD using variable bit-rate encoding can be visually identical to the original.

DVDs should also comply with the standards of the countries where they are to be used – NTSC for US, Canada, Mexico, Japan, etc., and PAL for most other countries. While most current NTSC players will also play PAL DVDs, their conversion for output to a standard TV set can cause considerable loss of quality. If your original show is SD at 30 fps (NTSC), you may want to use one of the software utilities (such as Apple Compressor or Sorenson Squeeze) to make a clean conversion to PAL before trying to burn PAL DVDs. The same is true for going from PAL originals to NTSC DVDs. Similarly, if your original project is at 24 fps, it should be converted to 25 fps for PAL release at 25 fps, and vice-versa. (Note: Most current computers will play either NTSC or PAL DVDs without quality loss.) Some (but not all) DVD authoring software will do these conversions automatically. For example, if you set up a DVD project as PAL, importing NTSC material will automatically create PAL files for inclusion in the final DVD.

DVDs are often authored for playback only in certain regions of the world, so they have a content protection system called *Region Coding*. A disk may be protected so that it only works in players designed for a specified region or regions. Manufacturers create DVD players that are hardware-enabled to play only selected region codes, though a few players are available which ignore the codes. These codes also apply to playback in computer DVD drives. Here are the standard regions:

- Region 0 - Plays world wide, no countries excluded
- Region 1 - US and Canada
- Region 2 - Most European and Mid-Eastern countries plus Japan.
- Region 3 - Southast Asia, Hong Kong, South Korea, Taiwan, Oceania
- Region 4 - Caribbean, Central and South America, Mexico
- Region 5 - Most African countries, Indian Subcontinent, Former Soviet Nations
- Region 6 - People's Republic of China except (Macau and Hong Kong)
- Region 7 - Reserved for future use; sometimes used for "screener" copies
- Region 8 - International use, as on airliners and cruise ships
- ALL - Disks authorized for all regions

Other DRM (Digital Rights Management) features may also be included on DVDs. These include CSS (Content Scramble System) and Macrovision, among others. Their purpose is to allow the DVDs to be played on computers without it being possible to copy the files. Most of these systems require a license fee or royalty to be paid where they are used.

DVDs can be very simple, with only a single movie file, to very complex, with a movie, behind-the-scenes features, chapter marks, multiple menus, multiple camera angles, still images, subtitles in multiple languages, closed captions and multiple soundtracks and formats. While it's (once again!) beyond the scope of this chapter to describe all the available options in DVD authoring, you should be aware that a wide variety of features and functions are available.

Manufactured (*replicated* or *pressed*) DVDs are the ones that are like you buy in the video store. They are manufactured in large volumes (thousands in a batch) and are produced by a different process where in a glass master disk is electroplated and the duplicates are literally stamped out of plastic. Because of this different process, the disks are cheaper to make, are somewhat more durable, and will probably last longer without deterioration. Also, this process allows disks to be dual-layer and also dual-sided (DL-DS, or DVD-18), which means up to about 18 GB of data can be held. For maximum quality, very long movies or those with a lot of "extra" content are sometimes delivered in this format.

If you need more than a few hundred copies of your DVD, you may want to consider one of the many replication houses to handle these for you. Ask for their instructions on how to create “master” DVDs that meet their particular specifications.

Disks for HD

For awhile, there were two competing technologies for delivering HD on DVD (or similar) disks. These were *HD-DVD*, created by Toshiba, and *Blu-ray* (also called Blue-ray Disk, or *BD*), developed primarily by Sony. Fortunately (except for the format’s backers and those who bought into it!), HD-DVD was discontinued, leaving Blu-ray as the preferred format for HD. Blu-ray is similar to DVD in concept, except it uses a blue-violet laser instead of an infrared laser to read the data on the disk. Because the laser has a much shorter wavelength (405 nanometers instead of 650 nanometers), it can pack in much more data per disk than DVD, about 25 GB per layer. Since there’s more data in an HD movie than as SD movie, it works out that Blu-ray has about the same capabilities and storage time for HD as a DVD does for SD. The same considerations apply to authoring for Blu-ray as for DVD. Of course you’ll need a read-write Blu-ray drive and authoring software that supports Blu-ray. In general, authoring for Blu-ray is similar to SD DVD authoring.

While Blu-ray has not yet achieved the near-universal acceptance of DVD, there are other ways to display HD content using a computer. Using more modern encoders such as MPEG-4, Windows Media 9, and H.264, excellent HD quality can be achieved at the bit rates of the older MPEG-2 used on SD DVDs. Using recordable DVDs, simply put the H.264 files on the disks as data. Standard software such as Quicktime or Windows Media Player will play these files beautifully on a reasonably fast machine.

Your Film on the Web

With improvements in broadband internet connectivity, it’s now possible to get high quality video (and even HD) on the web. Depending on the file formats you use and where you upload your video, you can allow users to watch or download your film with ease, creating a simple and low-cost distribution channel that didn’t exist even a few years ago.

There’s an ever-growing number of sites that let you upload videos for web viewing. YouTube is a great example. With some sites, you have to apply for “director” status (or its equivalent) to upload longer videos and some have file size restrictions. Most of these sites use Flash Video from Adobe, but will accept files in almost any format. What’s great about these sites is that there’s no cost for the disk storage space or used bandwidth, and the quality is getting better. You can also embed these videos on your own site, so viewers don’t have to go to the parent sites to see your film.

It's also possible to put your film on the web using any of the popular web hosting companies or even set up your own web server. For maximum quality and minimum bandwidth requirements, use one of the H.264-based codecs.

Going to Real Film

There's nothing quite as exciting as seeing your film on the big screen at the local Bijou. Most theaters still project plain old 35mm film —you know, the old fashioned kind of film with reels and sprocket holes. Several specialized companies can transfer your digital film to the kind they show in theaters. I warn you, however, that this is a very expensive process, and prices run in the hundreds of dollars *per minute*.

Earlier in the book we talked about shooting and editing considerations when you intend to transfer to film. In general, it's best to shoot HD at 24 (or 25) fps in one of the progressive formats (1080p 24 or 720p 24), although SD and interlaced HD formats can be successfully transferred to film. Most film transfer companies can accept your film as a "master" tape, though the preferred method is on an external hard drive, using the highest quality file you can output, preferably uncompressed. To make things easier, you should divide longer films into "reels", making each reel a separate file. Standard 35mm film reels for theatrical release are 22 minutes in length, so you should end each reel at a cut just before the 22-minute point. You may also want to include SMPTE countdown leader at the head of each reel. Consult your video-to-film transfer company for their recommended specifications.

4.6 Conclusion

"A movie is never any better than the stupidest man connected with it."
...Ben Hecht

At the risk of repeating myself: this book is only an introduction to filmmaking in the digital age. Since you've gotten this far, congratulations are in order. You're well on your way. I'll conclude with a short list of the key points you will want to remember in your filmmaking adventures. While nothing can guarantee the success of your film, these are the key takeaways:

- The STORY is EVERYTHING. Make the story good and your audience will overlook a multitude of flaws. Storytelling is more important than technique. Engage your audience. Meet their expectations. Delight them.
- LEARN all you can about the process, and learn by doing. Be intimately familiar with the techniques and technologies you'll be using.
- DESIGN your film to fit your story and your budget. RE-DESIGN as necessary and minimize any expenditures or efforts that don't advance the story. DESIGN it so you don't run out of time or money. Learn to make the best of any situation you encounter.
- On the technical side, ENGINEER your production for maximum efficiency and lowest cost.
- You can't do too much pre-production. The Boy Scouts say it best: Be Prepared. Don't shoot before you're ready.
- REFINE your concept and script. Re-write. Re-write. Re-write. Make it the best it can be.
- Crystallize your VISION. Have a clear picture of your film before you shoot, and make sure those working with you share your vision. Communicate and collaborate.
- Change the script BEFORE you shoot. It's a lot easier and much cheaper.
- The quality of your on-camera talent is more important than the quality of your images.

- The quality of your photography, lighting and composition are more important than the quality of your camera. Concentrate on the pictures, not the equipment; just keep in mind the limitations of the equipment.
- The quality of your soundtrack is every bit as important as the quality of your images.
- The quality of your film is only slightly related to the amount of money you spend.
- Good editing can make or break any film. Allow plenty of time and resources for this all-important phase of production.
- Resolve to FINISH your film. An unfinished film is a total waste.
- Get your film seen and elicit feedback and criticism. Learn how to make your next one even better.

A longtime friend tells the story of having the opportunity to have dinner with legendary film director, Frank Capra. During their conversation, my friend mentioned that he had been working on a film. "Is it a good film?" asked Capra. After an awkward pause, Capra asked his second question: "Is it finished?"

"Yes, it's finished," my friend replied.

"Then," quipped Capra, "it's a good film! Most of them aren't, you know."

The author is available to answer questions and for production consultation. Email me at ljgardner@digifonics.com.